Concerning the Prophets

Concerning the Prophets

True and False Prophecy in Jeremiah 23:9—29:32

DANIEL EPP-TIESSEN

☙PICKWICK *Publications* • Eugene, Oregon

CONCERNING THE PROPHETS
True and False Prophecy in Jeremiah 23:9—29:32

Copyright © 2012 Daniel Epp-Tiessen. All rights reserved. Except for brief quotations in critical publications or reviews, no part of this book may be reproduced in any manner without prior written permission from the publisher. Write: Permissions, Wipf and Stock Publishers, 199 W. 8th Ave., Suite 3, Eugene, OR 97401.

Pickwick Publications
An Imprint of Wipf and Stock Publishers
199 W. 8th Ave., Suite 3
Eugene, OR 97401

www.wipfandstock.com

ISBN 13: 978-1-61097-280-2

Cataloging-in-Publication data

Epp-Tiessen, Daniel.

    Concerning the prophets : True and false prophecy in Jeremiah 23:9—29:32 / Daniel Epp-Tiessen.

    xii + 224 p. 23 cm.—Includes bibliographical references.

    ISBN 13: 978-1-61097-280-2

    1. Bible—O.T.—Jeremiah—Criticism, interpretation, etc. 2. Prophecy—Biblical teaching. I. Title.

BS1525.52 E60 2012

Translations of biblical material are the author's own.

Manufactured in the U.S.A.

To Esther, Chris, Tim, Mark, and Melissa,
whose love and laughter nourish my scholarly work
and also place it in proper perspective.

Contents

Acknowledgments | ix
Abbreviations | x

Introduction | 1

1 Approaches to the Study of True and False Prophecy | 9
2 The Concentric Structure of Jeremiah 23:9—29:32 | 41
3 Section A: Condemnation of False Prophets in General (23:9–40) | 75
4 Section B: A Vision Regarding Exiles and Non-Exiles (24:1–10) | 107
5 Section C: The Symbolic Cup—Destruction of the Nations by Nebuchadnezzar (25:1–38) | 122
6 Section D: Proper and Improper Responses to True Prophecy (26:1–24) | 140
7 Section C': The Symbolic Yoke—All Nations Must Serve Nebuchadnezzar (27:1—28:17) | 162
8 Section B': A Letter Regarding Exiles and Non-Exiles (29:1–19) | 184
9 Section A': Condemnation of Specific False Prophets (29:20–32) | 195

Conclusion | 201

Bibliography | 211

Acknowledgments

ACKNOWLEDGING THOSE PERSONS ONE is indebted to is risky business because inevitably significant people will be omitted from the list, and yet giving thanks is essential because none of us is a self-made person, and few human projects are solo affairs. I am grateful to my parents, Nellie and Martin Tiessen, whose simple but faithful Christian life that included daily Bible reading and prayer inspired my own love of Scripture and taught me what it means to live by the Word. Of the many fine teachers who have shaped me over the years, I single out only two. My first Bible professor, Waldemar Janzen, who has also become mentor and friend, inspired my love for the Old Testament and the prophets, first encouraged me to explore the book of Jeremiah, and modeled how to combine solid scholarship with deep Christian piety. I am indebted to the late Gerald T. Sheppard for exposing me to canonical approaches to Scripture, and for supervising the doctoral thesis that let me test some of the central ideas that inform this book.

I am grateful to Canadian Mennonite University in Winnipeg, Canada, for giving me the best job in the world. Supportive and engaging colleagues, administrators, and students make teaching and writing a delight. I am also grateful to the university for granting me sabbatical leaves as well as a research grant that allowed me to complete this book.

My wife Esther has been a constant source of encouragement, and this project would not have reached fruition without her well-timed admonitions that "you need to get your book published." I am deeply grateful for the rich life that I share with Esther and our children, Chris, Tim, Mark, and Melissa.

Abbreviations

AB	Anchor Bible
ABR	*Australian Biblical Review*
AJSL	*American Journal of Semitic Languages and Literature*
ANQ	*Andover Newton Quarterly*
ASV	American Standard Version
AUSS	*Andrews University Seminary Studies*
BA	*Biblical Archaeologist*
BETL	Bibliotheca ephemeridum theologicarum lovaniensium
Bib	*Biblica*
BRev	*Bible Review*
BSac	*Bibliotheca sacra*
BTB	*Biblical Theology Bulletin*
BZ	*Biblishe Zeitschrift*
BZAW	Beihefte zur Zeitschrift für die alttestamentliche Wissenschaft
CBQ	*Catholic Biblical Quarterly*
CJT	*Canadian Journal of Theology*
ETL	*Ephemerides theologicae lovanienses*
EuroJTh	*European Journal of Theology*
HAR	*Hebrew Annual Review*
HSM	Harvard Semitic Monographs
HUCA	*Hebrew Union College Annual*
Int	*Interpretation*
JAAR	*Journal of the American Academy of Religion*
JBL	*Journal of Biblical Literature*

Abbreviations

JETS	*Journal of the Evangelical Theological Society*
JNES	*Journal of Near Eastern Studies*
JNSL	*Journal of Northwest Semitic Languages*
JR	*Journal of Religion*
JSOT	*Journal for the Study of the Old Testament*
JSOTSup	Journal for the Study of the Old Testament Supplement Series
JPS	Jerusalem Publication Society
KJV	King James Version
LXX	Septuagint
MT	Masoretic Text
NAB	New American Bible
NEB	New English Bible
NIV	New International Version
NJB	New Jerusalem Bible
NJPS	New Jerusalem Publication Society Translation
NKJV	New King James Version
NRSV	New Revised Standard Version
OBT	Overtures to Biblical Theology
OTL	Old Testament Library
OtSt	*Oudtestamentische Studiën*
RB	*Revue biblique*
RevExp	*Review and Expositor*
RSV	Revised Standard Version
RTR	*Reformed Theological Review*
SBLDS	Society of Biblical Literature Dissertation Series
SJOT	*Scandinavian Journal of the Old Testament*
TZ	*Theologische Zeitschrift*
VT	*Vetus Testamentum*
VTSup	Vetus Testamentum Supplements
WW	*Word and World*
ZTK	*Zeitschrift für Theologie und Kirche*
ZAW	*Zeitschrift für die alttestamentliche Wissenschaft*

Introduction

THIS BOOK CONTRIBUTES TO two very different areas of Old Testament scholarship even as it focuses on one block of text. It sheds light on the structure and composition of the book of Jeremiah, and it explores the portrayal of true and false prophecy in the largest block of biblical text that deals with this topic. Different proposals regarding the book of Jeremiah's structure and organization abound, while at the same time some scholars are convinced that the material in the book is for the most part a chaotic mess and therefore any order is largely a figment of scholarly imagination.[1] I will argue that Jer 23:9—29:32 displays a carefully crafted concentric structure, which illustrates that at least one significant section of the book of Jeremiah has been very deliberately organized. The intentionality behind this collection becomes all the more evident when the MT is compared to the LXX, which lacks the concentric structure. This book also contributes to the scholarly conversation about true and false prophecy. The structural features of 23:9—29:32 demarcate these chapters as a single block of text, which leads to the question of their purpose and theme. The content of 23:9—29:32 as well as the superscription in 23:9, "Concerning the Prophets," indicate that these chapters seek to reflect on the nature of true and false prophecy. Without recognizing the structure of 23:9—29:32, the material appears to be a miscellaneous and chaotic collection lacking any overarching theme or focus, a perception well illustrated by how most commentaries treat these chapters. Recognizing the structure permits one to see the order amidst the chaos, and to discern how editors forged originally disparate material into a thematic

---

1. The two commentators least inclined to see careful organization in the book are probably Carroll, *Jeremiah*; and McKane, *A Critical and Exegetical Commentary*. See also Carroll, "The Polyphonic Jeremiah."

unit focusing on the nature of true and false prophecy and the conflict between them.

The nature of true and false prophecy aroused considerable scholarly interest from the 1960s to the 1980s, but such interest has almost died out since, partly because the discussion reached something of a consensus. Much of the literature focused on whether or not there were adequate criteria for distinguishing between true and false prophecy. The emerging consensus was that there are no foolproof criteria that ancient (or modern) hearers could use to discern whether it was Jeremiah or Hananiah, Micah or his opponents who spoke the true word of the Lord. While I agree with this consensus, it does not do complete justice to the biblical material on true and false prophecy. The interest in criteria led scholars to focus on the original historical situation in which prophets with different messages confronted each other, a most worthy topic. Somewhat lost in the discussion was careful examination of how the biblical text actually portrays the nature of true and false prophecy. We still lack a comprehensive study of all the prophetic conflict texts in the Bible and how they depict the conflict between true and false prophecy. This book contributes to the discussion by analyzing the portrayal of true and false prophecy in the largest block of biblical text to deal with the issue.

Early on in my study I was determined to avoid the expression "false prophet" because of the erroneous images it conjures up and because there is no such word or expression in Hebrew. Hebrew knows only prophets, be they true prophets of YHWH, prophets of Baal, or prophets who claim to have a message from YHWH when they do not. The expression "false prophet" enters our vocabulary from the Greek. Ten times the LXX has some form of the word *pseudoprophetes* when the MT has only "prophet" (Jer 6:13; 26:7, 8, 11, 16; 27:9; 28:1; 29:1, 8; Zech 13:2). "False prophet" is problematic in English because it has metaphysical overtones, suggesting that the prophet in question is totally evil and can say or do little that is right. The Old Testament presents the matter somewhat differently. In 1 Kings 13, for example, the elderly prophet can in the same story speak both a lie and a genuine word of YHWH to the unwitting man of God from Judah. The Greek *pseudoprophetes* focuses on the character of the prophet, while the Hebrew is more interested in the truth or falsehood of the specific message that the prophet speaks.[2] Despite

---

2. Crenshaw, *Prophetic Conflict*, 47. So profoundly has the metaphysical understanding behind the expression "false prophet" entered the scholarly consciousness that it is responsible for a consistent mistranslation of Deut 18:22. "When the prophet

reservations about the expressions "true" and "false prophets," I have decided to use them anyway, for two reasons. The first is that unfortunately, the English language provides no suitable alternative. The second is that I have come to realize that it is no accident that nine of the ten occurrences of *pseudoprophetes* in the LXX are found in Jeremiah, and of these nine, eight are found in 23:9—29:32. The Hebrew may not have a word for false prophet, but the book of Jeremiah draws such a sharp contrast between Jeremiah, the authentic prophet of YHWH, and his prophetic opponents, who speak only falsehood and thereby lead the nation to its doom, that the LXX does not significantly distort the MT by using the term *pseudoprophetes* to designate these other prophets.[3]

Any major scholarly work on the book of Jeremiah must declare its convictions regarding the composition of the book, because such convictions are directly linked to convictions about how the book is best read and interpreted. Commentaries and monographs that believe the book has a simple compositional history and stems mostly from the historical Jeremiah read very differently than commentaries that see the book as an exilic or post-exilic creation designed to speak to the needs and concerns of a community struggling with the ongoing consequences of the Babylonian destruction of the nation. The world probably does not need yet another scholarly review of the massive body of literature that explores compositional issues, and so I will merely register my agreement with the growing number of scholars who believe that the book has a long and complex compositional history to which many interests

---

speaks in the name of YHWH, and the word does not happen or come to pass, that is a word which YHWH has not spoken. The prophet has spoken it presumptuously. Do not be afraid of it [מִמֶּנּוּ]." The question is whether the last word of the verse should be rendered "of it" (i.e., do not be afraid of that prophet's word), or "of him" (i.e., do not be afraid of the prophet). Most translations, including the KJV, NKJV, ASV, NAB, RSV, NJB, NEB, NJPS, and NIV, have "of him" and thereby imply that the issue is how to discern between the true and the false prophet, i.e., between the metaphysically good and the metaphysically evil prophet. But 18:21 clearly states that the key issue is, "How will we know the *word* which YHWH has not spoken?" In 18:21–22 the verb form דִּבְּרוֹ appears three times. The third-person masculine singular pronominal suffix is grammatically superfluous, yet it is included three times and each time it refers to "word," which also occurs three times. When this same suffix occurs in the last word of the verse, it once again refers to "word" and should be translated "of it" (i.e., the word) and not "of him" (referring to the prophet). The usual translation focuses on the person of the prophet, while the Hebrew is concerned about the truth or untruth of the prophetic message.

3. For a somewhat different rationale for retaining the expression "false prophet" see Crenshaw, *Prophetic Conflict*, 47.

groups and individuals have contributed.[4] The enormous effort expended on untangling compositional issues, in contrast to the paucity of agreed-upon conclusions, leads me to despair of making anything but general statements about the preservers and shapers of the Jeremiah tradition. The book appears too complex and multifaceted, and our knowledge of Second Temple groups and life too limited, to arrive at much certainty regarding the identity of the anonymous tradents and the specific nature of their work.[5]

While I believe that the book probably retains considerable material from both the historical Jeremiah and his early supporters that accurately reflects his prophetic ministry, I have less confidence in our ability to sort out the historical Jeremiah from the portrayal of Jeremiah flowing from the pen of later traditionists. I agree with Brueggemann that what we now find in the book is "an imaginative literary construct of the person of the prophet presented for interpretive reasons."[6] One major goal of the book, and especially of 23:9—29:32, is to present Jeremiah as a paradigm of the true prophet who courageously proclaims the divine word despite enormous hardship and opposition. The core of the book of Jeremiah emerged out of the crisis of exile, with its massive physical and spiritual dislocation. Thus, the book seeks "to help the community to endure its present suffering, to understand and absorb what has happened to it, and, finally, to reconstitute itself as God's covenant people."[7]

In keeping with this goal, the book uses "the heritage of Jeremiah to address the ongoing spiritual and religious needs of a devastated and questioning community."[8] When I speak of the prophet Jeremiah in this

---

4. Carolyn J. Sharp offers a helpful summary of some of the literature exploring compositional issues, grouping it according to three distinct approaches. See Sharp, *Prophecy and Ideology in Jeremiah*, 1–13. Some recent works still resist the near-consensus regarding the complexity of the compositional history. See for example Lundbom, *Jeremiah: A New Translation*; Leuchter, *Josiah's Reform and Jeremiah's Scroll*; Leuchter, *The Polemics of Exile*.

5. After noting the lack of concrete evidence regarding the existence of the supposed Jeremiah traditionists, Craigie observes, "These observations do not disprove their existence, yet they serve as a reminder that if Jeremiah himself is lost in the mists of history, the clouds of time that shroud the traditionists are no less dense" (Craigie et al., *Jeremiah 1–25*, xxxix). See also the reservations voiced by David M. Carr about scholarly ability to reconstruct complex compositional processes based on the limited evidence available, in Carr, "Moving beyond Unity," 62–64.

6. Brueggemann, "Meditation upon the Abyss," 341.

7. O'Connor, "The Prophet Jeremiah and Exclusive Loyalty," 137.

8. Fretheim, *Jeremiah*, 5. For additional comments along similar lines see Seitz,

book, I set aside questions of historicity and focus on the literary figure created by the text. The goal of my study is to explore how 23:9—29:32 presents true and false prophecy in such a way that it interprets the catastrophe of 587 and suggests ways in which the community can embrace the disaster and move forward as God's covenant people. The ongoing changes made to the book of Jeremiah in the Second Temple restoration period testify to the Jeremiah tradition's ability to address the needs and issues confronted by generations of Jews for whom the events of 587 had become a distant but still extremely powerful memory.

The field of Jeremiah studies is currently in a state of some methodological flux and confusion, not surprising given the perplexing nature of the book and the dizzying array of methods and approaches currently used in biblical scholarship.[9] The older diachronic approaches no longer seem adequate, and largely gone is the confidence displayed by the "biographers" of Jeremiah who believed it was possible to correlate the different passages in the book with the life experiences of the historical Jeremiah.[10] Newer diachronic approaches that seek to correlate different passages in the book with different redactions and/or different political and religious interest groups in exilic and Second Temple Judaism have achieved little consensus about the nature of these redactions beyond the conviction that Deuteronomists have had a major impact on the book. While providing much insight into the complexity of both the book and its compositional history, such studies have proved less useful in grasping the overall meaning and purpose of the final form of the book, including its various subsections.

The limitations of diachronic approaches and a desire for methodological purity make it tempting to adopt a purely synchronic approach and focus only on the world created by the text, thereby giving up any attempt to discern the historical context out of which the text arose and to which it was originally addressed. However, a purely synchronic reading

---

"The Place of the Reader," especially p. 73. O'Connor and Stulman have both written extensively on how the book of Jeremiah addresses the psychological and spiritual needs of the shattered post-587 community. See O'Connor, "Surviving Disaster"; O'Connor, "Jeremiah's 'Prophetic Imagination'"; O'Connor, "The Book of Jeremiah"; O'Connor, "Rekindling Life, Igniting Hope"; and O'Connor, "Lamenting Back to Life." See also Stulman, "Conflicting Paths to Hope"; Stulman, "Jeremiah as a Messenger of Hope."

9. For a discussion of the diversity of approaches and methodologies in Jeremiah studies see Diamond, "Introduction," 15–32.

10. See for example Skinner, *Prophecy and Religion*; and Welch, *Jeremiah*.

is never possible, nor is it entirely desirable. Even the meaning of words is linked to the historical and social context in which they are used, and so responsible interpretation of ancient texts requires attention to diachronic concerns such as the meanings that terms and concepts had in the original context. That is one reason concordances and lexicons are invaluable scholarly tools. An important term in Jer 23:9—29:32 is *Torah*, but what does it mean? As it was used by the historical Jeremiah (if it was), the term probably meant general instructions or guidelines from God about faithful living. Deuteronomistic editors who used the term may have been thinking of their Deuteronomistic law code, while later tradents living in the post-Ezra period would have thought of the Mosaic *Torah*, or Pentateuch. When encountering the word *Torah* the modern interpreter cannot adjudicate between the various possibilities without some attention to diachronic insights about the changing meaning of the term.

Another reason why a purely synchronic approach is inadequate for interpreting the book of Jeremiah is that the book is so closely linked to a particular historical situation. The book lives and breathes exile, and the physical, spiritual, and emotional crises set in motion by the disaster of 587 are everywhere evident. Whatever one believes about the book's origins, in its present form it is addressed to a particularly horrific situation and must therefore be interpreted in terms of this specificity.[11] A comparison with the book of Daniel is instructive. Daniel is set during the Babylonian exile, but the book does not breathe exile in the way that Jeremiah does. It so clearly addresses issues of the Maccabean period that it should at least partially be interpreted in light of that era rather than only in light of the Babylonian exile. As Brueggemann observes, the book of Jeremiah is profoundly in touch with the painful realities of the Babylonian crisis, and so a purely synchronic interpretation, "as though the 'book' floated in the air," is not adequate.[12] However, our knowledge of exactly how the content of the book connects with specific situations, issues, needs, conflicts, and interest groups in the post-587 era is very inadequate. Yet, since the text arose out of the experiences of real people and was written to address the real concerns of a flesh-and-blood community, interpretation should not entirely forgo attention to historical

---

11. Fretheim, *Jeremiah*, 4.
12. Brueggemann, "Next Steps in Jeremiah Studies?" 405.

context.¹³ Just as our appreciation and understanding of the book of Daniel is deepened by recognizing how it addresses issues of the Maccabean era, so our understanding of Jeremiah is deepened as we discern how it speaks to the needs and concerns of a community seeking to find its way through the Babylonian crisis and its aftermath.

The methodological flux and confusion within Jeremiah studies is partly caused by a recognition of the inherent limits of diachronic approaches combined with recognition that the nature of the book makes attention to diachronic issues at least somewhat necessary. Many interpreters adopt a both/and approach when it comes to synchronic and diachronic perspectives.¹⁴ Recently, the momentum in Jeremiah studies has shifted in the direction of synchronic approaches that concentrate on how the text construes its own reality and world irrespective of the historical context out of which it emerged. Interpreters focus on meaning that is based on internal features of the text and does not depend on external reference points such as authorship, historical context, and original audience. My own sympathies also move in this direction, and so I will focus on how 23:9—29:32 portrays the nature of true and false prophecy, including the ideas, convictions, polemics, and ideologies communicated by this portrayal.¹⁵ However, biblical prophecy is not divorced from historical realities, and this is rarely more true than in the case of Jeremiah. All biblical texts are addressed to some specific audience implied in the text, and therefore it is useful to discern who this audience is and what its concerns might be.¹⁶ Therefore, I will pay some attention to the historical, social, and theological particularities out of which the text may

---

13. For a discussion of the importance of historical context see Perdue, *The Collapse of History*, 296–97, and especially 186–92, where Perdue critiques Brevard Childs's canonical interpretation for being too ahistorical.

14. Brueggemann, "Next Steps in Jeremiah Studies?" 405. For an insightful discussion of why both synchronic and diachronic approaches are necessary, see Stulman, *Jeremiah*, 10–11. See also Carr's rationale for cooperation between synchronic and diachronic study, in "Moving beyond Unity," 92–93.

15. In his response to David Carr, Jacques Vermeylen agrees that synchronic and diachronic approaches are both necessary and can be complementary, but he calls for the chronological priority of synchronic study. Because reconstruction of a text's historical setting or compositional history always remains a hypothesis, the place to begin is at the synchronic level, with an exploration of the text's "structure, its internal moves, its evocative potentialities and its literary connections, before asking any question about its literary history" (Vermeylen, "Synchronic and Diachronic Perspectives," 96).

16. Habel, *The Land Is Mine*, 9.

have emerged, while at the same time remaining somewhat pessimistic about our ability to uncover more than general information about these historical particularities. I will seek to heed Habel's warning against the common circular approach of utilizing the ideas, allusions, and terms in a text to identify the historical audience, and then linking the meaning of the text to this hypothetical audience that has been identified using evidence almost exclusively internal to the text.[17] Readers of this book should be prepared for some methodological messiness (and perhaps inconsistencies) as I punctuate a largely synchronic study with a number of diachronic observations.

Although I am keenly aware of the differences between the MT and LXX versions of Jeremiah, and although I believe that the LXX witnesses to an older version of the book, I will focus on the MT. The LXX and MT are two different manuscripts, each with their own integrity and in many cases with somewhat unique theological emphases, and so they should be studied respecting their differences.[18] Therefore, I will not use one to "correct" the other, nor will I engage in text-critical exercises in an attempt to arrive at more pristine readings, but I will on occasion compare the two in order to shed more light on the nature of both, especially the MT.

---

17. Ibid., 8.

18. For an insightful example of this approach in action, see Sweeney, "The Masoretic and Septuagint Versions."

1

Approaches to the Study of True and False Prophecy

As indicated in the introduction, this book contributes to two different areas of Old Testament scholarship. One is the organization and composition of the book of Jeremiah, the other is the study of true and false prophecy. Before moving to a detailed discussion of the portrayal of true and false prophecy in Jer 23:9—29:32, I offer an analysis of selected previous studies of true and false prophecy, particularly as they relate to 23:9—29:32. The purpose of this discussion is to acknowledge the many points at which I am indebted to other scholars, to highlight how my approach is different from some previous work, and to demonstrate the need for some new directions. I have chosen to comment on only a limited number of earlier studies, focusing on those that are representative of approaches in the field and those that are most relevant for understanding Jer 23:9—29:32.[1]

GERHARD VON RAD

In his review of the literature, Armin Lange observes how two interests have dominated the scholarly discussion of true and false prophecy. One is concern with criteria for distinguishing between them, and the other is

---

1. For a more comprehensive review of the history of research, see Lange, *Vom prophetischen Wort*, 4–38.

the social and institutional setting of both true and false prophets.[2] Both these concerns come to the fore in the work of Gerhard von Rad, who surmises that conflict between true and false prophets centered on the fact that the false prophets proclaimed salvation while the true prophets announced primarily judgment.[3] Von Rad then seeks to discern the theological and institutional location of the false prophets by asking what other parts of the Old Testament contain promises of national well-being. He finds such promises in the book of Deuteronomy, which maintains the paradox that despite Israel's sin and unworthiness, God's covenant will ensure Israel's protection and well-being.

Of particular significance is God's promise to provide a continual line of Mosaic prophets to function as divine spokespersons, thereby ensuring the community's obedience and well-being (18:15–22). The people can know if such a prophet's message is true if it is fulfilled, and if not they can be sure that the prophetic word is false and they *need not fear it* (18:22). This concluding assurance has in mind prophets who proclaim words of doom, or else there would be no reason to fear their words. Deuteronomy knows two types of prophets, an institutional succession of prophets in the service of ensuring national well-being, and independent prophets whose words of doom needlessly unsettle the community. This represents a very different understanding of prophetic ministry than assumed by books like Amos and Jeremiah, where the true prophet announces primarily disaster. Von Rad also points out how Deuteronomy and numerous other texts envision the true prophet as an intercessor standing between YHWH and the people (18:15–18; see also Gen 20:7; 1 Sam 7:5; 12:19, 23; 2 Kgs 19:4; Jer 27:18; 37:3), and on this basis he concludes that the false prophets were attached more or less closely to the cult and saw intercession on the nation's behalf and announcing messages of well-being as integral to their role. This explains why Jeremiah's opponent Hananiah proclaims a message of deliverance by promising that the looted temple utensils will soon be returned from Babylon (Jer 28:2–4, 11).

Von Rad recognizes that ascertaining the theology and institutional position of prophets is not yet to answer the question of criteria for discerning between true and false prophecy, nor can this question be answered in a general way because even the canonical prophets provide no

---

2. Ibid., 4–33.
3. Von Rad, "Die falschen Propheten," 112.

comprehensive guidelines for separating the true from the false. When Jeremiah's message of judgment clashes with the prophet Hananiah's message of deliverance, Jeremiah cannot automatically declare Hananiah to be false, and so he deals with the matter in terms of history, which he asserts will discredit Hananiah (28:9). Von Rad concludes that after the optimistic times of Josiah, Hananiah, unlike Jeremiah, was not able to see that YHWH's will for the people had changed. If one abstracts the message of the false prophet from its historical context one can say little against it, because Hananiah's proclamation is no different than Isaiah's message in an earlier era. But true prophecy does not rely on unchanging dogmas such as God's defense of Zion, because it is attuned to a God who acts creatively within history.

Here von Rad touches on a point critical for understanding the portrayal of true and false prophecy in Jer 23:9—29:32. The truth or falseness of the prophetic message is determined less by reference to any theological doctrines than by its discernment of YHWH's plans for history. In some cases false prophecy is actually good theology proclaimed at or for the wrong time. Both Jeremiah and the false prophets are convinced that God's ultimate will for Israel is salvation, but the crucial difference is timing, because Jeremiah insists that there will be no deliverance on this side of horrible catastrophe.

Von Rad's approach to understanding true and false prophecy is to use a host of texts to reconstruct the historical situation and to describe two different lines of prophets in ancient Israel. Interestingly, von Rad implies that the book of Deuteronomy and the prophet Nahum are associated with the line of false prophecy. He notes how the prophecy of Nahum bears all the characteristics of false prophecy, but then he seems unable to take the next logical step and declare that Nahum is a false prophet.[4] I attribute this reluctance to the power of the biblical portrayal. The fact that Deuteronomy and Nahum are in the canon indicates that the community of faith has reckoned them to be true, whatever their historical origins. Even though von Rad operates out of diachronic historical-critical assumptions, with the goal of using the biblical text to shed light on historical developments in ancient Israel, his intuitive sense of the biblical portrayal of true and false prophecy prevents him from following some of his historical-critical arguments to their logical conclusion.

---

4. Ibid., 117.

Concerning the Prophets

MARTIN BUBER

In his brief essay on Jeremiah 28, Martin Buber follows in the footsteps of von Rad by stressing the crucial role that history plays in setting the true prophet apart from the false.[5] Buber notes that despite Jeremiah's powerful conviction of having received the divine word that all the nations must submit to Babylon, when Hananiah contradicts this message Jeremiah is silent and goes his way (28:10–11). Jeremiah realizes that the divine plan is not a rigid program but can change, and so the word that God speaks in one hour of history must not be touted as an unchanging doctrine.[6] Therefore, Jeremiah leaves the confrontation in order to wait for another word from the Lord. Hananiah, in contrast, does not know how to listen but only how to repeat the truths of the past, and so he imitates Isaiah, who had under similar circumstances asserted that God would break the yoke of the enemy. According to Buber, the essence of false prophecy is to repeat a message intended for one specific hour in history as if it were an eternal message.

Buber's diachronic study focuses less on how the text of Jeremiah 28 actually portrays the conflict between Jeremiah and Hananiah than on how the data supplied by the text can shed light on the historical situation which the text supposedly reflects. Like von Rad, Buber is correct in highlighting how true prophecy is attuned to God's plans for history, but in Jeremiah 28 the portrayal of true prophecy is quite different from Buber's construal. By ch. 28 the book has for twenty-seven chapters already portrayed Jeremiah as the quintessential true prophet who has consistently proclaimed that Babylon is God's agent to punish Judah, often in contrast to other prophets who promised a bright future. From the perspective of the text there is no possibility in ch. 28 that YHWH might now suddenly change his mind and reveal a radically different message to Jeremiah.[7]

GOTTFRIED QUELL

Gottfried Quell's insightful book was the first comprehensive study of true and false prophecy in the Old Testament and set the tone for much subsequent research. According to Quell, the problem of true and false

---

5. Buber, "False Prophets."
6. Ibid., 167.
7. For similar comments see Moberly, *Prophecy and Discernment*, 106–9.

prophecy will arise wherever people long for an authoritative word from God.[8] Because the prophet serves as divine spokesperson and claims to utter words of ultimate significance, some persons will inevitably doubt individual prophets and consider their messages to be false. Quell anticipates later sociological analysis when he astutely observes that a prophet is true only if some particular group of people regards that prophet to be true. This renders all criteria for distinguishing between true and false prophecy essentially useless, because these designations depend on subjective human opinion. The impossibility of solving the problem of true and false prophecy is rooted in the dual nature of prophecy. Prophets are human yet claim to speak for the divine, which means that by its very nature prophecy makes claims for itself that are not verifiable through normal rational means.[9] This is why Quell repeatedly asserts that only a prophet possessed by the divine spirit has the necessary insight to unmask another prophet as false.[10] Because the Israelites were confused by conflict between prophets there were attempts to establish criteria for discerning between the true and the false, but all such attempts were in vain because they could not grapple with the non-rational aspects of prophecy. This conclusion illustrates how Quell's focus on the historical context underlying prophetic conflict texts distracts him from seeing clearly the actual depiction within the text. One of the purposes of the biblical portrayal is to demonstrate unequivocally what the true prophetic word is, so that the community need no longer be confused or misled.

When Quell analyzes Jeremiah 28 he is not so much concerned with what the text itself says, but he uses the text in order to recreate the historical incident the text claims to recount. The key issue for Quell is how Jeremiah and Hananiah's audience could have discerned which of the two was the true prophet. He entitles his chapter on Jeremiah 28 "Chananja [Hananiah]," which reflects his attempt to rehabilitate Hananiah in the eyes of contemporary readers. Quell reacts to earlier simplistic understandings of prophetic conflict and to scholars who moralized and enhanced the Bible's already negative portrayal of so-called false prophets, a tendency that Quell can be credited with putting an end to.[11] According

8. Quell, *Wahre und falsche Propheten*, 40.

9. Ibid., 30.

10. Ibid., 33–34, 36–37, 193. Not surprisingly, Quell (ibid., 124–26) cites as evidence the role of the spirit in Mic 3:8 and in the story of Micaiah ben Imlah in 1 Kgs 22:19–23 (ibid., 76).

11. For Quell's critique of such commentators see *Wahre und falsche Propheten*,

to Quell, the Bible's description of false prophets should not be accepted at face value, because conflict stories do not yield accurate historical information. Quell avoids ascribing negative motives to Hananiah and observes that Hananiah and Jeremiah's audience had no easy way to discern which of the two spoke the truth. Hananiah's message is, after all, remarkably similar to Isaiah's in similar circumstances. Recognizing this leads Quell to conclude that Hananiah is really a true prophet, because he is only mistaken about the date he gives (two years) for the reversal of Judah's fortunes.[12] This conclusion is problematic because as von Rad and Buber demonstrate, the issue of timing is critical. There is a huge difference between a prophetic assurance that God's deliverance will arrive within two years, implying that Judah can avoid disaster, and the announcement that salvation will only arrive seventy years hence, long after catastrophe has befallen the nation.

Despite many insights, Quell's work is marked by a basic inconsistency also found in some subsequent studies. He is correct in observing that the audience to Jeremiah's and Hananiah's confrontation had no foolproof criteria for discerning who was true and who was false. However, if Quell concludes that no adequate criteria exist for discerning between true and false prophecy, then it makes little sense to declare Hananiah or any other prophet to be either true or false. If no criteria exist, then the categories of true and false prophecy become meaningless and should be abandoned. Whatever modern scholars may conclude about the lack of adequate criteria or their subjectivity, the biblical text does not share this skepticism but portrays some prophets as true spokespersons of God and others as false. Quell is unconsciously in tune with this biblical portrayal, and even though he fights it to some extent when he concludes, for example, that Hananiah is a true prophet, the biblical portrayal still influences him so profoundly that it prevents him from following through on the logic of his basic argument.

VARIOUS LEVELS TO THE ISSUE OF CRITERIA

The methodological inconsistency evident in the work of Quell and von Rad stems from a confusion about the various levels at which the issue of

---

50–54. Such moralizing is evident even in Buber's work when he claims that Hananiah thought he knew it all and did not know how to listen; "False Prophets," 167–68.

12. Quell, *Wahre und falsche Propheten*, 55.

criteria for true and false prophecy should be analyzed. There are at least four such levels that should be clearly differentiated:

1. What criteria were or were not available to the ancient Israelite audience that had to choose between conflicting prophetic voices?
2. What criteria did the community of faith use, consciously or unconsciously, for adopting certain prophetic words, texts, and stories as authoritative and eventually canonical, while rejecting others?
3. What criteria can contemporary readers use to decide who is a true or a false *biblical* prophet?
4. A fourth level, which goes well beyond the scope of this book, is what criteria are available to contemporary faith communities for discerning between conflicting "prophetic" voices today?

For persons who accept the authority of the canon, the third is the easiest of the three questions to answer, because the biblical portrayal becomes the criterion. The methodological inconsistency in Quell's work results from confusing the first and third levels of the issue. He discusses the issue of criteria as if we today are the ones who must decide who is a true or false biblical prophet, and so he seeks to rehabilitate Hananiah and declares him to be a true prophet. Brevard Childs has pointed out how the formation of the canon marks a watershed and forever changes the way the question of criteria should be asked.[13] We are no longer in the position of Jeremiah's hearers, who have to decide whether he or Hananiah is the true prophet. The canon has made that decision for us. We may choose to reject the verdict of the canon, but we should be aware of what the canon is seeking to do. Whereas the biblical texts reflect situations in which people were bewildered by conflicting prophetic claims, one of the driving forces behind the biblical portrayal is to put an end to precisely such uncertainty.

Quell deals primarily with the issue of criteria at the historical level, but the biblical portrayal is so powerful that it sometimes elbows its way into the discussion. On the historical level Quell recognizes with great insight that it was not easy for the people of Judah to determine if Hananiah's or Jeremiah's message was false, because there were no adequate guidelines. Yet, when he accepts that Jeremiah, Micah, and Isaiah were true prophets, he accepts the verdict of the canon and switches to the level of the biblical portrayal. But then he switches back to the historical

---

13. Childs, "True and False Prophets," 140–41.

level and speaks of Hananiah as also being a true prophet. This type of inconsistency is not uncommon in subsequent discussions of true and false prophecy. Largely because of the insights of Quell, a consensus has developed that none of the criteria suggested either explicitly or implicitly in the biblical text is effective in distinguishing between true and false prophecy.[14] Yet, numerous scholars continue to speak about true and false prophecy as if these are meaningful categories. This contradiction arises because the biblical portrayal of true and false prophecy is so powerful that it convinces even skeptical scholars who claim that there are no adequate criteria. This methodological confusion results from not adequately distinguishing the various levels at which the issue of criteria and true and false prophecy should be addressed.

FRANK LOTHAR HOSSFELD AND IVO MEYER

The works of Hossfeld and Meyer mark a somewhat new approach because they do not treat true and false prophecy as one homogenous theological issue but differentiate between different theological and redactional strands in the Old Testament.[15] Hossfeld and Meyer's studies are to a large extent source-critical and redactional analyses that seek to dissect the biblical text into its various layers and then reconstruct the original life situation that gave rise to the sources.[16] With respect to the book of Jeremiah, Hossfeld and Meyer sketch a picture of the historical Jeremiah and his conflict with other prophets, and then focus on how the two major redactional layers portray prophetic conflict.[17] In the case of Jeremiah 29, for example, they conclude that Jeremiah's letter originally had nothing to do with other prophets, but that the Deuteronomistic redactors have added the prophetic conflict material.[18] Hossfeld and Meyer unravel Jeremiah 27-28 into its supposed three original strands and describe the literary process behind the text. They regard 23:33-40 as a late addition, and because it does not belong to any of the major

14. For a thorough analysis of the many possible criteria by a scholar who accepts the basic conclusions of Quell, see Münderlein, *Kriterien*.

15. Lange, *Vom prophetischen Wort*, 19. The works in question are Hossfeld and Meyer, *Prophet gegen Prophet*; Hossfeld and Meyer, "Der Prophet vor dem Tribunal"; and Meyer, *Jeremia und die falschen Propheten*.

16. See Hossfeld and Meyer, *Prophet gegen Prophet*, 37.

17. Ibid., 112-13.

18. Ibid., 108-11.

redactions they do not discuss it in any depth.[19] It is not necessary to summarize further the specific findings of Hossfeld and Meyer except to mention that they follow Quell in expressing skepticism about the validity of any criteria for distinguishing between true and false prophecy. Even though many of their literary-critical judgments can be questioned, Hossfeld and Meyer do provide considerable insight into the formation of the text. However, the overall effect of their work is to draw attention away from the completed biblical text and its presentation of true and false prophecy.

JAMES L. CRENSHAW

Two of the most valuable features of Crenshaw's work are his survey of the history of research into true and false prophecy and his extensive discussion of all the possible criteria for discerning between the two.[20] Crenshaw identifies two major tendencies in the scholarly literature: a denial that there are any valid criteria for distinguishing between true and false prophecy, and an attempt to understand the reasons for false prophecy.[21] Both these tendencies illustrate how scholars have not focused on the biblical portrayal but have instead used the biblical text to reconstruct the situation in which prophetic conflict originally occurred, thereby regarding as significant something that stands outside the actual biblical account.[22] Crenshaw's work moves in the same phenomenological direction, as he seeks "to clarify the issues between the prophet and his adversaries, to illuminate the prophetic mode of self-vindication, and to determine the effect of this struggle upon the history of Israelite religion."[23]

Crenshaw begins with an observation similar to Quell's that the very nature of prophecy makes prophetic conflict inevitable. Because the prophet sought to formulate into words the realizations that had come to him from God while in a state of ecstasy or concentration, there were no

19. Ibid., 85.
20. Crenshaw, *Prophetic Conflict*, 13–22 and 49–61, respectively.
21. Ibid., 13.
22. A classic study of how biblical scholarship shifted focus from the portrayal within the text to what the text supposedly refers to is Frei, *The Eclipse of Biblical Narrative*.
23. Crenshaw, *Prophetic Conflict*, 4.

objective means to validate the prophetic word. The essential weakness of prophecy was this inability to validate its message, especially when different prophets made conflicting claims. This eventually led the community to distrust the prophets and turn to wisdom and apocalyptic for more "realistic" explanations of the pressing issues of life and faith.[24] In addition to arguing that false prophecy was inevitable, Crenshaw also asserts that there was a degree of fluidity between true and false prophecy.[25] In 1 Kings 13 the prophet sent from Judah with a message of judgment against the altar of Bethel is deceived by a false prophet, as a result disobeys his commission, and then receives a shattering word of judgment from this same "false" prophet who now delivers a genuine word from YHWH. Given this fluidity between true and false prophecy, Crenshaw believes it is worthwhile to explore various factors that might have tempted true prophets to become false.[26] Some prophets wished to be successful and so they proclaimed a message that was popular with the people. Kings sponsored prophets, and the person who pays the piper picks the tune. Some prophets were swayed by the theology of the masses and took their cues from it rather than from the word of YHWH. Some prophets were so firmly rooted in Israel's election traditions that they could not imagine how God could condemn the nation.[27] Some prophets wanted to see righteousness rewarded and so they could not envision a disaster that would sweep away the righteous with the unrighteous. On occasion God deliberately used false prophets to accomplish a certain purpose (1 Kgs 22:19–23; Ezek 14:9–11).

---

24. Ibid., 103–9. For helpful critiques of Crenshaw's hypothesis see Childs, "True and False Prophets," 140–42; Sheppard, "True and False Prophecy," 265–73; and Janzen, "Withholding the Word," 97–98.

25. Crenshaw, *Prophetic Conflict*, 62. The close connection between true and false prophecy is also stressed by Jacob, "Quelques remarques," 479, 483–86. Jacob cites as one piece of evidence the fact that Hebrew, unlike Greek, does not even have a term for false prophet.

26. Jacob also highlights the constant temptation that true prophets faced to become false; "Quelques remarques," 483–86. Crenshaw credits Jacob for first suggesting many of the temptations that he analyzes further; *Prophetic Conflict*, 65.

27. Crenshaw sees this factor as determinative for the confrontation between Jeremiah and Hananiah; *Prophetic Conflict*, 71–73. Hananiah is not an insincere, lying prophet but an orthodox prophet who takes his stand on the traditions that stressed YHWH's care and protection of Zion, the Davidic dynasty, and the chosen people. Jeremiah's message is that promises based on election traditions are inappropriate because this historical hour stands under the judgment of God.

From an historical perspective, Crenshaw's analysis is very helpful for understanding the nature of the prophetic conflict underlying the biblical texts. His work sheds less light on the actual biblical portrayal. Even if one accepts Crenshaw's theory that the prophetic movement was eventually discredited by prophetic conflict and by the inability to adequately explain the complexities of history, one should recognize that the biblical portrayal venerates true prophets for, among other things, their ability to explain the complexities of history (especially Jeremiah in 23:9—29:32). Crenshaw is correct in observing that the audience to Jeremiah and Hananiah's conflict had no foolproof criteria for distinguishing the true word from the false, but the biblical portrayal leaves no doubt about who is the true prophet. As De Vries observes, "Though many contemporaries allowed themselves to be deluded by those who were wrong, the community of faith that produced the Old Testament Scripture were [sic] able to say, sooner or later, which was which."[28] Wolff makes a similar point, claiming, "The biblical testimonies make it plain that the last word must not be left to the depression and resignation which laments that, when all is said and done, no one really knows what the right course is."[29]

When Crenshaw concludes that no adequate criteria exist for discerning between true and false prophecy,[30] he does not clearly distinguish between the various levels at which the question of criteria should be addressed. He projects what might be true for the historical level onto other levels of the issue as well, and in the process treats the historical level as the only one worthy of analysis. The statements by De Vries and Wolff remind us of two other levels of the issue. Those many anonymous persons whose decisions determined the content of the prophetic literature and the shape of the canon must have operated with conscious or unconscious criteria that guided their choices about whom to portray as true or false. After the closing of the canon, the biblical presentation provides the Jewish and Christian communities with a criterion for judging which Israelite prophets were true and which false. The biblical presentation asks us to accept its verdict rather than relive the historical situation so that we might make up our own minds.[31]

---

28. De Vries, *Prophet against Prophet*, ix.
29. Wolff, "How Can We Recognize False Prophets?" 67.
30. Crenshaw, *Prophetic Conflict*, 61.
31. See the comments by Childs, "True and False Prophets," 140–42.

Confusing the levels of the issue leads Crenshaw into the same methodological inconsistency noted earlier in the work of Quell. Immediately after Crenshaw concludes that there were no adequate criteria for distinguishing between true and false prophecy in ancient Israel, he moves to a lengthy chapter discussing factors that led to false prophecy.[32] But terms like "true" and "false" are meaningless if, as Crenshaw insists, there are no means to distinguish between them. The fact that Crenshaw describes some prophets as true and others as false illustrates that for the most part he unconsciously accepts the criterion of the biblical presentation. Ironically, inattentiveness to the powerful biblical portrayal allows it to exert such a strong influence that it prevents some modern scholars from fully realizing the logical consequences of their arguments.

JAMES A. SANDERS

The work of Sanders demonstrates a subtle shift in approach. Sanders still focuses largely on the history behind the text rather than the portrayal in the text, as he seeks to discern "the full, three-dimensional situation in antiquity necessary to understand the significance of the literary record or unit under study."[33] However, Sanders is aware of the verdict rendered by the biblical portrayal, and so he is less concerned with exploring how the original audience could have discerned between true and false prophets than in understanding what made the difference between those prophets whom the biblical record depicts as true and those it portrays as false.

Since true and false prophets came to very different conclusions, even though they addressed the same historical situation and in many cases utilized the same sacral traditions, the difference must lie in their hermeneutics, the way in which they brought their authoritative traditions to bear on a given situation. Sanders follows Buber when he asserts that the false prophets tended to use their traditions and employ typology in a static way. Since God had delivered the nation in the past, he would do so again in the future. Sanders also develops more fully von Rad's and Buber's point that often the historical context (i.e.,

---

32. Crenshaw, *Prophetic Conflict*, 61, 62–90.

33. Sanders, "Hermeneutics," 21. Many of Sanders's points in this article about the hermeneutics of prophets can also be found in an earlier essay, "Jeremiah and the Future of Theological Scholarship."

Approaches to the Study of True and False Prophecy

timing) was crucial in determining the validity of the message. A true prophet listened afresh for a new word of YHWH as the historical context changed, and he applied typology and the sacred traditions in a dynamic way. For example, Ezekiel rejects as false the people's typological argument that since they are numerous they can expect to possess the land, because Abraham had received the land even though he was only one person (Ezek 33:23–29). Yet, the similar typological argument in Isa 51:1–3 is reckoned as true prophecy. The hermeneutic is the same but the timing is different, which means that sometimes false prophecy may be good theology at the wrong time.[34]

One reason prophets facing the same historical circumstances could come to radically different conclusions is that while the true prophets affirmed Israel's election traditions, they also stressed that YHWH was creator of all the nations. This made true prophets sensitive to God's freedom to use other nations to punish the chosen people.[35] Jeremiah, for example, asserts that as creator of all, YHWH has the right to give what he has created into the hands of Nebuchadnezzar (27:5–7; cf. 28:14). To view YHWH as also God of the enemy is part of what Sanders terms the "canonical monotheizing process," and in canonical terms is one of the criteria for true prophecy.[36] This is the backdrop against which Sanders interprets Jeremiah 28. Hananiah's position as he broke Jeremiah's yoke must have been something like, one must have faith that the God who led Israel out of Egypt and delivered in the past will once again protect and deliver Israel. Jeremiah's response when he returned with the iron replacement yoke might have been that the God who was strong enough to lead Israel out of bondage in Egypt and grant her the land is strong and free enough to expel her from this land. Jeremiah is a true prophet because he exercises a monotheizing hermeneutic.

As mentioned above, Sanders demonstrates a slightly different approach than earlier studies in that he recognizes and accepts the biblical portrayal of who are true and false prophets, but he continues the

---

34. Sanders, "Hermeneutics," 31–33. This insight regarding timing is important for understanding the portrayal of true and false prophecy in Jer 23:9—29:32, where both Jeremiah and the false prophets believe that God will ultimately deliver the people, but they differ on the matter of timing. The false prophets proclaim that salvation lies in the near future, whereas Jeremiah insists that deliverance lies only on the other side of judgment.

35. Ibid., 37–38.

36. Ibid., 40–41.

tradition of using the biblical portrayal in an attempt to penetrate to the historical situation behind the text. His conclusions about a monotheizing hermeneutic are somewhat helpful in illuminating the historical differences between true and false prophets because in many cases the latter were more nationalistic and chauvinistic than the former (with some exceptions like Nahum). However, the concept also has its limitations. There is little reason to suggest that Hananiah was any less "monotheistic" than Jeremiah. If one reads the text historically one can easily imagine Hananiah concurring with Jeremiah that YHWH is creator of all peoples and can even use enemy nations to punish Israel. He could have added that YHWH has already used Babylon to chasten Israel (the defeat and deportation of 598), but now God will intervene to deliver the people he has chosen above all others. The issue at stake centers less on a monotheizing hermeneutic than on the question of what YHWH will do in this case with Israel. Moving from the historical level to the level of the biblical portrayal, one should note that the text is not interested in the theological thought process that brought Hananiah and Jeremiah to their respective positions, other than to assert firmly that Jeremiah received his message directly from God.

BURKE O. LONG AND ROBERT R. WILSON

Characteristic of the studies discussed so far is the assumption that the conflict between true and false prophets was primarily theological. In contrast, Long and Wilson look for the social forces underlying such conflict. Long's goal is to recover "hints of social, economic, and political currents helpful in giving us fuller historical understanding."[37] After studying anthropological literature on conflict between intermediaries, Long concludes that such conflict is typical of contexts where intermediaries exist and results from a complex interplay of social factors including competition for status and power. In his exploration of prophetic authority, Long begins by noting that by definition authority presupposes some degree of willing acceptance by other persons.[38] Therefore, true or false prophecy is not a matter of objective criteria but of social support or lack thereof (compare Quell). When the biblical prophets found themselves in conflict situations they adopted a variety of strategies to convince people

---

37. Long, "Social Dimensions," 33.
38. Long, "Prophetic Authority," 4.

of their authority, including claiming divine mandate for their words and actions, performing powerful deeds, conforming to accepted moral and religious values, and following prophetic role expectations. While actual prophets performed such actions, in many cases tradents ascribed such activities to the prophets they venerated in an attempt to persuade others to also accept the authority of these prophets. Even telling stories about prophets and collecting materials into a prophetic book constituted attempts to claim authority.[39] This last insight is significant for understanding the book of Jeremiah and its accounts of prophetic conflict. One of the central purposes of these stories is to assert that Jeremiah's word is authoritative for the community of faith in an ongoing way.

Wilson also stresses that the only way a prophet can be effective is to gain some measure of social support.[40] As soon as a prophet claims to have received a divine revelation the process of social validation begins, as society evaluates whether to accept the prophet's experience as genuine or not. The deciding factor in this validation process is whether or not the prophet conforms to social expectations of typical prophetic behavior. Prophetic conflict occurs when prophets emerge from different social support groups having different expectations regarding normative prophetic behavior. Such conflict frequently occurs between central and peripheral prophets. Society expects its central prophets to help ensure the stability and orderly functioning of society by providing supernatural legitimation for traditional religious, political, economic, and social ideologies and institutions.[41] In contrast, peripheral prophets are expected by their support groups to advocate for changes to the basic social, political, and religions institutions that will benefit the marginalized social groups for whom these prophets are spokespersons.[42] Thus, the conflict between central and peripheral prophets is really a conflict between the interests of different social groups for whom these prophets speak. Wilson applies this analysis to Jeremiah 28, arguing that Hananiah was a central prophet whose message was rooted in the Royal–Zion theology that provided legitimation for the Judean state and the Jerusalem cult. Jeremiah was a peripheral prophet representing adherents of the Deuteronomistic view that the election of Jerusalem and the Davidic dynasty was conditional

---

39. Ibid., 15–16, 20.
40. Wilson, *Sociological Approaches*, 73; Wilson, *Prophecy and Society*, 51–56.
41. Wilson, *Sociological Approaches*, 75–76; Wilson, *Prophecy and Society*, 83–85.
42. Wilson, *Sociological Approaches*, 75; Wilson, *Prophecy and Society*, 69–73.

upon adherence to *Torah*. Hence, the conflict between Jeremiah and Hananiah was not just a matter of differing theological views "but was also a confrontation between two prophets having different social locations and different supporters."[43]

Whether or not one agrees with all of Long's and Wilson's specific conclusions, they deserve much credit for promoting methods that can significantly enhance our understanding of prophetic conflict at the historical level, and in the case of Long, also our understanding of factors involved in the shaping of the biblical text. By recognizing that religious conflicts are a complex mixture of social, political, personal, and theological factors, Wilson and Long encourage a more realistic and holistic understanding of prophetic conflict in ancient Israel. In other ways Long and Wilson stand in continuity with earlier scholars, as they continue to use the biblical depiction as a means to get at something else, namely the social factors underlying prophetic conflict in ancient Israel. The actual biblical portrayal continues to be largely overlooked, and Long even regards it as part of the problem because it suppresses what he considers to be important, namely, the economic, political, and social features of prophetic conflict.[44]

ROBERT P. CARROLL

In his numerous writings on the book of Jeremiah, Carroll pays considerable attention to the biblical portrayal of the prophet while retaining a strong diachronic interest and interpreting the text in light of the historical context out of which it reputedly emerged. Carroll begins with the conviction that the book of Jeremiah contains nothing more from the historical prophet than a few isolated poems.[45] Various exilic and post-exilic editors and redactors, especially Deuteronomists, created the Jeremiah tradition as a way to support their own agenda and address

---

43. Wilson, *Sociological Approaches*, 79. Long disagrees with Wilson's characterization of Jeremiah as a peripheral prophet, citing as evidence Jeremiah's many connections in high places. He sees Jeremiah's struggles with other prophets as part of the conflict within the Judean court between the pro-Egyptian and pro-Babylonian parties, with Jeremiah emerging as spokesperson for the group advocating cooperation with the Babylonians. See Long, "Social Dimensions," 44–49.

44. Long, "Social Dimensions," 31–33.

45. See the chapter "The Quest for the Historical Jeremiah" in Carroll, *From Chaos to Covenant*, 5–30.

issues facing their own communities.[46] The relatively obscure Jeremiah was transformed into a colossus whose words were authoritative for life in the diaspora as well as in Jehud.

One of the major concerns Jeremiah is made to address is the community's need for an explanation of the catastrophe of 587. The person of Jeremiah becomes the linchpin in this theodicy, as it is the people's persistent failure to heed his pleas for repentance that finally leads to divine judgment. The tradition sharpens the tension between Jeremiah and the false prophets because it seeks to blame these prophets for preventing the repentance necessary to save the nation. The extremely negative portrayal of the prophets is a form of scapegoating that allowed the later community to vent its collective frustration and rage. "The dominant ideology has removed virtually every trace of what they were like and presented them as the conspirators who, by their deceit, lies and immorality, destroyed the people of God."[47] Besides being a psychological projection of the later community, the prophets are also a projection of sociological conflict in the Second Temple community. "The conflict between prophets suggests such warring sects of opinion and grouping that the matter may in fact be a case of different groups bolstering their own identity by abusing their opponents. To be a false prophet is to be a member of a different prophetic guild. *Our* prophets are good, *their* prophets are bad."[48] Conflicts in the community were so intense that opponents were caricatured and vilified as a way of discrediting the opposing party. "How do you distinguish between prophets? You do not even try, you abuse, accuse and denounce."[49]

Not surprisingly, Carroll is completely skeptical about the usefulness of any criteria for true and false prophecy, but he recognizes that the biblical text does not share his skepticism. The Deuteronomistic editors "knew" who the true and false prophets were and constructed the tradition in such a way as to provide norms and guidelines for discerning between the two, so that the Second Temple community would not fall prey to the same forces that had already once destroyed the nation. Carroll goes well beyond earlier scholars in paying attention to the biblical portrayal of true and false prophecy, even though he is still largely interested

---

46. Ibid., 256–59.
47. Ibid., 195.
48. Ibid., 196.
49. Ibid., 195.

in the origins of the text and how it is a deposit of the post-587 community's psychological projections and sociological conflicts. In this sense Carroll is similar to previous scholars, because for him also the text is significant largely in terms of what it reveals about the historical context out of which it emerged. What has shifted somewhat is that he identifies this context not as the time of Jeremiah but as the post-587 period.

BREVARD S. CHILDS

Childs agrees with Crenshaw and others that in ancient Israel conflicting prophetic voices caused much confusion, particularly during the time of Jeremiah. While some of this strife is reflected in Jer 23:9—29:32, Childs asserts that the canonical process has "shaped Jeremiah's oracles with a view to overcoming the confusion and setting up a scriptural norm for distinguishing the true from the false prophet."[50] The exilic and post-exilic tradents were convinced that history had demonstrated Jeremiah to be a true prophet, and so they collected and edited his words to serve "as an authoritative means for discerning the will of God and as a norm for distinguishing the true prophet from the false. If there had been confusion during Jeremiah's lifetime, there need be no longer."[51] Scholars may be correct in concluding that criteria are ineffective in specific historical situations, but Childs points out that the canonical text actually says something quite different. Scholars often approach the matter of criteria by asking how the audience of Jeremiah and Hananiah could have discerned who spoke the true prophetic word. Childs recognizes that the biblical text does not invite us to relive the historical moment in this way. "Future generations of Israel do not stand with those who lived before the fall of Jerusalem, but with those who lived after, and who now know to distinguish [sic] the true from the false."[52] Therefore, the formation of the canon marks a watershed in terms of how the issue of true and false prophecy ought to be discussed. Childs's encouragement to pay careful attention to the actual biblical portrayal marks a major shift in the study of true and false prophecy and provides the inspiration for this book.

One of the texts on which Childs tests his approach is Jeremiah 28. He critiques what he calls the "existentialist" interpretation of von Rad,

50. Childs, "True and False Prophets," 141–42.
51. Ibid., 140–41.
52. Ibid., 141.

Buber, Sanders, and others, according to which Hananiah's opposition makes Jeremiah so unsure of himself that he expresses a few mild reservations about Hananiah's optimistic prophecy and then goes his way (28:5–11). Although Jeremiah has in the past consistently announced God's judgment, he does not refute Hananiah on the basis of a past word from God because he refuses to abstract unchanging principles from such past messages. (Both Buber and von Rad identify Hananiah's falseness with his abstracting the principle of Zion's ongoing inviolability from the prophecy of Isaiah.) Childs pays attention to the larger editorial context of 23:9—29:32 and notes how closely Jeremiah's message in ch. 28 has been shaped to parallel his oracles in ch. 27, illustrating that according to the canonical portrayal there is ongoing consistency to the prophetic word. Therefore, Jeremiah's uncertainty cannot be rooted in existential concern about whether his past message is still valid.

Despite Childs's critique of the existentialist approach, his own interpretation is similar to it in that he too makes much of Jeremiah's supposed uncertainty and his departure in silence. The difference lies in what Jeremiah is supposedly uncertain about. Instead of experiencing doubt about the continuity of the prophetic message, Jeremiah is unsure because he is open to the possibility that God has changed his plan and therefore revealed a new word to Hananiah.[53] The issue at stake is theocentric, not psychological; what will God do, not how does Jeremiah know whether or not he is right.

In the case of Jeremiah 28 Childs has not quite followed through on his own insights about the importance of the canonical portrayal. By ch. 28 Jeremiah has for twenty-seven chapters and twenty-three years (25:3) already been announcing that divine judgment is coming at the hands of the Babylonians unless the people repent. In 23:9—29:32 Jeremiah is consistently portrayed as the quintessential true prophet, in contrast to unfaithful and lying prophets who lead the nation(s) toward doom (23:9–40; 27:9–10, 14–15, 16–18; 29:8–9, 21–23, 31). Given all this, the issue in ch. 28 can hardly be that YHWH has the prerogative to change his mind and as a result Jeremiah might now have to change his message. The consistent portrayal of Jeremiah as a true prophet means that the reader should recognize Hananiah's words as false prophecy the moment he opens his mouth. Jeremiah's departure in silence when confronted by Hananiah is part of the portrayal of Jeremiah as a true prophet. The false

---

53. Ibid., 139.

prophets are accused of speaking in YHWH's name without having been sent or commissioned (23:16, 21–22, 26, 32; 29:9, 23, 31), whereas the book repeatedly refers to how the word of YHWH came to Jeremiah. A true prophet is not a debater who can toss out authoritative words at will, but speaks in God's name only when commanded. When challenged by Hananiah, Jeremiah can only respond with some cautionary words calling attention to the tradition of judgment prophecy (28:7–9), but once YHWH speaks a new word then Jeremiah can deliver an oracle responding to Hananiah's false message (28:12–16).

GERALD T. SHEPPARD

Sheppard builds on the work of Childs and Wilson as he deals with true and false prophecy at both the historical and canonical levels, recognizing that these are two discreet levels that need to be kept separate. As a way to illuminate the historical level, Sheppard uses Wilson's social-scientific analysis of Israelite prophecy to point out that while scholars may claim that no criteria are valid for distinguishing between true and false prophets, adherents of prophetic groups in ancient Israel operated with criteria that they used to decide which prophets they would heed and which not.[54] These criteria functioned only in the context of such support groups and so they changed over time and from one social context to another. Thus, when dealing with the historical level scholars should not lift criteria out of their original social context and harmonize them into a single system applicable to all prophets.

At the canonical level, Sheppard points out how Jer 23:9—29:32 leaves little doubt about who are the true and who are the false prophets. But the biblical presentation is less interested in solving the older historical problem of distinguishing between true and false prophets than "it is to offer guides to the interpretation of the words and deeds of the true 'biblical' prophets in contrast to their adversaries."[55] "For the postexilic adherents to Scripture, the biblical prophets constitute a reliable and indisputable norm of God's word in ancient Israel; one that is continually applicable to future generations of believers."[56]

54. Sheppard, "True and False Prophecy," 267.
55. Ibid., 271.
56. Ibid., 270.

Sheppard's approach is extremely helpful because, on one hand, it encourages careful research into the original historical context in which prophetic conflict occurred. On the other hand, his approach also encourages serious examination of the biblical presentation of true and false prophecy, recognizing that even though this portrayal may shed some light on original historical situations, its primary purpose is to guide the community of faith in appropriating the message of true prophecy and avoiding the disastrous consequences of false prophecy.[57]

ARMIN LANGE

Lange stands in the tradition of Hossfeld and Meyer yet also goes beyond their approach in that he explores true and false prophecy from both a redactional and tradition-historical perspective. Lange shows little interest in examining the final biblical portrayal because he is concerned with a specific historical-developmental question: "how the inner prophetic conflict of pre-exilic times could evolve in the post-exilic period into a rejection of all contemporary and future prophecy in favor of interpretation of authoritative texts" (my translation).[58] Lange uses standard historical-critical methods to group the various prophetic conflict texts into their respective periods of origin: pre-Jeremiah, Jeremiah, between Jeremiah and the Deuteronomistic redaction, the Deuteronomistic redaction of Jeremiah, and the Second Temple period rejection of prophecy, treating each as a stage on the way toward the total rejection of prophecy in this last period.

Texts prior to the time of Jeremiah usually critique prophets attached to the cult or royal court for economic abuses and for belonging

---

57. At one point I disagree with Sheppard's analysis of the biblical portrayal of true and false prophecy in Jer 23:9—29:32. He accepts Childs's view that ch. 28 portrays Jeremiah as believing YHWH might change his mind about the coming judgment, which means that Hananiah may be speaking the truth even though he is portrayed as a false prophet. Sheppard concludes that the biblical presentation "seems to retain, even to build directly upon, the very recognition that a 'false' prophet may say a true word and a 'true' prophet may utter falsehood" (Sheppard, "True and False Prophecy," 270). As indicated in my discussion of Childs, the biblical portrayal leaves no possibility that Hananiah speaks the truth but presents him as a prime example of a prophet who is utterly false. Sheppard's conclusion does apply to a story like 1 Kings 13, where an old prophet initially lies to the unwitting man of God from Judah but then later delivers a genuine word from God.

58. Lange, *Vom prophetischen Wort*, 309. See also ibid., 4, 37.

Concerning the Prophets

to an unjust and corrupt upper class.[59] The historical Jeremiah replaces this critique with condemnation of prophets who adhere to Zion theology and therefore proclaim well-being to the nation without calling for the repentance necessary to avert catastrophe. Prior to Jeremiah, the true prophetic word could be distinguished from the false only on a case-by-case basis, but Jeremiah sets in motion a process with far-reaching consequences when he lumps all other prophets together and pronounces them all false.[60] The Jeremiah tradition carries this tendency forward, as an early editor added the heading in 23:9, "Concerning the Prophets," to Jeremiah's collection of oracles condemning prophets.[61] The editor venerated Jeremiah but was seeking to reject all future prophecy as false in favor of a textual prophetic tradition.

In light of the catastrophe of 587, Deuteronomistic editors understood Jeremiah's critique of other prophets as a rejection of all contemporary and future prophecy.[62] These editors sought to counter renewed hopes connected to the rebuilding of the temple by making Jeremiah say the same harsh things about salvation prophets like Haggai and Zechariah as he had said about the salvation prophets of his own day.[63] Deuteronomistic texts do not differentiate among prophets but hold them responsible as a group for the disaster of 587 because they did not call for repentance. The Deuteronomists made no effort to establish criteria for true and false prophecy, because their rejection of all present and future prophecy made criteria unnecessary. Because the Deuteronomists viewed Jeremiah as the last in a line of true prophets they sought to preserve and actualize the Jeremiah tradition in such a way that it would speak to the community in an ongoing way.

The process set in motion by the historical Jeremiah's sharp differentiation between himself and all other prophets, which received such a massive boost by the Deuteronomists, culminated in Second Temple-period texts like Jer 23:33–40; Ezek 22:28; Zech 10:2; and 13:2–6, which

---

59. Ibid., 81–83.

60. See ibid., 130–31, for Lange's summary of the historical Jeremiah's critique of other prophets.

61. Ibid., 161–62.

62. According to Lange, the Deuteronomistic redaction of prophetic conflict passages is evident mostly in 14:13–16, 23:9–23, and chs. 27–29; see Lange, *Vom prophetischen Wort*, 185. For Lange's summary of the Deuteronomistic editors' views see ibid., 261–68.

63. Ibid., 260. See also ibid., 199, 218–19, 222–23, 241–43, 266–67.

categorically reject all prophetic activity in favor of authoritative textual prophetic traditions.[64] The process of replacing new revelation with written traditions of past revelation provided a major impulse for a larger process that eventually led to the canonization of *Torah* and Prophecy.

Lange assumes that the meaning of prophetic conflict texts depends on assigning them to their proper redactional layer and correlating them with their original historical context. He demonstrates little interest in the completed text but gleans information from it to shed light on historical and theological developments in ancient Israel, particularly as these relate to the end of prophecy. Many of Lange's arguments are based on speculative literary-critical judgments or otherwise limited evidence. The claim that the Deuteronomistic portrayal of true and false prophecy was motivated by a desire to counter the hopes fostered by Haggai and Zechariah rests on the shaky foundation that critiquing Haggai and Zechariah is the most logical explanation for a Deuteronomistic rejection of all prophecy. In my opinion, we know too little about historical and theological developments in the Second Temple period to warrant such a conclusion. Some of Lange's arguments are circular. He extracts passages from their current context in the book of Jeremiah, and on the basis of their vocabulary, allusions, concerns, and content uses the texts to describe post-exilic developments like a Deuteronomistic rejection of prophecy, and then he interprets the passages in light of such a development.[65]

Like some other scholars, Lange does not clearly distinguish between different levels of the issue of prophetic conflict, although his concern is not with criteria for distinguishing between true and false prophecy. He observes that in the Second Temple period the prophetic movement ceased, and his goal is to explain the process that led to this demise. Laying aside the question of whether or not Lange's explanation is accurate,

64. Ibid., 306–8. For Lange's summary of the entire developmental process see 309–18. In my opinion Lange's description of a straightforward, linear process oversimplifies the situation and does not do justice to the presentation of true and false prophecy in the book of Jeremiah. I find more plausible John Hill's theory that the renunciation of prophecy in Zech 13:2–6 reflects a different estimation of prophecy than we see in the Jeremiah traditions. See Hill, "The Book of Jeremiah MT and Early Second Temple Conflicts"; and Hill, "The Book of Jeremiah (MT)," 163–67. Hill demonstrates how the MT version of the book highlights the person and role of Jeremiah much more than does the LXX, because the MT seeks to present prophecy and prophets, both true and false, as normal features of community life. See Hill, "The Book of Jeremiah MT and Early Second Temple Conflicts," 41.

65. For a helpful caution about such circular reasoning, see Habel, *The Land Is Mine*, 8.

it seems to me that he projects onto the biblical portrayal what he believes to be true at the historical level. Except perhaps for Zech 13:2–6, no biblical text clearly rejects all future prophetic activity in favor of written prophetic traditions. A passage like Jer 23:33–40 can only be made to reject all prophetic activity if extracted from its present literary context and read in light of some other scholarly reconstruction of historical or literary context. The book of Jeremiah certainly demonstrates a growing authority attached to textual prophetic traditions, as illustrated by the numerous references to documents reflecting the plans and purposes of God (25:13; 29:1, 3–9; 30:2; 36:2–3, 4, 32; 45:1; 51:60–63). However, by stressing the importance of a true prophet like Jeremiah, by referring positively to Jeremiah's contemporary Uriah (26:20), and by highlighting the importance of a long line of prophets sent by God (7:25–26; 25:4; 26:5, 18–19; 35:15; 44:4), the book creates the impression that since God has provided ongoing prophetic guidance in the past he will continue to do so in the future. Because Lange interprets texts in light of their reputed original historical context, not acknowledging that the meaning of these texts might change once they are incorporated into a new literary context, he seems unaware that the biblical portrayal is quite different than his historical reconstruction, which he then projects onto the biblical text.

MARVIN A. SWEENEY

Marvin Sweeney picks up numerous threads from previous studies of true and false prophecy. He too expresses skepticism regarding the validity of criteria, because true prophecy cannot be empirically verified any more than can the existence of God or any claim to speak on God's behalf.[66] This leads him to acknowledge along with Wilson, Long, and Sheppard that prophetic truth claims are contingent upon the willingness of an audience to accept such claims. Sweeney pays some attention to the biblical portrayal as he highlights how Deut 18:21–22 proposes non-fulfillment as a criterion for judging prophecies to be false. But he immediately pulls back from the biblical account when he emphasizes that this criterion renders aspects of the canonical books of the prophets false because they contain numerous unfulfilled prophecies, especially of restoration.[67]

---

66. Sweeney, "The Truth in True and False Prophecy," 9–11.
67. Ibid., 11–13.

The bulk of Sweeney's article deals with the issue of prophetic conflict at the historical level and explores the roots of such conflict. Building on points touched on by von Rad and others, Sweeney asserts that the prophets' diverse theological and sociological roots account for much of the conflict. Isaiah's prophecy is heavily informed by Jerusalem's David and Zion traditions, Jeremiah is a Levitical priest shaped by Deuteronomistic *Torah* traditions, and Ezekiel is a Zadokite priest rooted in traditions about the holiness of the temple.[68] Sweeney claims that one of the major differences between Jeremiah and his prophetic opponents lies in how they apply the Isaiah tradition to a new historical context. Jeremiah focuses on Isaiah's call to repentance and God's use of an enemy nation to chastise unrepentant Zion, whereas his opponents privilege the Isaianic theme of God's deliverance of Zion.[69] The confrontation between Jeremiah and Hananiah hinges on just such conflicting appropriation of Isaiah traditions in the context of the new threat of Babylon.

Following this analysis of historical, theological, and sociological factors that spawned prophetic conflict, Sweeney concludes that truth in prophecy lies not just in the issue of fulfillment but depends on when and how that fulfillment occurs. The conflict among prophets and the fact that the truth of earlier prophetic tradition is relative to how it is applied and realized in new historical circumstances means that truth must be recognized as a contingent category, both within the Bible and among its interpreters, with the consequence that we must always acknowledge that the canonical prophets might be false.[70]

Sweeney exhibits methodological imprecision similar to what we have seen elsewhere. He begins by noting that prophecy cannot be empirically validated, not even on the basis of Deuteronomy's criterion of fulfillment. Yet, under the influence of the powerful canonical portrayal Sweeney continues to operate within the categories of true and false prophecy even though his postmodern eschewing of valid criteria for distinguishing between them should render the categories meaningless. Sweeney accepts one feature of the biblical portrayal, namely the criterion of fulfillment, and uses it to challenge another feature of the biblical portrayal, namely the truthfulness of prophets like Jeremiah, without

---

68. Ibid., 13.
69. Ibid., 15–20, 25.
70. Ibid., 26.

explaining why one aspect of the biblical portrayal should be privileged over another.

In the postmodern context there is no question that truth is contingent, as Sweeney correctly notes, but this is not how the Bible presents prophetic conflict. Whether it be Jeremiah's confrontation with Hananiah or Micaiah's conflict with the four hundred court prophets of Ahab, the canon displays no postmodern doubt over who speaks divine truth and who does not. As is common among studies of true and false prophecy, Sweeney mines the actual biblical depiction for information to illuminate the historical situation behind the text. This focus on history shifts attention away from the biblical portrayal at the same time as it allows this portrayal to still exercise unconscious influence because it is the unacknowledged elephant in the room.

R. W. L. MOBERLY

Whereas most studies of true and false prophecy eschew explicit theological agenda, Moberly embraces such an agenda. His goal is to explore the issue of discernment with the theological and pastoral needs of the church in mind. He begins by discussing how the Bible presents its claim that prophets and other figures are able to speak for God. Christian faith rests upon both the claim that divine communication occurs through human mediation and upon the capacity to test claims that someone has spoken truthfully for God.[71] This issue extends well beyond the phenomenon of prophecy, but Moberly uses prophecy as a means to explore what is at stake in this larger issue. Discernment is critical because the claim that human beings can speak for God makes possible deception, manipulation, as well as conflicting views expressed in good faith. Moberly does not use the biblical text to reconstruct historical situations but searches the biblical portrayal for criteria to distinguish the true from the false word, with the ultimate goal of helping the contemporary faith community discern truth from falsehood.[72]

Moberly observes, as my review of the literature also does, that scholars normally engage the issue in terms of historical-critical categories with little concern for the Bible's own frame of reference. Moberly is

---

71. Moberly, *Prophecy and Discernment*, 12, 222.

72. Ibid. See for example p. 1, and the entire last chapter, titled "Prophecy and Discernment Today?" 221–54.

particularly critical of Crenshaw for marginalizing theological concerns by framing the issue in terms of prophetic conflict instead of discernment.[73] Moberly rejects the prevailing secular approach that seeks to explain prophetic conflict in terms of social, psychological, and cultural factors and thereby lacks the ability to speak about God and communication from God in theologically meaningful ways.[74]

Moberly also rejects the consensus that no criteria are valid for discerning between a true and false prophetic word. His survey of biblical texts finds two consistent criteria: the moral integrity of the prophet, and a message that challenges complacent self-will and calls for repentance and righteous living. These two are closely related in that the message and the messenger form a single communicative entity, because claims about the invisible divine realm are validated by the character, conduct, and priorities of the messenger who speaks for that realm. Moral failure on the part of an intermediary induces spiritual blindness and leads to a false message, because what is seen depends as much on the condition of the person seeing as upon the object of discernment.[75]

Moberly finds both criteria at work in the book of Jeremiah, which consistently challenges the people's complacency and summons them to repent and follow a *Torah* way of life.[76] Jeremiah 23:9–22 condemns other prophets for their adultery and immorality and for failure to turn evildoers from their destructive path, critiques illustrating that these prophets are self-willed and have not been sent by God or stood in the divine council. Standing in the council of YHWH does not involve some unusual visionary or psychological experience but involves a disposition responsive to God so that the prophet's character, conduct, and vision of the world are reshaped by appropriation of the divine will.[77] Moberly finds the same two criteria at play in 1 Kings 22. Unlike the four hundred prophets who utter what their patron wishes to hear, Micaiah is a prophet of personal integrity willing to suffer in the interests of speaking divine truth. Micaiah's words of judgment on Ahab cut through the king's self-serving desire to expand his territory and seek to alter his course of

---

73. Ibid., 15–17.
74. Ibid., 15–38, 221–22, especially 17, 31, 222.
75. Ibid., 147.
76. Ibid., 43–70.
77. Ibid., 81.

action so that he and his people might be spared defeat in war.[78] Moberly acknowledges that most texts that stress the morality of a prophet, including those in Jeremiah, remain quite vague in terms of the specifics of the moral life. He claims that such texts presuppose a more comprehensive vision of God and the faithful life that is not delineated in the narrative but is expressed in the larger biblical context.[79]

Because Moberly is interested in the issue of discernment from a Christian theological perspective, his study includes the entire Christian Scripture. In New Testament texts from Matthew, 1 John, and the Pauline letters he finds the same pattern and criteria at play as in the Old Testament, except that morality is now defined in terms of a Christ-centered mode of life.[80]

Moberly makes at least three significant contributions to the study of true and false prophecy. First, he highlights how prophetic conflict is part of a larger biblical issue, namely, how can human words communicate a word from God, and how can the faith community evaluate the truth or falsehood of claims to speak such a word? Second, Moberly models the benefits of paying attention to the actual biblical portrayal of true and false prophecy. Third, he demonstrates that personal morality and a message challenging complacency and calling for faithful living are central to the Bible's depiction of true prophecy. Christians might add a fourth contribution, the elucidation of an important biblical topic in such a way as to assist the contemporary faith community in its task of discerning true from false.

Moberly's focus on the biblical portrayal moves the conversation on true and false prophecy forward in helpful ways, but his focus on discernment and criteria for discernment means that significant features of the biblical depiction of true and false prophecy remain outside his interest. For example, he touches only lightly on Jer 23:9—29:32, which contains the largest block of prophetic conflict material in the Bible. Moreover, focusing on two criteria does not always illuminate the entire biblical depiction. For example, neither in the classic confrontation between Jeremiah and Hananiah nor in the preceding chapter containing three warnings about false prophets (27:9–10, 14–15, 16–18) is there any hint that the personal morality of the prophets is at stake. Moberly seems a bit

---

78. Ibid., 117–20.
79. Ibid., 233–35.
80. Ibid., 150–220, 225–26.

overconfident in the adequacy of the two criteria he identifies. As numerous scholars point out, truth and falsehood and criteria for distinguishing between them are always contingent upon an audience willing to accept such claims. Even definitions about what is moral are contested. Moberly does acknowledge that claims about truth cannot ultimately be proved but must be accepted in faith, but this point is important enough to merit more attention than one paragraph and a brief footnote.[81] Moberly's discussion could be enriched by greater attention to how conversations about truth and falsehood and criteria are meaningful only within the context of a community that already shares certain foundational convictions.[82]

ANTHONY CHINEDU OSUJI

Osuji approaches the issue of true and false prophecy somewhat indirectly. His major goal is to counter the readings of Robert Carroll and others who claim that the book of Jeremiah is so filled with ruptures, tensions, and disjunctions that it cannot be read as a coherent and meaningful whole. Osuji explores Jeremiah 26–29 using narrative criticism, which he describes as a synchronic approach that recognizes how a text may be composite in origins but nonetheless seeks meaning in the world created by the final text rather than in the reconstructed history of composition. Osuji pays attention to "the use, repetition, and arrangement of words, structural patterns, shifts in voices, deliberate verbal strategies that cause breaks, surprises, contrasts, comparisons, ambiguities, and open-ended marvel in the text."[83] His major conclusion is that Jeremiah 26–29 in its final form is a single literary unit demonstrating strong thematic coherence, held together by the central theme of true and false prophecy.[84]

---

81. See ibid., 226.

82. James E. Brenneman adopts a postmodern, reader-response approach to argue that all claims about truth and falsehood in relation to true and false prophecy can only be, and in practice always have been, adjudicated by interpretive communities who inevitably operate with prior faith commitments. See Brenneman, *Canons in Conflict*, 9, 43, 46–47, 90, 109, 140–43. Brenneman's study is not summarized here because he pays only minimal attention to the actual biblical portrayal of true and false prophecy and concentrates on the process of contemporary appropriation.

83. Osuji, *Where Is the Truth?*, 62. For a fuller discussion of Osuji's methodology see ibid., 61–74.

84. Ibid., especially 263–321.

Concerning the Prophets

While there is considerable overlap between Osuji's work and my own, in that we both offer a synchronic analysis of the portrayal of true and false prophecy, there are also significant differences. Osuji presents an exhaustive narrative exegesis of Jeremiah 26–29 and so his focus in on virtually all features of the text, not just the presentation of true and false prophecy. Secondly, Osuji accepts the common division of the book of Jeremiah into two parts, chs. 1–25 supposedly portraying the death and dismantling of the state of Judah and its cultic symbol system, and chs. 26–52 preparing for planting and rebuilding after the catastrophe of 587.[85] This leads him to treat Jeremiah 26–29 as a literary unit, rather than 23:9—29:32 as I do, which in turn leads Osuji to interpret the content of 26–29 largely in isolation from what precedes it. He claims, for example, that the focus of Jeremiah 26 is the legitimation of Jeremiah as YHWH's true prophet.[86] This conclusion overlooks how chs. 1–25, and especially 23:9—25:38, have already consistently confirmed that Jeremiah is a true prophet. In chapter 6 of this book I will demonstrate that by the time the reader arrives at Jeremiah 26 there is no further need to legitimate Jeremiah, but rather the focus in ch. 26 is squarely on proper and improper responses to the prophetic summons to repentance.

Osuji's inattention to the larger context also influences his interpretation of Jeremiah's confrontation with Hananiah. Like Buber and others, Osuji makes much of Jeremiah's supposed uncertainly when Hananiah contradicts his message that all nations must submit to the Babylonian yoke. Osuji claims that Jeremiah's initial withdrawal demonstrates his openness to the possibility that YHWH may have changed his mind and may now be speaking a new word through Hananiah.[87] Jeremiah needed to learn that YHWH was free and not bound even to a past divine word. Jeremiah believes in listening to the other, with whom he dialogues in a common quest for truth. One distinction between a true and false prophet is that the latter claims infallibility, while a true prophet like Jeremiah recognizes that God can speak through the other and that he himself can make mistakes.[88] This conclusion leads Osuji to observe that

---

85. Ibid., 5, 100–110.
86. Ibid., 121.
87. Ibid., 214–15, 387–91.
88. Ibid., 388.

human beings should always be reticent in matters pertaining to truth, and should cherish the contemporary benefits of religious pluralism.[89]

While I concur with Osuji's convictions about the value of humility, openness, and pluralism, I do not see such values reflected in the text. As already discussed, the book of Jeremiah's consistent portrayal of Jeremiah as YHWH's true prophet, especially in 23:9 and following, and the book's unwavering assertion that Babylonian hegemony is inevitable both indicate that in ch. 28 there is no possibility whatsoever that Hananiah could be speaking for God and that Jeremiah needs to learn that YHWH may change his mind. Moreover, in Jeremiah 26–29 all the prophets who contradict Jeremiah are condemned as false and consigned to their doom (Hananiah—28:15–17; Ahab and Zedekiah—29:21–23; Shemiah—29:31–32). Such features of the text hardly encourage pluralism or contribute to a depiction of Jeremiah as a prophet who doubts his message from YHWH and is interested in dialogue with the prophets who are portrayed as false. Reading Jeremiah 28 in the context of 23:9—29:32 can lead to greater clarity about the actual portrayal of true and false prophecy in the chapter.

Despite my disagreement with some of Osuji's conclusions, many of his fine exegetical insights make their way into my own analysis, and I am grateful for how he models the fruitfulness of a synchronic approach to the study of true and false prophecy.

CONCLUSION

This selective review of the research into true and false prophecy highlights how much of the scholarly literature is diachronic in orientation and uses the biblical text in order to shed light on the historical and social contexts that may have given rise to the text. Closely related to this is the preoccupation with the issue of criteria, often focused on how the original Israelite audience could or could not discern between true and false prophets. Given the limited amount of data to work with, the results of scholarly research have been truly impressive in providing insight into the nature of prophetic conflict in ancient Israel.

This review of the literature also demonstrates how little attention scholars have devoted to exploring the actual biblical presentation of true and false prophecy. Yet this portrayal is so powerful that even though

---

89. Ibid., 401–2.

some scholars do not consciously take it into account, they still come under its sway and continue to speak of true and false prophecy even when their arguments about the lack of criteria for distinguishing between the two should lead them to suggest that such categories are meaningless. Despite the positive start made by scholars like Childs, Sheppard, Moberly, Osuji, and to some extent Carroll, much remains to be done in terms of exploring the actual biblical presentation of true and false prophecy. The following chapters seek to move this agenda forward by exploring the portrayal of true and false prophecy in Jer 23:9—29:32.

2

The Concentric Structure of Jeremiah 23:9—29:32

JEREMIAH 23:9—29:32 AS A SINGLE EDITORIAL UNIT

A STATEMENT BY BREVARD CHILDS first led me to investigate whether Jer 23:9—29:32 might be a single editorial unit. In speaking of Jer 27-28 Childs writes, "There is general agreement that both chapters are part of a larger editorial unit which begins in 23:9 with the superscription 'concerning the prophets', and extends through ch. 29."[1] Great scholars sometimes have brilliant intuitive insights, even though in this case Childs has not backed up his insight with concrete evidence. In spite of Childs's observation, the vast majority of scholars do not consider 23:9—29:32 to be an editorial unit and many continue the tradition of viewing ch. 25 as a major break or hinge in the book of Jeremiah.[2] Also, the consensus among commentators is that the heading in 23:9, "Concerning the Prophets [לַנְּבִאִים]," applies only to the oracles against false prophets in 23:9-40.

---

1. Childs, "True and False Prophets," 137.

2. The only scholar I know of who concurs with Childs is Sheppard, in "True and False Prophecy," 263, 273. Moberly, *Prophecy and Discernment*, 101, cites Childs's opinion in a footnote with some approval but no supporting evidence.

Concerning the Prophets

Three pieces of evidence demonstrate that Childs's intuitive insight regarding 23:9—29:32 is correct. The first is that most of the material in these chapters deals explicitly with the portrayal of true and false prophecy and the conflict between them (23:9-40; 25:1-7; chs. 26, 27, 28, 29). The bulk of such material in the book of Jeremiah is now located in chs. 23-29, just as most of the salvation oracles are now found in chs. 30-33, which are easily recognizable as a thematic unit. Nowhere else in the Old Testament is there such a large amount of material dealing with true and false prophecy within the span of a few chapters or even an entire book. Other passages in the book of Jeremiah that condemn false prophets or deal with prophetic conflict are all brief and isolated from each other (2:8, 26; 4:9; 5:12-13, 30-31; 6:13-15; 8:1-3, 10-12; 13:12-14; 14:13-16, 18; 18:18; 20:1-6; 32:31-33; 37:18-19).

A second piece of evidence suggesting that 23:9—29:32 constitutes a single editorial unit is the heading "Concerning the Prophets" (23:9). This title is analogous to the one in 21:11, "Concerning the House of the King of Judah [וּלְבֵית מֶלֶךְ יְהוּדָה]," which stands over the material in 21:11—23:8 that consists of oracles concerning various kings and concludes with the promise of a future ideal king.[3] There are no similar headings or obvious introductions after 23:9 until 30:1-4, where Jeremiah is commissioned to record on a scroll words of hope for Israel and Judah, words of salvation now found in chs. 30-33. The lack of other headings in chs. 23-29 is significant but certainly not decisive, because if the book of Jeremiah always provided clear titles or introductions to new sections there would not be so much confusion and disagreement among scholars about the organization of the book.

Given that 21:11—23:8 (or perhaps 21:1—23:8) constitutes an editorial unit that very clearly focuses on kingship, and given that chs. 30-33 constitute a section that obviously focuses on restoration, each having a heading or introduction, it should not be surprising that in between stands another section with its own clear focus—prophets, as the heading in 23:9 indicates. The effect of joining material dealing with kings and prophets is to lay responsibility for the catastrophe of 587 at the feet

---

3. Commentators agree that 21:11—23:8 is a block of text focusing on the denunciation of Judah's kings. It appears that after 21:11—23:8 already existed as a unit, the section was prefaced by the story of how Zedekiah consults Jeremiah about the fate of the nation, a story that has affinities with what follows but is in some ways also quite different. Many commentators now treat all of 21:1—23:8 as a unit dealing with the kings of Judah.

of both the royal house and the false prophets.[4] Since the section on the prophets contains assurances of deliverance (24:5-7; 27:21-22; 29:10-14, 32) it leads quite smoothly into the following section, which consists mostly of such promises of deliverance interspersed with consistent reminders of the destruction foretold in the previous sections (30:5-7, 11-15, 23-24; 31:15; 32:1-5, 23-24, 28-36; 33:4-5, 10).

The third and most important piece of evidence for the editorial unity of 23:9—29:32 is structure. As chart 1 illustrates, the material is laid out in a concentric pattern consisting of seven parts.[5] Section A (23:9-40) condemns false prophets in general, while its counterpart A' (29:20-32) condemns several specific false prophets for some of the same offenses denounced in A. Section B (24:1-10) records the true prophet Jeremiah's vision of the good and bad figs; the good figs symbolizing the exiles who will receive God's grace and the rotten figs symbolizing the non-exiles who will experience divine wrath. In B' (29:1-19) Jeremiah writes a letter to the exiles in which he advises them to make the best of life in Babylon, and then he makes the same points as in section B about God's grace toward the exiles and God's wrath toward the non-exiles. Sections C (25:1-38) and C' (27:1—28:17) both describe symbolic actions by Jeremiah, predict Babylonian hegemony over Judah and the nations, and stress that Judah's fate is intertwined with the fate of the nations. At the heart of the concentric structure stands ch. 26, which deals with the central issue of the entire unit—how God's people should respond to the word of a true prophet.

---

4. This has long been recognized by commentators. See for example Nötscher, *Das Buch Jeremias*, 177; Weiser, *Das Buch Jeremia*, 201; Carroll, *Jeremiah*, 404.

5. Walsh asserts that it is important to distinguish between two forms of reverse symmetry: chiasm (ABCDD'C'B'A', with two parallel units at the center), and concentric structure (ABCDC'B'A', with one unit at the center). See Walsh, *Style and Structure*, 13-14. I will follow Walsh's suggestion even though many scholars are not so precise and do not make a significant distinction between chiasm and concentric structure.

Concerning the Prophets

Structure of Jer 23:9—29:32

A 23:9–40   Condemnation of false prophets in general

  B 24:1–10   Jeremiah's true prophecy—a vision regarding exiles and non-exiles
- hope for the exiles
- doom for the non-exiles

    C 25:1–38   Jeremiah's true prophecy

      The symbolic cup—destruction of Judah and the nations by Nebuchadnezzar king of Babylon

      D 26:1–24   Proper and improper responses to true prophecy

        26:1–16   Jeremiah is almost killed

          26:17–19   Micah inspires repentance

        26:20–24   Uriah is killed

    C' 27:1—28:17   Jeremiah's true prophecy

      The symbolic yoke—Judah and the nations must serve Nebuchadnezzar king of Babylon

  B' 29:1–19   Jeremiah's true prophecy—a letter regarding exiles and non-exiles
- instructions for living in exile
- hope for the exiles
- doom for the non-exiles

A' 29:20–32   Condemnation of specific false prophets

The Concentric Structure of Jeremiah 23:9—29:32

The LXX places the oracles concerning the nations after 25:13, thereby disrupting my proposed concentric pattern. A detailed comparison below of the MT and LXX versions of 23:9—29:32 will demonstrate that the MT contains numerous additions that enhance the parallels between corresponding panels, indicating that the Masoretic redaction has deliberately amplified the concentric features while the LXX redaction has disrupted the concentric structure by inserting the oracles concerning the nations into ch. 25.

Another objection to my outline of 23:9—29:32 might be that Jer 1–25 appears to form a unit or "book" of some sort. It seems that 25:1-13 may have been composed as a concluding summary to an earlier collection of Jeremiah material, as these verses offer a retrospective view on Jeremiah's already lengthy ministry (see especially 25:3-7, 13).[6] The dating of 1:1-3 is coordinated with that of 25:1-3 (compare especially 1:2 and 25:3), while 1:13-16 and 25:3-13 share thematic links and common vocabulary. The people have been evil (1:16; 25:5), have forsaken YHWH (1:16; 25:6), and worshipped the works of their own hands (1:16; 25:6-7), and therefore YHWH will summon enemy nations from the north against them (1:14-15; 25:9). In ch. 1 Jeremiah is called to be a prophet to the nations (1:5, 10), a commission he carries out in ch. 25.[7]

These connections between chs. 1 and 25 lead some scholars to suggest that the core material of these chapters at one time constituted a "book" concluded by 25:13, which states that YHWH will bring upon Babylon all that is recorded in this book that Jeremiah prophesied against all the nations.[8] On the basis of this hypothesis it is only a small step to propose that this collection, which included the words of Jeremiah spoken between his call and the fourth year of Jehoiakim (see 25:1, 3), is essentially the expanded scroll that Jeremiah dictated to Baruch, also in the fourth year of Jehoiakim (36:32).[9] Many recent scholars are more modest

---

6. In contrast to the views of many commentators, Aejmelaeus argues that 25:1-14 was not formulated as a summary of the first part of the book but represents a late composition designed to prepare the way for the insertion of the oracles concerning the nations into ch. 25. See Aejmelaeus, "Jeremiah at the Turning-Point of History," 475-76.

7. For a helpful discussion of how 25:1-14 "concludes" the first part of the book of Jeremiah see Stulman, *Order amid Chaos*, 36-38; Miller, "The Book of Jeremiah," 761; Hill, *Friend or Foe?*, 90-92.

8. See for example Bright, *Jeremiah*, lvii–lviii; Thompson, *The Book of Jeremiah*, 28; Albertz, *Israel in Exile*, 312-15.

9. See for example Holladay, *Jeremiah*, 1:664; and Miller, *Meet the Prophets*, 151-55.

in their claims and focus on how ch. 25 supposedly marks a major break in the completed book of Jeremiah, without linking this assertion to speculation regarding the history of the book's composition. Numerous commentators divide the book into two sections, chs. 1–25 and 26–52,[10] while others speak of ch. 25 as the hinge between major sections of the book or as one of the pillars upon which the book rests.[11]

I suspect that at some point in the complex compositional history of the book ch. 25 did mark the end of a collection of some kind, which would account for the retrospective character of 25:1–13 and for the significant parallels between chs. 1 and 25. At later points editors may have spliced material into these chapters and added material to the end as the book continued to grow. However, in the MT version of the book the break at ch. 25 is minimized, as later editors have incorporated the chapter into the larger unit 23:9—29:32 while at the same time not obscuring what might be elements of an earlier editorial scheme. These earlier elements, combined with the LXX's insertion of the oracles concerning the nations into ch. 25, encourage scholars to see ch. 25 as constituting a major break in the book.

David Carr suggests that the book of Isaiah is governed by more than one set of synchronic connections and that it has been edited on the basis of more than one macrostructure, with some tradents guided by the break between chs. 33 and 34 and others by the break between chs. 39 and 40, and still others essentially ignoring these breaks.[12] It is

10. It is common to publish commentaries in two volumes with the break falling between chs. 25 and 26. See Holladay, *Jeremiah*, 2 vols.; McKane, *A Critical and Exegetical Commentary*, 2 vols.; Brueggemann, *To Pluck Up, to Tear Down: A Commentary on the Book of Jeremiah 1–25*; Brueggemann, *To Build, to Plant: A Commentary on Jeremiah 26–52*. Stulman attaches considerable theological significance to the supposed break between chs. 25 and 26, asserting that chs. 1–25 focus on the death and dismantling of Judah's social and symbolic support systems while chs. 26–52 declare that God's grace and mercy ensure that the community will survive the ordeal of destruction and exile. See Stulman, *Jeremiah*, xix, 233–35; Stulman, *Order amid Chaos*, 23–71. Leuchter's two monographs argue on the basis of compositional and thematic grounds for dividing the book at ch. 25. See Leuchter, *Josiah's Reform and Jeremiah's Scroll*; and Leuchter, *The Polemics of Exile*. Yates finds structural and thematic features that link chs. 26–45 and demarcate them from the first part of the book, in Yates, "Narrative Parallelism and the 'Jehoiakim Frame.'"

11. Fretheim, *Jeremiah*, 18; Smelik, "An Approach to the Book of Jeremiah," 7, 9; Kessler, "Jeremiah 25,1–29," 44–70, especially pp. 63–64, 68–69; Kessler, "The Function of Chapters 25 and 50–51"; Kessler, "The Scaffolding of the Book of Jeremiah," 65–66.

12. Carr, "Moving beyond Unity," 92.

quite possible that the book of Jeremiah exhibits similar complexity and that some tradents treated ch. 25 as a major break in the book while the editorial activity of others minimized this break. Perhaps one reason that Jeremiah scholars have proposed so many different structural schemes for the book is that different tradents have in fact worked on the basis of different schemes.

Many of the parallels between the corresponding panels of 23:9—29:32 have been observed by numerous commentators, but the structural significance of these parallels has gone unnoticed, partly obscured by the conviction that ch. 25 marks a major break in the book. The concentric features in 23:9—29:32 are not as obvious as in some other examples of reverse symmetry, but these features are numerous, deliberate, and fairly obvious once highlighted, as the next section of this chapter demonstrates.

PARALLELS BETWEEN CORRESPONDING PANELS OF 23:9—29:32

B (24:1–10): Jeremiah's True Prophecy—A Vision Regarding Exiles and Non-Exiles and B' (29:1–19): Jeremiah's True Prophecy—A Letter Regarding Exiles and Non-Exiles

My detailed explanation of the concentric structure of 23:9—29:32 begins by focusing on sections B and B' because the parallels between these two sections are the most obvious. Jeremiah's vision of the good and bad figs (24:1–10) seems out of place within the larger unit of 23:9—29:32 because it does not relate thematically to the oracles against the prophets in 23:9–40, nor does it have significant connections to ch. 25. Chronologically, Jeremiah's vision of the figs occurs during Zedekiah's reign after the deportation of 598, while ch. 25 is dated earlier, to the fourth year of Jehoiakim. Such "disarray" can lead to judgments about how disorganized the book of Jeremiah is, or it can lead to probing questions about why editors would arrange the text in such an apparently odd way. There would seem to be little reason to place Jeremiah's vision of the good and bad figs in its present location except to balance Jeremiah's letter to the exiles within the larger concentric structure.

The similarities between 24:1–10 and 29:1–19 abound.[13] Both passages are unique in the book of Jeremiah in that they differentiate so

---

13. Commentators have noted many of these similarities. See for example Miller,

strongly between exiles and non-exiles and the respective fate that awaits each group. At the outset both texts are dated to the same time period and mention many of the same persons. Jeremiah sees his vision of the figs *after Nebuchadrezzar had taken into exile from Jerusalem King Jeconiah, the officials of Judah, and the craftsmen and smiths* (24:1).[14] In ch. 29 Jeremiah sends a letter addressed to the priests, prophets, and the rest of the elders in exile whom *Nebuchadnezzar had taken into exile from Jerusalem* after *King Jeconiah,* the queen mother, the eunuchs, *the officials of Judah* and Jerusalem, *and the craftsmen and smiths* had left Jerusalem (29:1–2). The interpretation of Jeremiah's vision is that the good figs represent the exiles whom YHWH will favor and restore to the land. In addition, YHWH will bring about their spiritual renewal and restore his covenant relationship with them (24:5–7). In 29:4–14 the focus is also on the exiles of 598 and here too YHWH promises them physical restoration upon their land and a spiritual renewal (29:10–14). In both sections the future salvation is designated as the "good" (טוב) that YHWH will do (24:5, 6; 29:10). One difference between Jeremiah's vision and his letter is that the letter begins by providing guidance for how to live in exile (29:5–9).

It appears that the message of hope for the exiles in 29:10–14, which parallels the message of hope in 24:5–7, is an addition.[15] The admonition in 29:8–9 not to heed the lying prophets and diviners in exile is continued by v. 15, which criticizes the exiles for listening to just such prophets. The intrusive verses about the deliverance of the exiles (29:10–14) may have been added to make Jeremiah's letter parallel more closely the interpretation of Jeremiah's vision of the figs. Recognizing the purpose of some of the editorial changes to the text uncovers the intentionality behind what might otherwise appear as disruptions.

Most striking is the insertion of vv. 16–19 into ch. 29, verses that most commentators recognize as intrusive and secondary. Jeremiah has been quoting the exiles to the effect that YHWH has raised up prophets for them in Babylon (29:15), which is nicely followed up in vv. 20–23 by

"The Book of Jeremiah," 793; Keown et al., *Jeremiah 26–52,* 67; Brueggemann, *A Commentary on Jeremiah,* 255–56; Lundbom, *Jeremiah 21–36,* 223, 349.

14. Unless otherwise indicated, all italics in cited biblical material are my own for purposes of emphasis.

15. After arriving at this conclusion, I discovered that I was not alone in my opinion. See Wanke, *Untersuchungen,* 50; Carroll, *Jeremiah,* 557. Most commentators recognize the "disturbed" nature of the text in the first half of ch. 29. Miller, "The Book of Jeremiah," 791, suggests that at one point the order may have been 29:1–14, 16–20, 15, 21–23.

condemnation of two such prophets. The off-the-topic insertion of vv. 16–19 is an oracle of judgment promising absolute annihilation of the non-exiles. The text offers its own clue as to why editors would disrupt a smooth-flowing text with this addition. In 29:17 YHWH promises to treat the king and the other non-exiles as *"disgusting figs that cannot be eaten because they are rotten,"* a direct reference to Jeremiah's vision of the good and bad figs where YHWH promises to treat Zedekiah and the other non-exiles as rotten figs that cannot be eaten.[16] In both chapters the judgment will entail, among other things, the triad of sword, famine, and pestilence (24:10; 29:17, 18). YHWH will make the people "a horror [an evil] to all the kingdoms of the earth" (וּנְתַתִּים לְזַוֲעָה [לְרָעָה] לְכֹל מַמְלְכוֹת הָאָרֶץ) (24:9; 29:18). Both 24:9 and 29:18 use a number of different terms, including "disgrace" (חֶרְפָּה), to describe the degradation YHWH will inflict on the people in the place to which he will banish (root: נדח) them. It appears that editors have added vv. 16–19 and 10–14 to Jeremiah's letter in order to make it parallel the figs vision in ch. 24:

24:1–3	Jeremiah sees two baskets of figs	29:1–3	Jeremiah writes a letter to the exiles
		29:4–9	instructions for living in exile
24:4–7	hope for the exiles	29:10–14	hope for the exiles
24:8–10	doom for the non-exiles	29:15–19	doom for the non-exiles

It is striking that the "awkward" insertion of 29:16–19 is entirely lacking in the LXX, and so sections B and B' do not correspond nearly as closely in the LXX as they do in the MT. Also, the MT of 24:1 and 29:1 mentions the name Nebuchadnezzar, while the LXX has the name only in 24:1. In 24:1 both the LXX and MT mention the officials of Judah, but only the MT contains the parallel phrase in the corresponding panel, "the officials of Judah and Jerusalem" (29:2). Already on the basis of this limited evidence it appears that the concentric features of 23:9—29:32 are more pronounced in the MT than in the LXX.[17]

---

16. Some scholars have long noted that 29:16–19 is an addition based on 24:8–10, but they have not recognized the full significance of this observation. See for example Weiser, *Das Buch Jeremia*, 255; Lindblom, *Prophecy in Ancient Israel*, 228; Schmidt, "Einsicht und Zuspruch," 397. Allen, *Jeremiah*, 326–27, asserts that 29:17–18 is derived from 24:8–10 and that the connection was sparked by the similarities between the two respective promises of deliverance (24:5–7; 29:10–14).

17. By no means all or even the majority of the differences between the LXX and

A (23:9–40): Condemnation of False Prophets in General
A' (29:20–32): Condemnation of Specific False Prophets

Section A (23:9–40) consists of once-independent units of material that condemn unnamed prophets for a variety of offenses and stress that YHWH will inflict harsh punishment upon them (23:12, 15, 30–32, 33, 34). Section A' (29:20–32) names three specific prophets (Ahab, Zedekiah, and Shemaiah), accuses them of some of the offenses mentioned in 23:9–40 (prophesying falsehood, prophesying in YHWH's name without being commanded or sent, making people trust in falsehood, and committing adultery), and pronounces a gruesome fate for all three (29:21–22, 32). Thus, these three prophets serve as concrete examples of the kind of prophets condemned in a general way in 23:9–40.

In addition to these general similarities, sections A and A' display a number of specific verbal parallels. Five times 23:9–40 accuses the prophets of prophesying *sheqer* ("falsehood") (23:14, 25, 26, 32, 32), while 29:20–32 levels the same accusation three times (29:21, 23, 31). As Overholt has demonstrated, *sheqer* is an important term in various strands of the Jeremiah tradition.[18] It occurs fourteen times in 23:9—29:32 and so its appearance in sections A and A' is not particularly remarkable. However, 23:9–40 and 29:20–32 contain some of the highest concentrations of this term in the entire book of Jeremiah. This is even slightly more striking if one looks only at instances where *sheqer* appears in reference to false prophets.[19] Within 23:9—29:32, section A has five occurrences, A' has three, C' has five, while B' has one. Outside of 23:9—29:32, the only time *sheqer* occurs more than once in a chapter is 14:14, where it appears twice.

If one compares the use of *sheqer* in the MT versus LXX of A and A', then it becomes evident that the term has been added several times to the MT, most likely as part of the attempt to enhance the parallels between A and A'. The LXX contains all five occurrences of *sheqer* in 23:9–40 but has only one in 29:30–32, versus the three occurrences in the MT (29:31; absent in 29:21, 23). This "omission" by the LXX is significant because out of the thirty-seven occurrences of *sheqer* in the MT of Jeremiah, the

MT of 23:9—29:32 relate to the presence or absence of concentric features. My interest is primarily in those differences that do touch upon this matter.

18. Overholt, *The Threat of Falsehood*.

19. 5:31; 6:13; 8:10; 14:14, 14; 20:6; 23:14, 25, 26, 32, 32; 27:10, 14, 15, 16; 28:15; 29:9, 21, 23, 31.

only other instance where the LXX lacks the term is in 8:10c, which is a doublet of 6:13 and is part of a larger "omission" by the LXX (8:10b–12). The LXX has no pattern of omitting the term *sheqer*, nor does the MT have a habit of adding it. This suggests that the two "additions" of *sheqer* in 29:21, 23 represent an attempt by the MT to enhance the parallels between sections A and A'. In the MT of 29:21 the two prophets Ahab and Zedekiah are described as "prophesying to you in my name *sheqer*," a clause lacking in the LXX. This parallels nicely the clause in section A, "who prophesy in my name *sheqer*" (23:25). In the case of the other LXX "omission" of *sheqer* (29:23), it appears that the single word *sheqer*, which is all that is absent from the LXX, is an insertion into the MT, which now results in some awkwardness. "And they proclaimed a word in my name *sheqer* which I did not command them [וַיְדַבְּרוּ דָבָר בִּשְׁמִי שֶׁקֶר אֲשֶׁר לוֹא צִוִּיתִם]." This apparent addition of *sheqer* makes 29:23 correspond closely to 23:25, "who prophesy in my name *sheqer*."

Another verbal parallel between A and A' is that 29:23 accuses the prophets Ahab and Zedekiah of both speaking *sheqer* and committing adultery (וַיְנַאֲפוּ—piel preterite), echoing God's assertion in 23:14 that he has seen in the prophets both adultery (נָאוֹף—qal infinitive absolute) and walking in *sheqer*.[20] Referring to prophets and priests, 23:10 describes the land as being full of adulterers (מְנָאֲפִים—piel participle), a line missing in the LXX. The verb נאף (to commit adultery) and its various forms occur only three times in the MT of 23:9—29:32, twice in A (23:10, 14) and once in A' (29:23).[21] Despite the extensive critique of the prophets in 23:9—29:32, only sections A and A' condemn them for adultery (23:10, 14; 29:23). Everywhere else the prophets are judged to be false on the basis of their message.

In 29:24 the prophet Shemaiah is called a "Nehelemite [הַנֶּחֱלָמִי]," perhaps intended as a reference to his hometown or membership in a group by that name, although we know of no such place or group. Scalise observes that the root consonants are נחל, which means to dream, and that Shemaiah's designation is a pun on the word "dream," intended to recall the deceptive dreams of the prophets condemned earlier in 29:8.[22] It is also possible that calling Shemaiah a "dreamer" or designating him

---

20. Lange claims that the accusation of adultery leveled against Ahab and Zedekiah in 29:23 is based on 23:14. See *Vom prophetischen Wort*, 252–53. Plant speaks of how 29:13 echoes the accusations in 23:14. See *Good Figs, Bad Figs*, 124.

21. Elsewhere in the book forms of נאף appear only in 3:8, 9; 5:7; 7:9; 9:1 (Heb.).

22. Keown et al, *Jeremiah 26–52*, 78.

as being from "dreamland" is a reference to section A's blistering attack on the prophets for their false dreams that lead the people astray (23:25–32).[23] Section A' may portray Shemaiah as a specific example of the kind of dreaming prophets who are so harshly condemned in a general way in section A.

Another verbal parallel between sections A and A' is that in 23:32 the prophets prophesy *sheqer* without being commanded (צִוָּה), just as Ahab and Zedekiah speak *sheqer* without being commanded (29:23). The only other reference in the book to prophets speaking without being commanded is in 14:14. Shemaiah prophesied even though he was not sent (29:31) (שׁלח), just as did the prophets castigated in 23:21, 32. This parallel is not that striking because similar accusations against false prophets appear three additional times in 23:9—29:32 (27:15; 28:15; 29:9), and twice more elsewhere in the book (14:14, 15). After accusing the prophets of prophesying without being commissioned, 23:23–25 stresses that YWHW sees all that these prophets do and say. After Ahab and Zedekiah are accused of committing adultery and speaking *sheqer*, YHWH declares that he is the one who knows and is witness (29:23b). The idea is similar even though there is no overlap in vocabulary.

A significant difference between the MT and LXX is that the LXX lacks 29:20, which is the introduction to section A' in the MT. This "omission" is not surprising because the LXX also lacks 29:16–19, which has been added to the MT in order to make B' (29:1–19) correspond more closely to B (24:1–10). Because of this addition, 29:20 or something like it is needed in the MT in order to introduce section A'. In the LXX this verse is not required because the break between the two sections of ch. 29 comes after 29:14, with 29:15 providing a very suitable opening to A'.

	MT B'		LXX B'
29:1–3	introduction to the letter	29:1–3	introduction to the letter
29:4–14	concerning the exiles	29:4–14	concerning the exiles
29:15–19	concerning the non-exiles		
	MT A'		LXX A'
29:20–32	against the prophets	29:15, 21–32	against the prophets

23. Lange believes that Deuteronomistic redactors may have understood "Nehelemite" as meaning "dreamer" and as an allusion to 23:25–28 and 27:9. See *Vom prophetischen Wort*, 256.

From a logical and stylistic perspective the LXX reads more smoothly than does the MT. It appears that editors in the MT tradition were willing to make a few sacrifices in order to include additions that amplify the concentric features of the text.

One last significant difference between the LXX and MT is that in the LXX, section A concludes with an oracle of salvation after 23:9-40. Since section A' contains no such oracle its presence in A creates a significant difference between the two sections. The MT includes the same oracle but places it immediately before section A, in 23:7-8, so that here again the concentric features are more evident in the MT than in the LXX. The MT redaction may have changed the order of an earlier version to which the LXX still bears witness, although there are only two pieces of circumstantial evidence to support this suggestion. One is that the MT redaction has made other changes in order to enhance the concentric features of 23:9—29:32. The other reason for believing that the LXX order may be original is that an inclusio involving the name Zedekiah brackets the section dealing with kingship (21:1—23:8). The desire to create an inclusio may explain why the material dealing with Zedekiah has been inserted at the beginning of ch. 21, as a way of balancing the messianic oracle containing a pun on the name Zedekiah (23:5-6), which now concludes the kingship section in the LXX. In the MT the presence of another oracle of deliverance after the inclusio (23:7-8) lessens its force somewhat, and suggests that originally 23:7-8 may have stood after 23:40 as it still does in the LXX.

C (25:1-38): Jeremiah's True Prophecy—The Symbolic Cup and C' (27:1—28:17): Jeremiah's True Prophecy—The Symbolic Yoke

Sections C and C' both focus on symbolic actions by Jeremiah. In 25:1-38 Jeremiah makes the nations drink the cup of wrath, which leads to their destruction at the hands of Babylon, while in 27:1—28:17 he makes yokes for himself and a group of nations to symbolize servitude to Nebuchadnezzar king of Babylon. Although the book of Jeremiah contains numerous accounts of symbolic actions, the only examples found in 23:9—29:32 are in sections C and C'. Moreover, these two symbolic actions are the only ones in the book that involve the fate of both Judah and foreign nations.[24] The emphasis on Jeremiah as a prophet to the na-

---

24. A number of symbolic actions foretell the destruction of Judah (13:1-11;

tions, highlighted in his call (1:5, 10), is a significant theme in the book, yet the early chapters do not develop it in any significant way until it comes to the fore twice in 23:9—29:32, in sections C and C'. Chapter 25 is the first passage in the book to portray other nations as victims of Babylon,[25] a portrayal continued in chs. 27–28, but not highlighted anywhere else in 23:9—29:32. Another important theme in the book of Jeremiah, especially in the early chapters, is the enemy from the north who will attack Judah. One of the major purposes of both sections C and C' is to stress that Babylon is this enemy through whom God will punish both Judah and the nations.

At the surface level, section C contains material that is very different from C', yet the basic thrust of both sections is remarkably similar. Chapter 25 opens with a retrospective look at Jeremiah's twenty-three-year ministry, stressing the people's refusal to heed God's persistent call to repent as delivered by Jeremiah and a succession of faithful prophets (25:1–7). This refusal leads YHWH to pronounce horrendous punishment on Judah and the nations using Nebuchadnezzar as his agent (25:8–12), and he commands Jeremiah to set this punishment in motion by making the nations drink the cup of wrath (25:15–38). The juxtaposition of material in ch. 25 places Judah's fate squarely into the context of earth-shattering disasters affecting all the other nations of the region, and stresses that the sins of Judah have initiated a chain of events that will suck the nations into a maelstrom of destruction (25:7–11).

Section C' revolves around Jeremiah's symbolic action of making thongs and yoke bars, which he wears and which he sends to various kings of nearby nations (27:2–3) with the message that all nations must submit to Babylon (27:5–11). Jeremiah then delivers the same message to Zedekiah king of Judah (27:12–15) and to the priests and all the people of Judah (27:16–22). Both sections C and C' highlight YHWH's sovereignty over the nations, stress that God has granted Babylon temporary dominion over Judah and all the nations, and set the fate of Judah squarely into the context of the fate of the nations.

The emphasis in chs. 27–28 on the fate of the nations is particularly evident in the portrayal of the conflict between Jeremiah and Hananiah. At one level this conflict focuses on the future of the temple utensils, which have been carted off to Babylon, and hence the conflict is about

16:1–4; 16:5–7; 16:8–9; 18:1–11; 19:1–13), while two predict the defeat of individual foreign nations (Egypt—43:8–13; Babylon—51:59–64).

25. Aejmelaeus, "Jeremiah at the Turning-Point of History," 471–72.

the fate of Jerusalem, Judah, and the exiles (28:3-4). However, ch. 28 consistently presents the issue as the fate of the nations and how Judah's situation is encompassed by this fate. Hananiah's claim that YHWH will restore the temple utensils to Jerusalem depends on God breaking the *yoke of Babylon* (28:2, 4). Jeremiah's initial response to this optimistic announcement is to remind Hananiah that the prophets of old prophesied war and disaster "against *many lands and great kingdoms*" (28:8). When Hananiah breaks the yoke that Jeremiah has been wearing his interpretation does not even mention Judah, even though the future of Judah is clearly at stake. "Just so I will break the yoke of Nebuchadnezzar king of Babylon from the neck of *all the nations*, within two years" (28:11). Jeremiah departs and later returns with a new message from YHWH that also does not mention Judah. "A yoke of iron I have put upon the neck of *all these nations* that they may serve Nebuchadnezzar the king of Babylon" (28:14).

Section C explicitly states that Judah's failure to heed the message of Jeremiah and the other prophets leads YHWH to raise up Nebuchadnezzar as his agent of judgment upon the world (25:7-11). The same assumption underlies section C', although in a somewhat more subtle way. Chapter 26 has highlighted how Jeremiah's contemporaries rejected the message of true prophets like Jeremiah, Micah, and Uriah, even though Jeremiah warned that failure to repent would lead to catastrophe (26:3-6, 13; compare 25:3-7). When chs. 27-28 speak of Babylonian domination the clear implication is that Judah's sin has led YHWH to raise up Nebuchadnezzar, who will wreak devastation on the nations as a byproduct of YHWH's punishment of Judah. Thus, in C', just as in C, the nations are caught up in YHWH's punishment of the people of Judah.

In addition to the general correspondence in theme and content between sections C and C', there are a number of specific verbal parallels. Jeremiah sends yokes to the kings of Edom, Moab, Ammon, Tyre, and Sidon (27:3). In ch. 25 the list of nations who must drink from the cup of wrath is much longer, but these five occur in the middle of the list in precisely the same order (25:21-22). This list of five peoples is not found anywhere else in the Old Testament. In both C (25:11) and C' (27:7) YHWH decrees that all the nations will serve (עבד) the king of Babylon. In both cases a prediction about the eventual reversal of Babylon's fortunes immediately follows, indicating that Babylonian domination is but for a limited period of time.[26] Both these verses are lacking in the LXX.

| For *many nations and great kings will enslave* even them [the Babylonians] and I will recompense them according to their deeds and the works of their hands. (25:14) | All the nations will serve him [Nebuchadnezzar] and his son and his grandson until the time of his, even his land comes, then *many nations and great kings will enslave* him. (27:7) |

Commentators frequently point out that the LXX lacks all explicit references to Babylon in 25:1–14, while in the MT the role of Babylon is central to the passage (25:1, 9, 11, 12).[27] In 25:1 the LXX simply "omits" the MT's reference to the accession year of Nebuchadnezzar. In 25:11 the LXX states that "they will serve among the nations," presumably a reference to the dispersion of the people of Judah, while the MT states that *these nations* will serve *the king of Babylon*. In the MT there is a subtle but significant change in meaning as the target of the prophecy shifts from just Judah to Judah and the nations, and as the punishment changes from exile to domination by Babylon.[28] These changes fit precisely with the central message of chs. 27–28 that Judah and all the nations must serve Nebuchadnezzar. In the MT of 25:9 and 27:6, YHWH designates Nebuchadnezzar as "my servant." To ascribe such an honorific title, normally reserved for a person consciously committed to doing YHWH's will, to a pagan emperor, especially one responsible for inflicting such enormous suffering on Judah, is truly astounding. Only one other Old Testament text uses such remarkable language (Jer 43:10). In all three instances the title is lacking in the LXX. This analysis of the differences between the LXX and MT of C and C' illustrates again how the parallels between corresponding panels of 23:9—29:32 are more extensive in the MT than the LXX.[29]

---

26. Allen, *Jeremiah*, 307, notes that 27:7b repeats 25:14.

27. For a detailed analysis see Hill, *Friend or Foe?*, 113–17. Aejmelaeus, "Jeremiah at the Turning-Point of History," 465, 474, is probably correct in concluding that the LXX represents a more original text which, in keeping with the early chapters of the book of Jeremiah, does not reveal the identity of the foe from the north.

28. Applegate, "Jeremiah and the Seventy Years in the Hebrew Bible," 94.

29. There are other differences between the MT and LXX of C and C' that I have not discussed and that cannot be explained on the basis of the concentric structure.

D (26:1–24): Proper and Improper Responses to True Prophecy

An axiom of studies in chiasm and concentric structures is that the center almost always contains the most theologically important material or marks the major turning point in the passage.[30] Jeremiah 23:9—29:32 is no exception, as its center focuses on the key issue of how God's people should respond to the true prophetic word.[31] The chapter is composed of three sections:

26:1–16   Jeremiah is almost killed in response to his temple sermon
    26:17–19   Hezekiah repents in response to Micah's pronouncement of judgment
26:20–24   Uriah is killed by Jehoiakim for prophesying the same words as Jeremiah

Scholars are sometimes puzzled by the fact that Jeremiah's temple sermon is recorded in ch. 7 while the audience's response is found in ch. 26. This peculiarity indicates that in 26:1–16 the focus is not on the content of the sermon but on how God's people should respond to the true prophetic word. Chapter 26 depicts three incidents that all highlight the community's reaction to a true prophet. The key concerns of the chapter are laid out in 26:2–6, where YHWH instructs Jeremiah to proclaim a message at the temple intended to encourage the people to repent, obey the *Torah*, and heed the prophets whom God has persistently sent to warn them. If the people are obstinate then divine punishment will surely follow. The crowd is so incensed by Jeremiah's threat of doom that it seeks to lynch him (26:8), but royal officials intervene to rescue him and convene a proper judicial hearing (26:10). Jeremiah presents no evidence in his defense except to issue another plea for repentance (26:13) and to insist that he has been commissioned by YHWH (26:12, 15). The hearing concludes with the officials and the people declaring their verdict that Jeremiah does not deserve death (26:16).

---

30. For comments stressing the importance of the center see Lund, *Chiasmus in the New Testament*, 40; Parunak, "Oral Typesetting," 165; Welch, introduction to *Chiasmus in Antiquity*, 10; Welch, "Criteria for Identifying and Evaluating," 165–66; Lundbom, *Jeremiah: A Study in Ancient Hebrew Rhetoric*, 95; Breck, "Biblical Chiasmus," 71, 73; Stock, "Chiastic Awareness," 23; Eslinger, "More Drafting Techniques," 223; Man, "The Value of Chiasm," 147–48; Walsh, *Style and Structure*, 14.

31. This point will be demonstrated more fully in chapter 6, which discusses ch. 26 in detail.

Many scholars do not recognize that a new unit of material begins in 26:17.[32] The officials and the people have already rendered their verdict (26:16), and the next verse introduces a new set of characters, the elders of the land and the assembly of the people. This means that the Micah incident of 26:17–19 does not belong to the original trial scene but has been attached secondarily, indicating that its presence here might be all the more deliberate and significant. At the center of ch. 26 and at the center of the entire concentric unit stands an account of people responding appropriately to the message of a true prophet. The text reports that after Micah delivered his blistering attack on Jerusalem, Hezekiah and all of Judah repented, and therefore YHWH changed his mind about the catastrophe he had decreed. Then follows the ominous statement that closes this brief section, "But we [Jeremiah's contemporaries] are bringing a great disaster upon ourselves" (26:19). This is the central message of all of 23:9—29:32—the people are bringing disaster upon themselves by not heeding the message of true prophecy.

Hezekiah's positive example contrasts with the actions of the wicked Jehoiakim. When another prophet named Uriah prophesies "just like all the words of Jeremiah" and then flees to Egypt to escape the wrath of Jehoiakim (26:20–21), the king is not content simply to be rid of this troublesome prophet. He illustrates his total rejection of the true prophetic word by extraditing Uriah from Egypt, executing him, and then desecrating his corpse (26:22–23). This story demonstrates how the nation was indeed in the process of bringing disaster upon itself by refusing to heed the true prophets.

IMPLICATIONS FOR UNDERSTANDING THE COMPOSITIONAL HISTORY OF 23:9—29:32

The parallels between the corresponding panels of 23:9—29:32 are created by repetition of words, phrases, key ideas, and general content. Parallels between units that are not corresponding panels in the concentric structure also exist. For example, both 25:11–12 (C) and 29:10 (B') speak of Babylonian domination lasting seventy years, while 25:4 (C), 26:5

---

32. See Weiser, *Das Buch Jeremia*, 234; Holladay, *Jeremiah 2*, 107–8; Brueggemann, *To Build, To Plant*, 8–9; Miller, "The Book of Jeremiah," 774; Lundbom, *Jeremiah 21–36*, 294. Failure to observe the break in the text sometimes leads commentators to assert that the precedent of Micah saved Jeremiah's life, an interpretation that misconstrues the purpose of the Micah incident.

The Concentric Structure of Jeremiah 23:9—29:32

(D), and 29:19 (B') all mention YHWH's servants the prophets, whom he has persistently sent. Sections D and C' begin with virtually identical chronological introductions (26:1; 27:1). Such parallels do not mean that the concentric structure is a mirage, since it is common to find parallels between non-corresponding sections in a concentric structure. Some similarities in content and vocabulary may be necessary in order to carry ideas and themes forward across several sections of a larger unit. The significant factor is which sections display the majority of parallels in vocabulary, phrasing, and subject matter.

In the case of 23:9—29:32 some of the similarities between non-corresponding panels are due to the nature of the material utilized by the editors. Both sections B' and A' speak of letters being sent between Jerusalem and Babylon. Chapter 29 was, and still is, a single narrative that should be read as a whole, even though it falls into two distinct parts. It is not surprising, then, to observe significant parallels between the two halves of the chapter.[33] One of the similarities across all of chs. 27–29 is the peculiar spelling of the names Jeremiah, Nebuchadnezzar, and Zedekiah, in comparison to the rest of the book of Jeremiah. Also, these chapters are linked to a similar time period and the theme of prophetic conflict is central.[34] These factors suggest that at some point the perhaps originally independent material of chs. 27–29 became a unit that was then incorporated into a larger Jeremiah collection. The main purpose of the unit was to reflect on Jeremiah's conflict with the false prophets in the midst of the Babylonian threat.[35]

---

33. Some of the features that tie all of ch. 29 together are Jeremiah's sending of letters to the exiles (vv. 1, 31), his advice to the exiles to make the best of life in Babylon (vv. 5–7, 28), the critique of false prophets in exile (vv. 8–9, 15, 21–23, 31–32), and the designation of the future salvation as the "good" (טוב) that YHWH will do (vv. 10, 32).

34. For a more detailed discussion of the evidence pointing to the unity of chs. 27–29 see Volz, *Der Prophet Jeremia*, 255; Rudolph, *Jeremia*, 157–58; Overholt, "Jeremiah 27–29," 242; Carroll, *Jeremiah*, 523–24, 566–67; Keown et al, *Jeremiah 26–52*, 35–36; Lundbom, *Jeremiah 21–36*, 304; Lange, *Vom prophetischen Wort*, 224–26; Plant, *Good Figs, Bad Figs*, 96–100; Osuji, "True and False Prophecy," 438–52.

Assuming that the beginning of ch. 26 marks a major break in the book, Osuji argues that chs. 26–29 function as a single unit to introduce the second half of the book. See "True and False Prophecy," especially pp. 437–38; Osuji, *Where Is the Truth?*, 111–16. Allen also believes that chs. 26–29 function as a literary block but claims that ch. 26 has been prefixed to the preexisting unit composed of chs. 27–29. See *Jeremiah*, 295.

35. Thiel claims that it was Deuteronomistic redactors who combined the material of chs. 27–29 and then supplemented it in such a way that it came to focus on Jeremiah's

In the process of creating the larger unit of 23:9—29:32, editors probably began with chs. 27-29, which already focused on Jeremiah's conflict with false prophets. Editors had available to them other Jeremianic material dealing with matters like a critique of other prophets (23:9-40), the fate of the exiles and non-exiles (ch. 24), the Babylonian threat and its meaning (ch. 25), and stories about the nation's response to true prophecy (ch. 26). Out of a desire to present the nature of true and false prophecy, particularly in light of the Babylonian threat, editors probably chose, arranged, and altered their material in such a way that it balanced the existing content of chs. 27-29, which already focused on true and false prophecy. Quite possibly the editors also made changes to chs. 27-29 in order to make this material better balance the other panels of their concentric structure. For example, the promise of deliverance for the exiles in 29:10-14 (B') may have been included in order to balance the similar promise in 24:5-7 (B). Editors placed ch. 26 in the center so as to leave no doubt about how people should respond to the message of a true prophet. After the material in 23:9—29:32 received its overall shape, editors continued to make additions and changes for a variety of reasons, as is illustrated by the significant differences between the MT and LXX. Editors in the MT tradition continued to be aware of the concentric structure and deliberately sought to enhance the parallels between corresponding panels by adding individual words, sentences, and in one case even a whole paragraph (29:16-19).

As a way of testing some of these hypotheses it is helpful to explore in a bit more detail the relationship between the LXX and MT versions of 23:9—29:32. How might one account for the fact that the concentric features are more evident in the MT than the LXX? Does the MT represent the more original text, from which the LXX has deliberately sought to eliminate some of the concentric features? Or does the LXX represent the more original text, which the MT has altered in order to create the concentric structure? Or did a common *Vorlage* to both the LXX and MT contain the concentric structure, which the MT augmented and which the LXX distorted by inserting the oracles concerning the nations into ch. 25?

The first possibility, that the LXX deliberately eliminated the concentric structure of the MT, is unlikely, since it is not clear why editors would want to disrupt such a carefully constructed text. Also, in the LXX

---

conflict with false prophets. See *Die deuteronomistische Redaktion*, 100-101.

many of the key parallels between corresponding panels still exist, and so it makes little sense to argue that editors sought to eliminate the concentric features when their efforts were so half-hearted. The second possibility, that the concentric structure is entirely the creation of the Masoretic tradition, is also unlikely. Except for the oracles concerning the nations, the order of material in the LXX is essentially the same as in the MT. It is unlikely that this arrangement is purely coincidental, and that only after the LXX and MT diverged did editors in the Masoretic tradition first see the potential of making 23:9—29:32 concentric. The most logical conclusion is that the material was already arranged concentrically in the common *Vorlage* to the LXX and MT. The LXX has disrupted the concentric structure by inserting the oracles concerning the nations into ch. 25, while the Masoretic tradition has enhanced the concentric features by adding parallels to corresponding panels. One way to test this hypothesis further is to examine briefly the LXX version of 23:9—29:32 minus the oracles concerning the nations, to see if even the LXX contains features that make the text concentric (see chart 2).

Concerning the Prophets

Structure of LXX Jer 23:9—29:32
(minus the oracles concerning the nations)

A   23:9-40,   Condemnation of false prophets in general
       7-8

   B   24:1-10   Jeremiah's true prophecy—a vision regarding exiles and non-exiles
- hope for the exiles
- doom for the non-exiles

     C   25:1-13, 15-38   Jeremiah's true prophecy
          (25:1-13; 32:15-38)[A]

                           The symbolic cup—destruction of Judah and the nations by the enemy from the north

       D   26:1-24   Proper and improper responses to true prophecy
            (33:1-24)

               26:1-16   Jeremiah is almost killed
               (33:1-16)

                       26:17-19   Micah inspires repentance
                       (33:17-19)

               26:20-24   Uriah is killed
               (33:20-24)

     C'   27:1—28:17   Jeremiah's true prophecy
          (34:2—35:17)

                           The symbolic yoke—Judah and the nations must serve Nebuchadnezzar king of Babylon

   B'   29:1-19   Jeremiah's true prophecy—a letter regarding exiles
        (36:1-14)
- instructions for living in exile
- hope for the exiles

A'   29:15, 21-32   Condemnation of specific false prophets
      (36:15, 21-32)

A. References in parentheses refer to the LXX.

The Concentric Structure of Jeremiah 23:9—29:32

A (23:9-40, 7-8) and A' (29:15, 21-32)

The LXX indicates that the heading in 23:9 "Concerning the Prophets" (לַנְּבִאִים), which it translates ἐν τοῖς προφήταις, was already in the *Vorlage* of the LXX and MT. This illustrates that from early on editors signaled that the material following 23:9 was a new editorial unit focusing on prophets. Virtually all the similarities between A and A' in the MT are also present in the LXX, and these need not be listed again. There are some differences between the LXX and MT but these are minor. In 23:9-40 the MT and LXX both accuse the prophets five times of prophesying *sheqer*. The MT repeats this accusation three times in 29:20-32 (vv. 21, 23, 31) while the LXX includes it only once (v. 31). In both sections A and A' the MT and LXX accuse the prophets of committing adultery (23:14; 29:23), but the MT contains one additional such accusation (23:10).

B (24:1-10) and B' (29:1-14)

In the LXX Jeremiah's vision of the good and bad figs is as out of place topically and chronologically as it is in the MT, and there seems to be little logical reason to place the vision here except to balance 29:1-14. Both 24:1 and 29:1-2 focus on the same group of people, and in both B and B' the exiles receive a hopeful promise of physical and spiritual restoration (24:5-7; 29:10-14). In ch. 29 this promise appears to be a later addition to the text, since the material in 29:8-9 is continued by v. 15 and then v. 21. It appears that already before the LXX was translated editors added a promise of salvation to B' in order to make it parallel B more closely. In the MT redaction a prediction of doom for the non-exiles (29:16-19) has also been added to heighten even more the correspondence between B and B'.

C (25:1-38) and C' (27:1—28:17)

If one removes the oracles concerning the nations from the LXX, then C and C' are similar in the same ways in the LXX as they are in the MT. In both the fate of Judah is announced against the backdrop of the devastation that will befall the nations. In C the MT consistently adds that it will be Nebuchadnezzar and the Babylonians who will devastate the earth, whereas the LXX speaks of a "family from the north" (25:9), "that people" (25:12), and "that land" (25:13). In the larger context of the book of Jeremiah these expressions can only refer to Babylon, and so the MT only makes explicit what is implicit in the LXX. Another indication that C parallels C' in the *Vorlage* already is that the five nations mentioned in 27:3 (Edom, Moab, Ammon, Tyre, and Sidon) appear in the same order in 25:21–22, even though in this context they are part of a longer list of peoples forced to drink the cup of wrath.

This brief analysis of the LXX text of 23:9—29:32 minus the oracles concerning the nations demonstrates that the concentric structure existed already in the *Vorlage* to the LXX. The differences between the LXX and MT are not the kind one would expect if the LXX were deliberately seeking to eliminate the concentric features. Rather, the nature of these differences indicates that the Masoretic tradition attempted to enhance a pattern that was already present in the common *Vorlage*. This adds yet another piece of evidence in favor of the growing consensus that the LXX of Jeremiah represents a more original text than the MT.[36]

The previous discussion raises the question of how to account for the position of the oracles concerning the nations in the LXX, where they disrupt the concentric structure. Not only is the position of these oracles different in the LXX and MT, but so is the order of the individual oracles. These and other factors have led some scholars to surmise that the oracles circulated independently until they were incorporated into the book of Jeremiah, which already consisted of most of chs. 1–45.[37] Numerous commentators assert that the LXX placement is more original than the MT, partially because the LXX generally appears to preserve a more original text. Also, the books of Isaiah and Ezekiel both contain

---

36. The priority of the LXX over the MT is one of the major conclusions of Janzen, *Studies in the Text of Jeremiah*; see for example pp. 127-28. Since Janzen's study most scholars have concurred with his conclusion. See Tov, "Exegetical Notes," 73–77; Tov, "The Literary History of the Book of Jeremiah," 212–14; Tov, "The Book of Jeremiah," 32–38, 45; McKane, *A Critical and Exegetical Commentary*, 1:l–li; Carroll, *Jeremiah*, 50–55; Stulman, *Jeremiah*, 8; Hill, "The Book of Jeremiah MT and Early Second Temple Conflicts," 30–31; Aejmelaeus, "Jeremiah at the Turning-Point of History," 460; Allen, *Jeremiah*, 7–8; Sweeney, "The Masoretic and Septuagint Versions," 66–67.

For a dissenting view see Soderlund, *The Greek Text of Jeremiah*, 193–248; Craigie et al, *Jeremiah 1-25*, xli–xlv. When commenting on individual passages Lundbom repeatedly argues that the LXX is an inferior text and much has dropped out because of haplography; *Jeremiah: A New Translation*.

37. See for example Bright, *Jeremiah*, cxxiii.

oracles concerning the nations in the middle of the book, and so it is reasonable to assume that Jeremiah would follow the same pattern. A third factor is how the statement in 25:13 that YHWH will bring to pass all the words "written in this book which Jeremiah prophesied concerning all the nations" provides an excellent segue into the oracles that follow immediately in the LXX.[38] Despite these plausible reasons, other scholars continue to insist that the MT position of the oracles is original, for reasons that need not concern us here.[39]

My findings regarding the concentric structure of 23:9—29:32 indicate that the position of the oracles concerning the nations in the MT cannot be entirely accidental, since the MT has good reasons for not placing them in ch. 25. Also, these oracles were probably not situated in ch. 25 before the LXX and MT parted ways. Otherwise, one would have to make the unlikely argument that the concentric structure existed in the common *Vorlage*, only to be disrupted by the addition of the oracles, and that after the MT and LXX diverged, editors in the Masoretic tradition observed the disruption and moved the oracles to the end of the book, thereby restoring the concentric structure.[40] More plausible is Bright's suggestion that the oracles concerning the nations were inserted independently into the MT and LXX after the two had parted company.[41] If this is the case, then talk about an "original" or "secondary" position is somewhat inappropriate. However, it is also

---

38. Aejmelaeus, "Jeremiah at the Turning-Point of History," 473, 479, argues that 25:1–13 was not originally composed as a conclusion to or summary of the first part of the book, but rather as an introduction to the oracles concerning the nations. The latter part of ch. 25 functioned as the conclusion to these oracles, and when the MT removed the foreign nations oracles the framing material remained in place but lost its original function. Other scholars who claim that the LXX position of the oracles is original include Rudolph, *Jeremia*, 153; Janzen, *Studies in the Text of Jeremiah*, 115; Tov, "The Literary History of the Book of Jeremiah," 217; Carroll, *Jeremiah*, 53–54; Holladay, *Jeremiah*, 2:5; Lundbom, *Jeremiah 21–36*, 240–41; Parke-Taylor, *The Formation of the Book of Jeremiah*, 101–2.

39. See for example Haran, "The Place of the Prophecies against the Nations," 704–6; Leuchter, *The Polemics of Exile*, 146–48.

40. Allen, *Jeremiah*, 11, 283, does propose something like this process. He claims that the LXX "bulldozed" apart a carefully arranged composition by inserting the oracles into ch. 25, but then later MT editors repaired this disruption by moving the originally independent oracles to the end of the book.

41. Bright, *Jeremiah*, cxxiii.

possible that in this case the MT represents an older version of the text that the LXX has deliberately altered.[42]

Another question raised by this discussion is why the editors of the LXX inserted the oracles concerning the nations into ch. 25, thereby destroying the concentric structure. One piece of evidence suggests that the LXX editors or translators did not observe the concentric structure. The LXX translates the heading to the entire section לַנְּבִאִים as ἐν τοῖς προφήταις and connects it to the preceding oracle of salvation (23:5–6). Thus, in the LXX 23:6 reads, "In his [the future king's] days both Judah will be saved and Israel will dwell securely, and this is his name which the Lord will call him, Josedec *among the prophets*."[43] The LXX does not seem to recognize the Hebrew לַנְּבִאִים as the superscription to a new section entitled "Concerning the Prophets" but understands the phrase as modifying "Josedec." If the LXX understood לַנְּבִאִים as a heading then it would probably read περί τῶν προφήτων.[44] If the LXX tradition did not recognize the title, then it was probably also unaware of the larger unit and its concentric structure. It should be remembered that the concentric features of the unit were somewhat less obvious in the *Vorlage* than they currently are in the MT. If the LXX tradition did not recognize the concentric structure, then it had good reasons to add the oracles concerning the nations to ch. 25. The chapter's focus on YHWH's devastation of the nations, and especially the reference to a document proclaiming disaster on the nations (v. 13), invited such an insertion, and the books of Isaiah and Ezekiel provided a model to follow.

ORDER AT THE CENTER?

The book of Jeremiah's bewildering array of material from different sources and time periods, representing a variety of genres and often lacking in thematic coherence, has led more than one scholar to despair

42. See Haran, "The Place of the Prophecies against the Nations," 704–6; Albertz, *Israel in Exile*, 320–21.

43. This is the reading of LXXB. Other manuscripts have slightly different wording.

44. The LXX does not seem to have understood the similar heading in 21:11 either.

וּלְבֵית מֶלֶךְ יְהוּדָה
שִׁמְעוּ דְּבַר־יְהוָה

(Concerning the house of the king of Judah; hear the word of YHWH). The LXX renders these lines Ὁ οἶκος βασιλέως Ἰούδα ἀκούσατε λόγον Κυρίου (The house of the king of Judah, hear ye the word of the Lord).

of finding any overarching structure or organization in the book.[45] Yet before concluding that the book of Jeremiah lacks discernible principles of organization, we do well to consider Lundbom's observation that the coherence of an ancient composition may follow "an inner logic that is still quite alien to the modern Western mind."[46] It should humble us to recognize that while scholars have by now identified hundreds if not thousands of examples of chiasm and concentric structures in the Bible, a mere eighty years ago, before the pioneering work of Nils Lund, scholarship was oblivious to chiasm as a major structuring device in biblical literature.[47] There may be much more order than we expect lurking amidst the chaos of Jeremiah, just waiting to be discovered. A positive trend in recent Jeremiah studies is the attempt to discern both large and small editorial units or organizing schemes in the book. Given the complexity of the book and its composition history, it is not surprising that little consensus has yet emerged regarding larger structures, and perhaps none will because the book is just too complex and the evidence points in too many diverse directions. The observations that follow are an attempt to contribute a few insights and questions to the conversation.

It is widely recognized that a significant section of the book of Jeremiah comes to a close with ch. 20.[48] The account of Jeremiah's early ministry concludes with the last of his confessions, in which the despairing prophet utters a curse upon the day of his birth and the man who announced his birth (20:14–18). While it is also widely recognized that 21:11—23:8 focuses on kingship, there is no agreement about larger sections of material following 21:1. Brueggemann lumps together 21:1—25:38 for the sake of convenience because it is difficult to detect any intentional ordering, and he provides the general title "Judgment and Hope."[49] Miller adopts the same grouping of chapters and calls it "Against Kings

---

45. McKane's theory of a "rolling corpus" leads him to caution against looking for evidence of structure and organization in the book. See McKane, *A Critical and Exegetical Commentary*, 1:xlix–l. For a description of the "chaos" in the book by someone who still seeks to discern order amid this chaos, see Stulman, *Jeremiah*, 11.

46. Lundbom, *Jeremiah 1-20*, 85.

47. The groundbreaking works on chiasm by Lund include "The Presence of Chiasmus in the Old Testament"; "The Presence of Chiasmus in the New Testament"; "Chiasmus in the Psalms"; and *Chiasmus in the New Testament*.

48. See for example Hill, *Friend or Foe?*, 55, 72–73; Lundbom, *Jeremiah 21-36*, 94–95. Fretheim, *Jeremiah*, 303, includes a discussion of some of the differences between chs. 20 and 21 that mark the break between sections.

49. Brueggemann, *A Commentary on Jeremiah*, 188.

and Prophets."⁵⁰ Lundbom describes chs. 21–23 as a king and prophet appendix and claims that ch. 24 begins a unit that concludes with ch. 36.⁵¹ Hill, Plant, and Allen all treat chs. 21–24 as a block that should be distinguished from what precedes and follows.⁵² Allen's title is "Doomed Kings and Discredited Prophets." Because of the disparate nature of the material, scholars who group together chs. 21–23, 21–24, or 21–25 must give the section a somewhat general heading or call it an appendix to the previous section.⁵³

The concentric structure of 23:9—29:32 demonstrates that there is very careful organization at the center of the book of Jeremiah. Chapter 20 concludes a major section of the book, and then three collections of topical material follow: 21:11—23:8, "Concerning the Kings of Judah"; 23:9—29:32, "Concerning the Prophets"; and 30–33, "The Book of Consolation." One question is what to make of 21:1–10, the story of how King Zedekiah sends Pashhur and the priest Zephaniah to inquire of Jeremiah regarding divine intervention to end Nebuchadnezzar's siege of Jerusalem. Since this pericope deals with King Zedekiah many scholars see it as an addition to the kingship section, but the Zedekiah story comes before the heading in 21:11, "Concerning the House of the King of Judah." Also, in terms of content this story is quite different than the judgment oracles in 21:11—23:8 that target various kings for acts of injustice. It is striking that immediately following the "Book of Consolation" stands another Zedekiah story (34:1–22), which is also curiously out of place in some ways. Chapter 34, the story of how Zedekiah and the upper-class citizens renege on the release of their slaves, does not follow from the promises of salvation in chs. 30–33 nor does it fit chronologically with ch. 35, which reverts to a prior time when Jehoiakim is still king.⁵⁴ Chronologically, ch.

50. Miller, "The Book of Jeremiah," 731.

51. Lundhom, *Jeremiah 1–20*, 94, 222, 253–54.

52. Hill, *Friend or Foe?*, 72–74; Plant, *Good Figs, Bad Figs*, 55–57; Allen, *Jeremiah*, 234–78.

53. See Fretheim, *Jeremiah*, 303; Lundbom, *Jeremiah 21–36*, 94, 222; Craigie et al., *Jeremiah 1–25*, 283.

54. Stulman, *Jeremiah*, 286–87, provides a helpful discussion of how ch. 34 is thematically connected to ch. 35. If editors were determined to keep chs. 34 and 35 together, they could still easily have done so by placing both after ch. 36, and by reversing the order of chs. 34 and 35. Then Jehoiakim's unfaithfulness in ch. 36 would contrast with the faithfulness of the Rechabites during his time (currently ch. 35), which would contrast with the unfaithfulness of Jerusalem's leading citizens during Zedekiah's time (currently ch. 34), which would lead nicely into the account of the Babylonian siege

34 belongs after 37:5, especially since the reference in 37:5 to the temporary lifting of the Babylonian siege of Jerusalem provides the reason why the wealthy citizens would take their slaves back. During siege times being responsible to feed slaves was a liability, but once life returned to normal then slaves were valuable again.

Perhaps editors utilized 21:1–10 and 34:1–22 to create an inclusio around the kings, prophets, and salvation sections. Both passages are set during Nebuchadnezzar's siege of Jerusalem, and in each Jeremiah delivers a harsh word from YHWH regarding the ultimate success of the Babylonian campaign. In both the language of making war is prominent (root לחם) (21:2, 4 [twice], 5; 34:1, 7, 22), and God promises to give the city of Jerusalem into the hand of Nebuchadnezzar, who will burn it with fire (21:10; 34:2). YHWH also promises to deliver Zedekiah, his officials, and the people to the Babylonians and "into the hand of their enemies and into the hand of those who seek their life" (21:7; 34:21). Perhaps most significantly, in both passages the withdrawal of the Babylonian army is a key issue. In 21:1–10 Zedekiah dispatches messengers to ask Jeremiah if perchance YHWH might force Nebuchadnezzar to withdraw (וְיַעֲלֶה מֵעָלֵינוּ [21:2]). In 34:1–22 God sends Jeremiah to Zedekiah with the message that God will hand over the city to the Babylonians, and then Jeremiah condemns Zedekiah and the leading citizens for their despicable treatment of Hebrew slaves. No context or rationale is given for why the elite would take back their slaves after having entered into a covenant a short time before to release them. Only at the very end of the story do we read that the Babylonian army has withdrawn (הָעֹלִים מֵעֲלֵיכֶם [34:21]) but that this withdrawal will only be temporary (34:21–22). After the mention of Babylonian withdrawal the whole story makes greater sense as the reader comes to understand the self-centered motives of Judah's leading citizens. Perhaps these two Zedekiah stories that both highlight the question of Babylonian withdrawal and stress that Judah should place no hopes in such a withdrawal form an inclusio around the kings, prophets, and salvation collections. In ch. 34 the mention of Babylonian withdrawal may be withheld until the end so as to form an inclusio with the mention of Babylonian withdrawal at the beginning of 21:1–10.

If chs. 21–34 form some kind of unit, then what might be its overall focus or purpose? Fretheim observes how the book of Jeremiah as a whole does not present an argument in a systematic or logical manner,

---

during Zedekiah's reign (ch. 37).

but rather explores a complex situation from a variety of different angles.[55] Perhaps the purpose of chs. 21–34 is to present different perspectives on the catastrophe of 587, and perhaps it merits a title something like "Concerning the End of Judah." Zedekiah appears in 21:1 for the first time in the book since the introduction (1:1–3), and he wishes to know if the fall of the nation might yet be averted even though the Babylonians are now at the gates. The appearance of Judah's last king, Zedekiah, and the mention of the Babylonian siege both signal that the end is near, and the devastating word of YHWH delivered by Jeremiah leaves no doubt about this. The section on kingship (21:11—23:8) explores how the unfaithfulness of Judah's kings is partly to blame for the coming disaster and how these kings squandered opportunities to lead the nation in healthy directions. The section concludes with YHWH's promise to restore the exiles and raise up a new Davidic king who will reign with righteousness and justice (23:1–8). While horrible punishment is imminent, it will not mark the end of God's dealings with Israel. The section on prophets explores how false prophecy has filled the people with false hopes, lulled them into complacency, prevented them from repenting, and has thus brought disaster crashing down. This section also proclaims that things could have turned out very differently had the people heeded Jeremiah and the other true prophets and repented. Here too promises of salvation affirm that YHWH's punishment is not the final word, but the section emphasizes that there is no deliverance this side of disaster. Then follows the "Book of Consolation," which reverses many facets of the judgment proclaimed in the first part of the book,[56] and unambiguously affirms that God's ultimate will for the people is restoration and renewal. Once the text establishes that God's graciousness will overcome judgment, then it can return in ch. 34 to the agony of the siege and the coming destruction. Shortly before the fall of the nation the people have yet another opportunity to act faithfully, but they fail miserably, providing yet further reason for God's punishment. The section ends with a temporary reprieve from the Babylonian siege (34:21), which makes it possible for the following chapters to tell further stories of unfaithfulness and to describe the final end of the nation.

---

55. Fretheim, *Jeremiah*, 22.
56. For an excellent chart demonstrating this, see Stulman, *Jeremiah*, 260–61.

HERMENEUTICAL IMPLICATIONS

How significant is awareness of the concentric structure for interpreting the once-disparate material that editors have combined in 23:9—29:32? A minimalist response might be that texts have to be organized in some way, and the concentric structure of 23:9—29:32 is an esoteric editorial technique that is but a minor surface feature of the text and need not have a major impact on the interpretation of the passage. There is some validity to such a response, because some biblical passages display obvious concentric features yet the structure may exert little impact on the meaning of the text. Psalm 8 is probably one such example where the basic content of the text can easily be grasped without observing the structure.[57]

    A   Benediction (v. 2ab, Heb.)
        B   God's dominion (vv. 2c–4)
            C   Human lowliness (v. 5)
            C'   Human greatness (v. 6)
        B'   Human dominion (vv. 7–9)
    A'   Benediction (v. 10)

There are other instances where recognizing the chiasm or concentric structure is key to understanding the meaning and purpose of a passage. By itself Genesis 34 is a story glorifying the violence and duplicity of Jacob's sons as they murder the men of Shechem to avenge the rape of their sister Dinah. However, the Jacob Cycle is organized as a chiasm, and the editors have in the chiasm matched this story with Isaac's peaceful and much more exemplary way of relating to non-Israelites (Gen 26). By pairing these two stories the editors present two paradigms of how to relate to non-Israelites, and Isaac's actions function as a critique of the model presented by Jacob's sons.[58] In order to discern this meaning, interpreters must be attuned to the structure and how the two corresponding panels create a composite meaning when compared that does not emerge if each section is read in isolation.[59]

    57. The outline of Ps 8 is taken from Alden, "Chiastic Psalms," 13.

    58. For this analysis of the Jacob Cycle see Walters, "Jacob Narrative," especially pp. 605–6.

    59. For more on how chiasm and concentric structures invite comparison of corresponding panels and how these panels illuminate each other and create composite meanings through similarity, contrast, and elaboration, see Man, "The Value of Chiasm," 148.

This example illustrates the truth of Porten's assertion that "structure is not simply artificial device or literary elegance. It is a key to meaning. Oversight of structure may result in failure to grasp the true theme."[60]

Porten's comment raises the question of how much the hermeneutical significance of a concentric structure depends on whether or not the reader or hearer recognizes the structure. Perhaps an analogy can illuminate the issue. English literature frequently utilizes esoteric and not-so-esoteric symbols and allusions that the average reader may never notice or understand, but which the literary critic may find very significant for interpretation. Similarly, the average reader can understand much about the Jacob Cycle without ever realizing how the cycle is organized. However, recognizing the chiastic structure of the cycle may provide additional insights and allow new meanings to emerge. As illustrated by the contrasting examples of Psalm 8 and Genesis 34, the hermeneutical weight of a structure can vary significantly from text to text, and so the particularities of a given passage should determine how much hermeneutical significance to attach to the structure, not preconceived notions about the importance of structure. In the case of Jer 23:9—29:32 the concentric features are not immediately obvious, nor does comparing the similarities and differences between corresponding panels reveal major new meanings. One might be inclined to suggest that the hermeneutical weight exerted by the concentric structure is more akin to what we observe in Psalm 8 than in Genesis 34. However, there are significant ways in which recognition of the structure should impact interpretation of 23:9—29:32.

One of the most obvious hermeneutical impacts of chiasm or concentric structures is to demarcate the boundaries of a passage, even if the structure appears to be only a surface feature of the text.[61] This simple fact has major hermeneutical implications, because if a block of material is a unit then the interpreter should be attuned to connections, similarities, contrasts, and other features of order and unity. Individual passages acquire some of their meaning from the larger whole in which they are embedded, at the same time as they also contribute to the meaning of that larger whole. Thus, placing a story or other type of material into a new

---

60. Porten, "The Structure and Theme of the Solomon Narrative," 95. For similar comments about the significance of structure for interpretation see Man, "The Value of Chiasm," 154; Bar-Efrat, "Some Observations on the Analysis of Structure," 172–73.

61. Bar-Efrat, "Some Observations on the Analysis of Structure," 172. Bar-Efrat makes this comment about literary structures in general, not just chiasm or concentric structures.

context can significantly change its meaning. The story of how Jacob's sons murder the men of Shechem was probably at one time a chauvinistic tale celebrating Israel's dominance over its Canaanite neighbors, but the new context of the story alters its meaning.

On the surface the diverse material in 23:9—29:32 appears to deal with a variety of topics, and if one is not attuned to the structure then the material may appear disjointed and even chaotic, a fact well illustrated by how many of the commentaries treat these chapters. The existence of a large concentric structure encourages the interpreter to ask what the purpose is behind organizing such apparently disparate material into a single unit. The superscription and the bulk of the content provide the answer. The text seeks to portray the nature of true and false prophecy, the conflict between them, and the effects of each upon the community of faith. This means that interpreters should not read the individual sections of 23:9—29:32 in isolation from each other, but should discern how each contributes to the meaning of the larger whole, and how each is in turn impacted by this larger whole. For example, read in isolation, the figs vision in ch. 24 and the cup of wrath passage in ch. 25 say little about the nature of true or false prophecy. However, read in light of the larger unit, this material contributes to a portrayal of the quintessential true prophet Jeremiah and provides guidance for how to appropriate the message of true prophecy and how to distinguish it from false prophecy.

Recognition of the concentric structure also makes the interpreter attuned to the significance of the material in the center. At the heart of the concentric structure stand three stories all focusing on faithful and unfaithful responses to the word of true prophets. At the center of the center is the incident of how Micah's proclamation of disaster on Jerusalem inspired Hezekiah and his people to repent, so that catastrophe was averted (26:17–19). This stands out as one of the central messages of the entire editorial unit—true prophecy in any age calls for repentance, and such repentance is the only way to avoid divine punishment.

One of the major ways in which 23:9—29:32 deals with the issue of true versus false prophecy is by depicting Jeremiah as the paradigmatic true prophet who speaks the authoritative word of God, in contrast to his prophetic opponents who are presented as paradigms of misleading and dangerous prophecy, which brings disaster upon the nation. These paradigms attempt to guide the community of faith in the ongoing task of discerning between the true and the false prophetic word, they offer guidelines for how to appropriate the words of true prophecy, and they encourage faithful living as defined by the true prophet Jeremiah.

As Long has pointed out, the very act of collecting prophetic materials into a book represents an attempt to claim authority for the prophet and his message.[62] Chapters 23–29 employ a variety of other strategies to legitimate Jeremiah and to claim ongoing authority for his word: asserting that YHWH is the source of his message, highlighting the close relationship between Jeremiah and God, setting Jeremiah and his message in the context of a venerable tradition of past prophets, and sharply contrasting Jeremiah with other prophets who are immoral, lack divine inspiration, and proclaim a false and dangerous message. As mentioned in chapter 1, a significant contribution of Lange's study is to highlight how written prophetic traditions gradually acquired increasing authority in the Second Temple period. The community became increasingly convinced that YHWH no longer communicated directly with human beings but that the divine will had been revealed through past communications, the significance of which needed to be spelled out for the present.[63] A driving force behind the production of prophetic books like Jeremiah was the work of scribes in the Second Temple period, who prolonged the prophetic process of communication by preserving, shaping, and interpreting older prophecies in ways that addressed the socio-religious crises related to the destruction and rebuilding of Jerusalem.[64] Jeremiah 23:9—29:32 seeks to present and interpret prophetic conflict so as to make authoritative claims upon future generations of the faithful community.

---

62. Long, "Prophetic Authority," 20.

63. See Blenkinsopp, *A History of Prophecy in Israel*, 256.

64. See Nissinen, "How Prophecy Became Literature," especially p. 157. For a somewhat different description of how the prophetic literature transmitted older traditions so as to make authoritative claims on the faith community, see Childs, "The Canonical Shape," 48–49.

3

Section A
Condemnation of False Prophets in General (23:9–40)

SECTION A (23:9–40) is a complex of originally independent sayings in prose and poetry that heaps up a series of condemnations of false prophets. The rhetorical effect of beginning the larger editorial unit with such a long and harsh list is to stress the grave danger that false prophecy poses for the community. By the time the reader reaches 23:9 the book has for twenty-two chapters already portrayed Jeremiah as a faithful true prophet, and so the sharp critique of other prophets serves to illustrate the huge gulf between such false prophecy and the true prophecy represented by Jeremiah. The critique also stresses how false prophecy prevents the true word of God from being heard with force and clarity,[1] and the harsh fate predicted for the false prophets functions as a dire warning about the disastrous consequences of heeding such prophecy. By seeking to describe the nature of false prophecy the passage also indirectly characterizes the nature of true prophecy and thereby provides guidance for discerning between them. The catastrophe foretold in 23:9–40 is clearly the Babylonian destruction of Judah, and so another impact of the chapter is to place a good share of the blame on Jeremiah's prophetic opponents.[2] This gives the section a "you shall know them by their fruits"

---

1. Clements, *Jeremiah*, 143.
2. Carroll observes how one of the strongest elements running through Jeremiah 2–24 is a "discourse of blame" targeting the priests, prophets, people, kings, wise men,

perspective.³ The text portrays the kind of prophecy that leads to catastrophe, and thereby creates a paradigm that can help the future community avoid the sort of prophecy that has already once brought utter calamity.⁴ The depiction of false prophecy in 23:9–40 mentions no specific prophets and remains somewhat general, but later incidents in 23:9—29:32, especially in section A' (29:20–32), will provide specific illustrations of the offenses and prophets condemned in a general way in 23:9–40.

PROPHETS AND PRIESTS ARE GODLESS (23:9–12)

Immediately after the superscription "Concerning the Prophets," Jeremiah launches into a lament describing how personally devastated and incapacitated he is as a result of the divine words (23:9). His heart is crushed, his bones tremble, and he experiences the disorientation and weakness of drunkenness, all because of YHWH and his holy words. This deep level of emotional and physical involvement in the divine purpose is typical of Jeremiah, illustrated especially by his laments, and it serves to validate his message and ministry, in contrast to the false prophets who have no such experience of God and are not so passionately involved in their ministry.⁵ So powerful are the divine words he must speak that they

and Jerusalem. See Carroll, "Halfway through a Dark Wood," 75–76.

3. Fretheim, *Jeremiah*, 331.

4. Because of the critical stance toward prophets, and because no positive model of prophecy is presented in 23:9–40, Carroll suggests that the entire passage belongs to a late period when prophecy per se was held in disrepute (compare Zech 13:2–6), and that it seeks to condemn all prophecy as false and misleading. See *Jeremiah*, 449–50. Lange's view is that Jeremiah himself collected the material in 23:9–32 but then a later editor added the heading in 23:9, "Concerning the Prophets," as a way to turn the entire section into a rejection of prophecy as a whole. See *Vom prophetischen Wort*, 162. Such observations may or may not shed light on the origins of the text, but its current function is not to discredit all prophecy but only a certain kind of false prophecy. Carroll and Lange assume that the original or some earlier meaning of the text is the one it continues to have in its present context.

5. Stulman, *Jeremiah*, 216; Fretheim, *Jeremiah*, 332. For more on Jeremiah as tormented and consumed by his ministry see O'Connor, "The Prophet Jeremiah," 135–37. On 137 she observes, "[Jeremiah] appears as one who lives in profound intimacy with God and knows that intimacy in his whole being. This intimacy distinguishes the true prophet from the false, for the latter has not stood in the council of God to see and hear the divine word (23:18)." Hill, *Friend or Foe?*, 40–46, describes how Jeremiah frequently becomes a metaphor for YHWH, especially in passages that portray the suffering of a speaker whose identity is ambiguous. Perhaps 23:9 is also a text that melds into one the suffering of Jeremiah and the suffering of God over the sad state of

overwhelm his being. The devastation Jeremiah experiences indicates that God's words must be ones of horrible judgment, and the rest of the unit is in fact an invective-threat oracle, with vv. 10–11 specifying the reasons for punishment and v. 12 describing its nature.

Since the opening description of Jeremiah's personal devastation follows the superscription "Concerning the Prophets" and leads into a scathing critique of false prophets, this devastation is more than just a response to YHWH's holy words but is also a response to everything that is said about the prophets, and a response to the sad state of the nation which is led by unfaithful priests and prophets (23:10–11). Similar to how the opening statement in the book of Amos, "YHWH roars from Zion" (1:2), casts a pall over the rest of the book, the description of Jeremiah's shattered being sets the tone for the rest of 23:9–40 and all of 23:9—29:32 and dramatizes the depth of the calamity.

It is not immediately apparent that a change in speaker occurs in v. 10, but by the end of v. 11 the reference to the temple as "my house" indicates that vv. 10–11 constitute a divine speech and must be the holy words of YHWH that have brought such distress to Jeremiah. Verse 10 begins to explain what is so drastically wrong: the land languishes under a drought brought on by the adulterers in its midst; the land has become so overburdened with human evil that it grieves under a curse and can no longer function normally.[6] The identity of the adulterers is not immediately clear, and it is tempting to think that the entire population is indicted when the text states, "the land is *full* of adulterers." Verse 11, which targets the priests and prophets for the first time, reads, "Even prophet and even priest are defiled," making it sound as if the religious leadership is corrupt *in addition to* the adulterers who fill the land. However, in the larger context of 23:9–40 the focus is almost exclusively on the sins of the false prophets and there is little interest in highlighting the sins of the people, which is very different from other parts of the book. Also, 23:14 explicitly condemns the Jerusalem prophets for committing adultery. Therefore, "the land is *full* of adulterers" should probably be read as hyperbolic language stressing the all-encompassing moral decay caused by the sins of the prophets and priests.

---

affairs in Judah.

6. Brueggemann, *A Commentary on Jeremiah*, 209. The suffering of the natural world because of human sin is a theme in the book of Jeremiah (3:2–3; 4:23–28; 9:10; 12:4, 10–11; 14:1–6), based on the conviction that human morality affects cosmic order. See Fretheim, *Jeremiah*, 333.

"The unholy alliance between prophet and priest"[7] occurs here for the fourth time in the book (cf. 5:31; 6:13=8:10; 14:18), as Jeremiah once again issues a sweeping condemnation of the nation's entire religious leadership. The exact nature of the priests' and prophets' sins remains vague, as it is not clear if the adultery of 23:10 designates sexual offenses or participation in fertility cults. In 29:23 the adultery committed by the prophets is unambiguously sexual, but elsewhere in Jeremiah and the prophetic literature adultery can be a metaphor for the worship of other gods (3:1–3, 8–9; 5:7–8; Hosea 1–3; 4:13–14; Ezek 16:32, 38; 23:37, 43–45). The accusation in 23:13–14 that Jerusalem's prophets are even worse than Samaria's prophets who prophesied by Baal is further reason to believe that the adultery involves apostasy. The ambiguity in 23:10 suggests that the point is not the exact nature of the sin but an attempt to tarnish priests and prophets with the social abhorrence associated with adultery, one of the Old Testament's most shameful of sins.[8] If adultery does refer to participation in fertility cults then the irony is that such participation has resulted in drought, the exact opposite of the desired outcome.

The priests and prophets are also accused of being חָנֵפוּ, often translated as "godless" or "defiled." חנף is a relatively rare verb used to describe how the land is polluted or defiled by human sins such as murder (Num 35:33), sexual misconduct (Jer 3:1–2), the worship of other gods portrayed as adultery (Jer 3:9), child sacrifice and worship of Canaanite gods (Ps 106:38), or covenant-breaking and general disobedience of God's laws (Isa 24:5), always with devastating consequences for the land and its inhabitants. While Jer 23:11 does not specify any particular offense, the use of חנף tarnishes prophets and priests with the most damaging type of misconduct. This wickedness has even infiltrated YHWH's temple, which suggests that the security and well-being associated with the temple will become the opposite.[9]

The לָכֵן (therefore) of v. 12 introduces the description of YHWH's punishment, which is portrayed only in very general terms. The judgment contains some poetic justice. The prophets and priests ran after evil (23:10—רָעָה) and so God will bring evil (רָעָה) upon them (23:12). Blaming the prophets and priests for their own downfall is also to blame

---

7. Lundbom, *Jeremiah 21–36*, 183.

8. See Domeris, "When Metaphor Becomes Myth," 258. Sharp, *Prophecy and Ideology in Jeremiah*, 117–18, argues that adultery in 23:9–15 refers to the promotion of foreign political alliances.

9. Moberly, *Prophecy and Discernment*, 71.

them for the downfall of the nation, because from the perspective of the completed book it is the catastrophe of 587 that constitutes the punishment decreed here for prophets and priests.

THE PROPHETS CAUSE AN "EPIDEMIC OF IMMORALITY"[10] (23:13–15)

The second unit of material in section A flows very smoothly from 23:9–12 and is another invective-threat oracle that no longer mentions the priests but zeroes in on the prophets and some of their specific offenses. The two units are similar in vocabulary and theme. Both vv. 10 and 14 speak of adultery (root נאף) and evildoers (root רעה), while vv. 11 and 15 use forms of חנף to stress the defilement that emanates from the prophets (and priests in the case of v. 11). Both oracles hold prophets responsible for the sad state of the nation and predict a horrible fate for them.

The oracle of 23:13–15 begins by calling attention to the prophets of Samaria who prophesied by Baal and thereby led the people of Israel astray. The verb תעה can mean to wander or be lost in a literal sense, but it can also refer to straying from faithfulness to YHWH,[11] or in the hiphil, enticing others to forsake the ways of YHWH,[12] and so use of the term here casts the prophets in an extremely negative light. Accusing the prophets of encouraging worship of Baal affirms the first commandment as a central criterion for distinguishing between true and false prophecy (compare Deut 13:2–6 [Heb.]). By omitting any other reasons for the fall of the northern kingdom besides the apostasy and false teaching of its prophets, the text lays the blame squarely on them. The focus then shifts immediately to the prophets of Jerusalem as a way to compare and contrast them with their northern counterparts.

---

10. This expression is borrowed from McKane, *A Critical and Exegetical Commentary*, 1:576.

11. See Ps 58:4 (Heb.); 95:10; 119:110, 176; Isa 28:7; 53:6; Ezek 14:11; 44:10, 15; 48:11.

12. See 2 Kgs 21:9; 2 Chr 33:9; Isa 3:12; 9:15 (Heb.); 63:17; Jer 23:32; 42:20; 50:6; Hos 4:12; Amos 2:4; Mic 3:5.

Concerning the Prophets

> Now [ו] in the prophets of Samaria
> I have seen something repulsive:
> They prophesied by Baal
> and led my people Israel astray.
> (23:13)

> But [ו] in the prophets of Jerusalem
> I have seen something horrible:
> Committing adultery and walking in *sheqer*,
> and strengthening the hands of evildoers,
> so that no one turns from his wickedness.
> (23:14ab)

The way in which the opening bicolon of v. 14 follows the structure and vocabulary of the first bicolon of v. 13 signals that in God's eyes the offenses and impact of the two groups of prophets are similar. The only accusation leveled at Samaria's prophets is promoting Baal worship, which implies that the offenses of Jerusalem's prophets are similar in nature and gravity. If the northern prophets were responsible for the destruction of their nation more than a hundred years earlier, then surely the southern prophets of Jeremiah's time are in the process of leading their nation to its doom. Such a dire warning signals how disastrous the consequences of false prophecy are and how much the community of faith has at stake in discerning and rejecting it.

Juxtaposing descriptions of Samaria's and Jerusalem's prophets highlights the similarities between them but also calls attention to some differences. The initial *waw*s in 23:13 and 23:14 create somewhat of a contrast between the prophets of the two capital cities.[13] The text levels more accusations against the Jerusalem prophets, thereby making them look even worse than the prophets of Samaria. The horrible thing that YHWH has seen in the Jerusalem prophets is adultery, walking in *sheqer* (falsehood or lies), and strengthening the hands of evildoers so that no one turns back from his wickedness (23:14). The text is only minimally interested in the northern prophets but uses them as a foil to portray the southern prophets as being even worse than their apostate northern counterparts.

Here too commentators are divided as to whether the adultery of the prophets in 23:14 is sexual or refers to participation in fertility cults. Given the parallels that the text creates between the Jerusalem prophets and the pagan northern prophets, and given that worship of other gods is elsewhere in the book of Jeremiah described as adultery (3:6–10; 5:7–8; cf. 3:1–2), the adultery here must at a minimum allude to participation in the worship of other gods.[14] However, this does not rule out reference

---

13. Lundbom, *Jeremiah 21–36*, 186.

14. Lange claims that the text clearly associates the Jerusalem prophets with paganism. See Lange, *Vom prophetischen Wort*, 129.

to sexual impropriety. The text is less interested in spelling out the fine points of prophetic misconduct than in issuing a blanket condemnation of false prophecy by describing it with vocabulary that will evoke feelings of revulsion. The term "adultery" functions similarly in 9:1 (Heb.), where Jeremiah accuses the entire population of adultery. Here too the text does not specify if the adultery is sexual, religious, or both, but seems primarily interested in painting the accused as totally depraved.

The fact that adultery can be a metaphor for participation in the fertility cult leads some scholars to assert that the second accusation against the prophets in 23:14, "walking in *sheqer*," means following Baal, *sheqer* being a code word for Baal.[15] The text does not seem quite this specific, but numerous passages in the book of Jeremiah link *sheqer* to the worship of other gods (3:23; 10:14; 13:25-27; 16:19-20; 51:17), and so the accusation of *sheqer* does create an association between the prophets and paganism. However, this reading does not exhaust the meaning of the text. Overholt suggests that in the present context the accusation means that the prophets live and carry out their ministry in a way that is false and misleading.[16] The precise nature of the prophets' falsehood is spelled out more clearly in the rest of ch. 23, but already it is evident that their actions encourage evil rather inspire repentance. *Sheqer* is a key term in the polemic against false prophets in 23:9—29:32 and frequently designates false assurances of well-being (27:10, 14, 15, 16; 28:15; 29:9, 21, 23, 31). Elsewhere in the book *sheqer* can designate hopes for God's protection, sometimes delivered by prophets (14:13-14; see also 6:13-14 = 8:10-11) and sometimes not (7:4, 8). Earlier texts in the book have already condemned the prophets for proclaiming *shalom* when there is no *shalom* (5:12-13; 6:13-15 = 8:10-12; 14:13-16; see also 37:19). The book portrays such assurances as extremely dangerous because they distort reality, lead to complacency in the face of sin, and prevent repentance. The declaration of 23:14 that the prophets strengthen the hands of evildoers so that no one turns back (root: שוב) from their wickedness is at the heart of the book of Jeremiah's critique of the false prophets. The *sheqer* in which they walk is a false worldview that results in active unfaithfulness to YHWH and therefore disaster.[17] The activities of the false prophets are

---

15. Thompson, *The Book of Jeremiah*, 495. Holladay, *Jeremiah 1*, 631-32, also sees this as a possibility.

16. Overholt, *The Threat of Falsehood*, 54. See also Macholz, "Jeremia in der Kontinuität der Prophetie," 307.

17. Lange, *Vom prophetischen Wort*, 112. This is particularly evident in texts like

so deplorable because their actions and message contribute to the moral decline of the nation, which is precisely the opposite of what prophetic ministry is supposed to accomplish. Over and over 23:9—29:32 stresses that true prophecy uncovers the people's sin and calls for repentance and obedience, so that the nation might yet avert God's wrath (23:17, 22; 25:3–6; 26:2–6, 12–13, 18–19, 20; 27:12–15, 16–17; 29:4–9, 19).[18]

The book of Jeremiah looks back from the other side of the Babylonian conquest and asks how such a horrendous disaster came about. One response is that the nation was lulled into complacency by false assurances of God's grace and protection. Such hopes were rooted in traditions regarding Zion as God's chosen city and the Davidic kings as YHWH's vice-regents on earth.[19] The prophets and priests attached to temple and court played a significant role in promoting these royal and Zion traditions and so they become a special target of Jeremiah's critique. The book of Jeremiah is determined to convince the community that it should never again blindly trust such assurances, but that it should instead heed the ongoing prophetic summons to faithful living.

The last couplet of 23:14 indicates that the prophets are responsible for an "epidemic of immorality,"[20] since their activity has made YHWH regard the people like those of Sodom and Gomorrah. Some commentators see the comparison to Sodom and Gomorrah as less an assertion of the people's depravity than a message of judgment, since these two cities are elsewhere archetypes of God's complete destruction of a people.[21] Sodom and Gomorrah are indeed archetypes, but since their depravity is what leads to their destruction, they are archetypes of both moral depravity and destruction. Thus, the comparison to Sodom and Gomorrah

---

27:12–15, 16–17, and 28:13–16, where promises of deliverance are depicted as creating a distorted view of reality that leads to active rebellion against YHWH, culminating in catastrophe.

18. For a discussion of how prophecy, which was originally quite a diverse phenomenon, came to be viewed primarily as a call to repentance, see the analysis below of Jer 25:3–7.

19. See Overholt, *The Threat of Falsehood*, 1–23, for a discussion of the false sense of security in Judah during the time of the historical Jeremiah. For a discussion of how critique of royal and Zion traditions is central to the book of Jeremiah, see Brueggemann, *A Commentary on Jeremiah*, 6, 14.

20. McKane, *A Critical and Exegetical Commentary*, 1:576.

21. See for example Overholt, *The Threat of Falsehood*, 55. Texts that treat Sodom and Gomorrah as archetypes include Deut 29:22 (Heb.); 32:32; Isa 1:10; Jer 49:18; 50:40; Ezek 16:46–58; Amos 4:11.

functions as an accusation of immorality and an announcement of judgment all rolled up into one.[22]

Jeremiah 23:13-15 closes with an announcement of judgment couched in the metaphorical language of a banquet. As host YHWH will feed the prophets a meal of poisonous herbs and then wash it down with poisonous drink, turning the event into an "anti-banquet." Then the text adds one more reason for the punishment of the prophets, as a way of summarizing the effect of their offenses. From them חֲנֻפָּה (defilement) has spread to the entire land. As discussed in relation to 23:11, forms of חנף generally refer to serious sins such as worship of other gods, murder, sexual immorality, child sacrifice, and covenant-breaking, all of which have a devastating impact on the land and the community. In this instance חֲנֻפָּה does not designate any particular offense but refers to the ruinous corruption that the prophets spread over the entire land.

Both sections A and A' assert that immorality is one of the identifying features of false prophecy, accusing the prophets of personal moral failings and blaming them for the moral decline of the entire people (23:10-11, 14-15, 17; 29:23). This raises the question of whether immorality automatically invalidates the message of a prophet. Not necessarily, Carroll claims, since "this is the old problem of 'would a good man make a better pair of shoes than a good cobbler?'"[23] To frame the issue this way is to misunderstand prophetic ministry as envisioned by the book of Jeremiah and the Bible as a whole. According to prophetic understanding, YHWH is a God of righteousness and justice who will not tolerate evil among his people, and so prophets must be attuned to the divine will so that they can point out breaches in the covenant relationship between God and Israel. In order to perform this role the personal lifestyle and message of prophets must embody the divine will and promote adherence to it.[24] As Moberly puts it in his critique of Carroll, prophecy is not like shoemaking because it is not involved in the production of material objects but in the formation of human lives.[25] Because the message and

---

22. Hossfeld and Meyer, *Prophet gegen Prophet*, 76; Meyer, *Jeremia und die falschen Propheten*, 121.

23. Carroll, *When Prophecy Failed*, 193.

24. For a discussion of why personal morality is central to prophetic ministry, see Mowinckel, "'The Spirit' and the 'Word,'" 219-26; Lindblom, *Prophecy in Ancient Israel*, 215; Long, "Prophetic Authority," 18.

25. Moberly, *Prophecy and Discernment*, 94.

the messenger form a single entity,[26] 23:9—29:32 assumes that prophets who lead immoral lives or overlook the sins of their people cannot possibly be YHWH's spokespersons.

Moberly argues that morality is the primary criterion that the Bible uses to discern between the truth and falsehood of a message or messenger (prophetic or non-prophetic) claiming to speak for God. "The reality of YHWH may be discerned in public life when His character and priorities are appropriately enacted in the words and deeds of His human representatives."[27] Because YHWH is interested in the character of the faith community as a whole, prophetic speech is response-seeking speech that must call for repentance and faithful living.[28] Moberly even interprets prophetic announcements of disaster as summons to repent, arguing that their intent is to convict the hearers to change course so that YHWH will not follow through with judgment.[29] On this point Moberly overstates his case somewhat and fails to distinguish adequately between different prophets and between what in some cases may have been the initial intent behind a prophecy versus the intent behind a prophetic book. In the case of Amos, for example, there seems little evidence that summoning people to repent stood at the core of his ministry, although the book of Amos was preserved so that it would function in the faith community as an ongoing call to repent. Moberly makes a valuable contribution by highlighting the significance of morality and the summons to repent, both of which are central to Jer 23:9—29:32. However, there is more at stake in the portrayal of true and false prophecy than these two issues.

Moberly observes that despite the centrality of morality as a criterion of discernment, many texts remain vague in terms of what specifically constitutes morality or immorality on the part of God's spokespersons. It is not unusual to see similar vagueness with respect to what people should repent of and what kind of lifestyle they should embrace. We see precisely such vagueness in what 23:9–15 says about the false prophets and their failure to turn people from wickedness. Such texts, Moberly notes, presuppose an unstated vision of the faithful life that can only be fleshed out on the basis

26. Ibid., 187. This is especially true of the book of Jeremiah, which is unique among prophetic books in providing such an extensive portrayal of the prophet's life. Jeremiah devotes himself so fully to his ministry that his life becomes the message.

27. Ibid., 82.

28. Ibid., 52.

29. Ibid. See for example 115–25.

of the community's traditions and Scriptures.[30] Realistically it can hardly be otherwise, because it would be impractical to insert lengthy moral codes into Jeremiah 23 or similar texts. The material in 23:9–15 (and all of 23:9—29:32) is intended to be read in light of the larger book of Jeremiah and all its specific points regarding the nature of faithfulness, as well as its more general appeals to live a *Torah* way of life (26:4), however the content of that *Torah* is defined.

DO NOT LISTEN TO THE PROPHETS (23:16–24)

There is no consensus among translators and commentators about how to divide 23:16–24 into smaller units, and so I will analyze these verses as a whole, focusing on the progression of ideas rather than on how best to partition the text. The core message is that the other prophets have absolutely no access to God or God's word. With the opening words, "Thus says YHWH of hosts" (23:16), Jeremiah makes authoritative claims for himself and his speech, in keeping with the account of his call where YHWH promises to place the divine word in his mouth (1:9).[31] That Jeremiah is God's spokesperson is central to the portrayal of true prophecy in 23:9—29:32 and the book as a whole.

The messenger formula here identifies the condemnation of the prophets that follows as the direct word of YHWH, except for 23:18–20 where Jeremiah is the speaker. After the initial depiction of the prophets and their devastating impact on the community (23:9–15), God now addresses the community directly with a warning not to heed these prophets. The stinging critique begun in 23:9–15 continues, but with a subtle shift. In the previous units it is primarily the immorality of the prophets that demonstrates their falseness, whereas in 23:16–24 the focus is the falseness of their message, rooted in their lack of divine inspiration.[32] Following the exhortation not to listen to the prophets, most of the pericope provides reasons why the prophets are not to be heeded. They delude the people because their prophecies originate within themselves and do not come from YHWH (v. 16b). This delusion entails a message of *shalom*, which leads to complacency in the midst of great evil (v. 17). Had the

---

30. Ibid., 235.

31. See ibid., 43–47, for a discussion of how the book portrays Jeremiah's word as word of YHWH.

32. Rudolph, *Jeremia*, 139.

prophets stood in the divine council (v. 18) they would have realized that YHWH's plan was for destruction (vv. 19–20). Instead, they prophesied without being commissioned (vv. 21–22a) and as a result failed to call the people to repent (v. 22b).

The first accusation against the prophets is that they are deluding the people (23:16b). מַהְבִּלִים is a denominative verb from הֶבֶל, which is usually a figurative noun for that which is a delusion, worthless, empty, or fruitless. The hiphil form used here is a *hapex legomenon*, but the meaning seems to be that the prophets are making people trust in that which is a delusion and has no power.[33] What the prophets utter is worthless and misleading because it is the product of their own minds and does not come from YHWH (23:16b). The text does not accuse the prophets of deliberately uttering lies, but they confuse their own thoughts with the word of YHWH.[34] The prophets delude the nation with their repeated proclamation of *shalom* to persons who despise the word of YHWH and persist in their evil ways (23:17). In this context the word of YHWH that people despise must be the consistent message of Jeremiah that judgment is in the offing unless the nation begins to follow the divine will. False prophecy leads to complacency because its promise of well-being removes the necessary incentive for repentance. The conviction that the catastrophe of 587 was YHWH's punishment dominates the book of Jeremiah, and so it depicts the complacency caused by false prophetic assurances of well-being as one of the gravest dangers that the community must guard against.

Jeremiah is not purely a prophet of doom, in contrast to his opponents, who are prophets of salvation, because Jeremiah too announces future deliverance (24:5-7; 27:22; 29:10-14, 32; chs. 30-32). However, two things distinguish him from the other prophets. The first is that false prophets announce deliverance without reference to the moral demands of the covenant relationship with YHWH.[35] The second is that Jeremiah does not envision salvation this side of judgment. The nation's sin has enormous consequences, and only after these consequences have run their course can the people expect a time of divine favor.[36]

---

33. For a more detailed discussion see Overholt, *The Threat of Falsehood*, 57.

34. McKane, *A Critical and Exegetical Commentary*, 1:578-79.

35. For a helpful discussion of this point, see Reventlow, *Liturgie und prophetisches Ich bei Jeremia*, 121-26.

36. This point will be discussed in more detail in connection with ch. 24.

The critique of the false prophets continues by denying that they are in touch with divine revelation in any way (23:18-22). Verse 18 is a rhetorical question, "But who has stood in the council of YHWH to see and hear his word, who has given heed to his word and heard?"[37] The implied answer is, "Jeremiah has but certainly not the prophets who are the topic of discussion." True prophets were sometimes transported into the divine council, where YHWH commissioned them and gave them a message to announce (1 Kgs 22:19-23; Isa 6:1-13). Duhm and other scholars since have argued that v. 18 is an editorial addition claiming that no one has ever stood in the divine council.[38] It is difficult to know what the original author may have intended, and placing material into a new literary context can alter its meaning. In its present context the verse is not a blanket denial of prophetic access to the divine council but is part of the text's denial of the false prophets' access to God. This is made clear by v. 22, which asserts that had the prophets stood in YHWH's council they would have proclaimed his word and called the people to repent. The fact that Jeremiah does precisely this—announce YHWH's word and call for repentance—indicates that he at least has access to the divine council.

Moberly suggests that the "council [סוֹד] of YHWH" may imply more here than just the court of YHWH as heavenly king. The term *sod* can refer to a gathering of people, and by extension the kind of understanding shared by people in an intimate relationship (Prov 25:9). In Amos 3:7 *sod* designates the divine purpose/plan revealed to faithful prophets. "Surely Lord YHWH does nothing without revealing his plan/counsel [סוֹדוֹ] to his servants the prophets." Moberly claims that Jer 23:18 does not root the authenticity of a prophet's word in some kind of "supernatural" experience but in appropriation of the divine will/plan in such a way that it shapes the character, vision, actions, and message of the prophet.[39]

---

37. A change of vocalization of the last word would yield the form וַיַּשְׁמַע ("announced [it]"), which would suit the context very well but would not significantly alter the gist of the question.

38. Duhm, *Das Buch Jeremia*, 187. See also Quell, *Wahre und falsche Propheten*, 38-39; Münderlein, *Kriterien*, 63. On the basis that Zech 3:1-10 depicts a scene in the divine council, Lange argues that Jer 23:18 represents a Deuteronomistic critique of Zechariah and his hopes for salvation associated with the rebuilding of the temple. See *Vom prophetischen Wort*, 218.

Lundbom points out that "to stand" in the divine council means to stand ready as messenger to the one who presides over the council. For a fuller discussion of the divine council, see Lundbom, *Jeremiah 21-36*, 195-96.

39. Moberly, *Prophecy and Discernment*, 74, 80-81.

Concerning the Prophets

The fact that the verses that follow report a vision (23:19–20) suggests that in the present context *sod* does refer to an extraordinary revelatory experience, but Moberly is certainly correct in his articulation of a key assumption underlying this passage and all of 23:9—29:32. In 23:18-22 it would have been easy to make grandiose claims regarding Jeremiah's access to the divine council, but in terms of legitimating Jeremiah as a true prophet, dramatic religious experiences take a back seat to the content of his message, both here and in all of 23:9—29:32.

Lundbom and others are probably correct in pointing out how 23:18 is continued by 23:21-22 and that the intervening verses, a doublet of 30:23-24, have been inserted secondarily.[40] The effect of including these verses is to describe a vision of the divine wrath and judgment that the prophets would have seen had they stood in the divine council. In contrast to the optimistic announcements of the false prophets, this hour in history stands under God's wrath that will not relent until God's purpose is accomplished. Jeremiah is authenticated as a true prophet because he announces just such a message, but the other prophets are discredited because they know nothing of YHWH's impending punishment of the wicked. Another effect of these verses is to pronounce judgment on the false prophets. In a passage condemning such prophets, the announcement that YHWH's whirling tempest is about to overwhelm the wicked must mean that God will also sweep away these prophets. The conclusion of 23:20 gives the passage a retrospective "I told you so" quality: "In the days to come you will perceive it clearly." The early readers of the book knew all too well that God's storm had blown through, and that Jeremiah had been right and the false prophets wrong. The conclusion legitimates the message of Jeremiah and suggests that since his words have proved to be so true in the past, the community of faith should heed these words in an ongoing way.

The next two verses return to specific denials that the false prophets have any access to revelation, with the two perfectly parallel statements of 23:21 emphasizing that the prophets have no mandate to speak for God.

> I did not send the prophets
>   but they ran;
> I did not speak to them
>   but they prophesied.

---

40. Lundbom, *Jeremiah 21-36*, 193-94.

This explains why the prophets can only recount the visions of their own minds (23:16) and why they announce *shalom* when God's plans are for destruction (23:17). YHWH can only stress that he has no relationship with such prophets who announce horribly misleading messages in his name. This stands in sharp contrast to Jeremiah, who is throughout the book portrayed as being divinely commissioned and having a close relationship with YHWH.[41] The prophets' lack of divine inspiration is stressed further by the next verse, which claims that had the prophets been privy to deliberations in the divine council they would have announced YHWH's words to the people, leading them to turn from their evil ways and practices. The argument is not that had the prophets stood in the divine council they would have been successful in turning people away from evil and averting calamity.[42] Jeremiah is depicted as the quintessential true prophet even though he had minimal success in this area. The issue is the fundamental nature of true prophecy, which always issues a call to forsake every form of evil and unfaithfulness.

Another effect of 23:22 is to link the fate of Judah to the failure of a certain kind of prophecy. The book of Jeremiah stresses over and over that refusal to repent resulted in the nation's doom. Here that refusal is attributed to the failure of prophecy to call for such a turnaround in people's lives. One reason 23:9—29:32 repeatedly emphasizes that true prophecy calls for repentance is because the stakes are so high. A text like Ezra 9:6-15 illustrates how at least some later Jews believed that the danger of history repeating itself was very real, and therefore the community of faith must adopt a repentant attitude and be continually vigilant in matters of faith and morality.

Jeremiah 23:23-24 consists of a series of three rhetorical questions whose meaning in the present context is not immediately obvious.[43] Because these verses focus not on the false prophets but on the nature of God, they seem out of place and some commentators treat 23:23-24 as an independent unit whose meaning is not connected to its present literary context.[44] I will read the text holistically and ask what these verses contribute to the portrayal of true and false prophecy. The first question,

---

41. For a more detailed discussion of how Jeremiah's message is legitimated by his close relationship to God, see O'Connor, "The Prophet Jeremiah," 135-37.

42. Fretheim, *Jeremiah*, 337-38; Moberly, *Prophecy and Discernment*, 83-88.

43. For a detailed discussion of the difficulties in these verses, see Carroll, *Jeremiah*, 464-68.

44. See for example McKane, *A Critical and Exegetical Commentary*, 1:587.

"Am I a near God, declares YHWH, and not a distant God?," would seem to highlight YHWH's transcendence.⁴⁵ In the present context this implies that he is not a familiar and comfortable patron deity who is easily accessible to the prophets who claim to speak in his name,⁴⁶ which fits with the previous assertions that the prophets have no divine revelation (23:21) and have not stood in the divine council (23:18, 22). Perhaps the question is also a subtle critique of false assurances from prophets and priests that YHWH will be near to Zion, the Davidic king, and the nation, in contrast to the true prophetic message of Jeremiah highlighting God's distance from Judah's sacred institutions.⁴⁷ Two further rhetorical questions follow, the import of which is that God is both omniscient and omnipresent. The implication of these assertions in the present context must be that even if the prophets are able to deceive their fellow citizens, God can see exactly what they are up to and will hold them accountable. The combined impact of the three rhetorical questions is to suggest that God is not a domesticated patron deity but is keenly aware of human sin and will hold accountable the false prophets whose view of God is too small and localized.⁴⁸ The impact is similar to that of the doxologies that have been inserted into the book of Amos (4:13; 5:8–9; 9:5–6). YHWH is the sovereign and all-powerful deity who is not to be trifled with, because he has the power to fulfill what he has spoken through his faithful prophet.

Translators and commentators frequently connect 23:23–24 with the verses that follow (23:25–32) rather than the verses that precede, as I have done. Either possibility can be defended. If 23:23–24 is read in light of what follows, the meaning and impact are not significantly different. The rhetorical questions would then imply that YHWH can see the

---

45. Craigie et al., *Jeremiah 1–25*, 346, interpret the question somewhat differently, claiming that it has no single answer, since YHWH is both close to the people and yet distant at the same time.

The LXX and some other ancient versions read somewhat differently than the MT: "'I am a near God,' says the LORD, 'and not a distant God.'" See Herrmann, "Jeremia 23,23f als Zeugnis der Gotteserfahrung," 156–57. The difference is merely that the *Vorlage* of the LXX must have lacked the interrogative particle at the beginning of the sentence. For a fuller discussion of the differences between the MT and LXX see Lemke, "The Near and the Distant God," 541–42, 551–55.

46. Lemke, "The Near and the Distant God," 554; Kraus, *Prophetie in der Krisis*, 47; Brueggemann, *To Pluck Up*, 205–6.

47. See Brueggemann, *A Commentary on Jeremiah*, 213–15; Brueggemann, *Theology*, 48–49.

48. Stulman, *Jeremiah*, 217; Lundbom, *Jeremiah 21–36*, 201.

falseness of the prophets and their dreams, and that he is not at their beck and call. YHWH is a distant God who invades human experience with the power of fire or a hammer that shatters rock (see 23:29).[49]

LYING DREAMS (23:25–32)

The next two pericopes (23:25–32 and 23:33–40) constitute one long divine speech, and both focus on the forms in which the prophets receive and/or communicate their message. The first of these falls into two closely related sections, with 23:25–29 using a series of three rhetorical questions to undermine the authority of the false prophets, while in 23:30–32 YHWH three times declares his enmity toward the prophets, each time citing a different reason.[50]

YHWH begins by declaring that he has heard the prophets "who prophesy *sheqer* in my name saying, 'I have dreamed, I have dreamed'" (23:25). This opening follows smoothly from the previous verse, which stresses that nothing is hidden from God, implying that he is not about to stand idly by while prophets proclaim a false message in his name. The direct quotation and repetition of the prophets' words, "I have dreamed, I have dreamed," may be a form of satire or sarcasm. The prophets proclaim these dreams in YHWH's name, indicating that they consider him to be the source of their revelation. YHWH, however, declares that these dreams represent *sheqer* (falsehood), and the next two verses spell out how and why these prophetic dreams are false. "How long will there be in the heart of the prophets who prophesy *sheqer*—the prophets of their own deceitful heart[51]—the plan to make my people forget my name, by means of their dreams which they tell to each other, just like their fathers forgot my name for Baal" (23:26–27). The opening "how long" is an expression of lament, found elsewhere in Jeremiah (4:14, 21; 12:4; 13:27; 31:22; 47:5) and frequently in the Psalms. Here it expresses YHWH's deep pain resulting from the false dreams of the prophets. Earlier in 23:14, and at numerous other points in 23:9—29:32 and the rest of the book, *sheqer* designates prophetic assurances of well-being that create a distorted view of reality (see the discussion above of 23:14). Here the prophets are accused of an additional type of falsehood, undermining

---

49. Lemke, "The Near and the Distant God," 554.
50. Hossfeld and Meyer, *Prophet gegen Prophet*, 81.
51. The translation is awkward because the original Hebrew is awkward.

loyalty to the one true God and promoting worship of Baal. The *sheqer* that the prophets utter is spoken in YHWH's name (v. 25), yet the ultimate effect is to entice people to forsake YHWH for Baal (v. 27). The prophets are portrayed as promoters of syncretistic practices that blur the distinction between YHWH and Baal, something already hinted at when the prophets of Jerusalem are compared to the prophets of Samaria, who are active promoters of paganism (23:13–14). The charge of paganism also functions as a rhetorical strategy to discredit the prophets. The linking of prophets, dreams, and worship of other gods is also evident in Deut 13:2–6 (Heb.), which warns the community to be on guard against prophets and "dreamers of dreams" who can produce impressive signs but use their powers to divert the community's loyalty away from YHWH. Both texts affirm one of the central criteria for distinguishing between true and false prophecy—any prophet who encourages less than full devotion to YHWH is automatically false (cf. 23:13).

There is considerable debate about the interpretation of 23:28–29. "The prophet who has a dream, let him report the dream, and the one who has my word, let him speak my word truthfully. 'What does straw have in common with wheat?' declares YHWH. 'Is not my word like fire?' declares YHWH, 'and like a hammer that shatters rock?'" Because of the strong contrast between dreams and YHWH's word, numerous interpreters read these verses as ruling out dreams as a legitimate means of revelation.[52] Lundbom points out that dreams play only a very limited role in Old Testament prophecy, in contrast to the much more frequent vision.[53] Carroll maintains that the condemnation of dreams is part of a late postexilic attempt to ban prophetic activity as a whole.[54] The text might well be late but in its current context it does not denounce prophetic activity as a whole, because it encourages the prophet who has YHWH's word to speak it truthfully. Overholt marshals a host of examples that illustrate, despite a few disparaging remarks about dreams being insubstantial, that the Old Testament as a whole accepts dreams as a legitimate form of revelation.[55] One might still argue that Jer 23:25–29 represents an exception to the rule, especially since 27:9 and 29:8 also condemn false prophetic dreams, but it seems to me that Overholt is correct in claiming that the

---

52. See for example Osswald, *Falsche Prophetie*, 13; Thompson, *The Book of Jeremiah*, 500–502; McKane, *A Critical and Exegetical Commentary*, 1:588–91.

53. For a fuller discussion of the issue see Lundbom, *Jeremiah 21–36*, 204–6.

54. Carroll, *Jeremiah*, 474.

55. Overholt, *The Threat of Falsehood*, 64–65.

text is primarily concerned with condemning the dreams of a particular group of prophets rather than denying the validity of dreams in general. As Moberly points out, the dreaming should not be decontextualized as though this passage were a theoretical discussion regarding appropriate channels of revelation.[56] The text stresses that the dreams of the prophets are false because of their content and consequences—they divert people's loyalty away from YHWH (23:27, 32). All of 23:9-40 seeks to discredit the false prophets, one of the primary critiques being that they have no access to divine revelation. No matter what these prophets say or how they claim to have received their message, the text would judge them to be false. A legitimate means in the hands of the wrong persons becomes illegitimate; that is, the falseness of the prophets makes their techniques false.[57]

The straw-wheat analogy of 23:28 is not between the dream and the word as means of revelation, but between the content of the true prophetic word and the content of false prophetic dreams that lead people astray, the two having no more in common than wheat and straw. To emphasize the power of YHWH's word the next verse compares it to fire and to a hammer that shatters rock. The translation "word" is far too weak to capture the power of the Hebrew term *dabar*, which designates a speech act with power to destroy or create and set events in motion.[58] The book portrays Jeremiah's word, especially his message of disaster, as such a speech act that does not just predict the future but provokes it, in contrast to the anemic words of false prophecy, which promise a deliverance they are powerless to provoke because God does not stand behind the words.

In vv. 30-32 YHWH declares his threefold opposition to the prophets, each time listing a different offense, although all three involve some type of prophetic announcement without divine commission. YHWH declares that he is against the prophets who "steal *my* words from one another." It appears that genuine words of YHWH are being stolen, yet borrowing or sharing prophetic material is not considered problematic elsewhere, as the almost identical oracle of salvation in Isa 2:2-4 and Mic 4:1-3 illustrates. Some commentators note an apparent contradiction in

---

56. Moberly, *Prophecy and Discernment*, 75.

57. Carroll, *Jeremiah*, 473. For an interpretation similar to mine see Münderlein, *Kriterien*, 56-59; Miller, "The Book of Jeremiah," 752-53; Fretheim, *Jeremiah*, 338-39.

58. See Lundbom, *Jeremiah 21-36*, 208-9. For a discussion of the prominence of the word of YHWH in the book of Jeremiah as a whole, see Stulman, *Jeremiah*, 27-29.

23:25–32, in that the text accuses the prophets of having no access to divine revelation but then also castigates them for stealing genuine words of YHWH from each other.[59] Holladay's solution is to point out that the prophets claim to speak the words of YHWH but in fact only utter the words of their own deceitful hearts (23:26, 32). The assertion that they steal "my words" is ironic and should be in quotation marks, because they are only stealing the words of fellow false prophets.[60] Lundbom, who like Holladay reads the text historically, suggests that since prophets like Jeremiah sometimes announced salvation for Judah and destruction for her enemies, the *shalom* prophets could have appropriated these oracles and used them improperly to give the impression that Judah could avoid disaster.[61] My own approach is to begin by noting how the conclusion to the passage emphasizes that YHWH did not send the prophets even though they claim to prophesy in his name (23:32). This is the crux of the matter—the prophets have spoken purely on their own initiative, and the text provides three examples of how they have done this: by devising oracles with their own tongues (23:31), reporting their deceitful dreams (23:32), and stealing YHWH's words from each other (23:30). The issue in v. 30 is not so much the truth or falseness of what is spoken, but that the prophets have not been commissioned. Thus, if they happen to speak genuine words of YHWH this can only be because they have stolen these words. The accusation of stealing YHWH's words is not part of an attempt to discern between true and false prophecy but is part of the rhetorical effort to discredit all of Jeremiah's prophetic opponents.

Following YHWH's opening charge that the prophets steal his words, he declares that they "take their tongue and oracle an oracle [וַיִּנְאֲמוּ נְאֻם]" (23:31). This is the only example in the Old Testament of the denominative verb נאם, which suggests that it may have been coined for this occasion.[62] The text satirizes prophets who have no revelation and so must use their tongues to mimic the proper form of prophetic speech, another example of rhetorical strategy used to disparage Jeremiah's opponents. Six times in 23:28–32 Jeremiah uses the expression "oracle of YHWH [נְאֻם־יְהוָה]," thereby claiming his legitimate right to use the

---

59. Werblowsky, "Stealing the Word," 105; Carroll, *From Chaos to Covenant*, 175.
60. Holladay, *Jeremiah 1*, 645.
61. Lundbom, *Jeremiah 21–36*, 209.
62. Bright, *Jeremiah*, 153.

oracle formula and highlighting the contrast between himself and the false prophets.

The concluding verse of the unit returns to the topic with which 23:25–32 opened, the false dreams of the prophets. "Indeed, I am against those who prophesy dreams of falsehood [*sheqer*] declares YHWH, and report them and lead astray [וַיַּתְעוּ] my people with their falsehoods [*sheqerim*] and their wantonness; I did not send them and I did not command them; and they do this people absolutely no good, declares YHWH" (23:32). This verse provides a summary of 32:25–32. In the strongest terms YHWH disassociates himself from the prophets who have claimed divine authority by prophesying in his name. The prophets are charged with leading the people astray (root תעה) by means of their *sheqer*, a horrible offense that can only lead to disastrous consequences for them and the nation. (See the discussion above of the similar accusation in 23:13.) In this context the *sheqer* of the prophets refers to their promotion of paganism, since their false dreams make people forget YHWH (23:27), but the text also rings with overtones of the close association between *sheqer*, false prophets, and false hopes of salvation so prominent in other Jeremiah texts.

According to 23:25 and 30, the prophets speak in YHWH's name, which is presumably why he uses such strong language to disavow any connection to them. The prophets steal YHWH's words from each other and they oracle oracles, indicating that they employ accepted forms of prophetic speech. The text acknowledges the difficulty of discerning between true and false prophecy, since both claim divine authorization and use the same speech forms. Yet the community of faith must discern, because the *sheqer* of false prophecy undermines the truthfulness essential for survival, whether it be truthfulness about whom the community must worship, or truthfulness about the community's moral fiber, or truthfulness about the community's future.

NO MORE MASSOTH (23:33–40)

Textual difficulties and confusing grammar, syntax, and terminology make 23:33–40 a challenging passage to interpret, the result being that there are almost as many interpretations as interpreters.[63] I will briefly

---

63. See the helpful summary of different interpretations in Lange, *Vom prophetischen Wort*, 280–85.

engage several of these interpretations and then offer one of my own that pays closer attention to the literary context in which the text is embedded. The first verse is generally considered to be a clever wordplay on the term *massa* (מַשָּׂא), which can mean either burden or oracle.[64] The verse sketches a scenario in which lay people or a prophet or a priest ask Jeremiah what the *massa* (oracle) of YHWH is, and he is instructed to respond with a proclamation usually translated, "you are the burden [*massa*] and I will cast you off." Verse 33 is sometimes regarded as genuinely Jeremianic, in contrast to the reputedly late midrashic commentary in 23:34–40, which develops the pun in a different direction by means of a diatribe against anyone who dares ask for or utter a *massa*.

The key question is, what specific prophetic activity does the text seek to prohibit? Lundbom explains the prohibition of *massoth* as due to the people's misuse and desecration of what was once an appropriate term. "Whenever language suffers abuse, becomes empty by mindless repetition, or is compromised in some other way by people not using it properly, there is justification for banning it and replacing it with meaningful language."[65] The difficulty with this interpretation is that the harshness of the rhetoric against the use of *massa* suggests that the issue is about more than outworn theological language. Nicholson believes that the passage stresses the seriousness with which the prophetic office must be taken. Because so many persons were claiming to be prophets the office had been brought into disrepute, and so the text asserts that imposters who utter oracles of YHWH without being commissioned will be punished.[66] Thompson's view is similar. The people may only ask what YHWH has answered or spoken (v. 35), but to utter a *massa* is a privilege reserved for the person actually entrusted with proclaiming the word of YHWH.[67] The weakness of this interpretation is that the text does not

---

64. The noun derives from the verb נשׂא, which means "to lift up" or "to carry." There is debate about what the two meanings of the noun have in common, or even if there are two meanings, but it is possible that *massa* designates that which is lifted up either in speaking (i.e., as a declaration) or in carrying (i.e., as a burden). See Holladay, *Jeremiah 1*, 650; Floyd, "The מַשָּׂא (*MAŚŚĀ'*) as a Type of Prophetic Book," 401–2. De Boer concludes that *massa* has only one meaning, an imposed literal or figurative burden. See "An Inquiry into the Meaning of the Term מַשָּׂא," 214. In contrast, McKane argues that *massa*, "burden" and *massa*, "utterance" are two separate words that happen to be homonyms. See McKane, "מַשָּׂא in Jeremiah 23:33–40," 40.

65. Lundbom, *Jeremiah 21–36*, 217.

66. Nicholson, *The Book of the Prophet Jeremiah*, 1:202.

67. Thompson, *The Book of Jeremiah*, 503–5.

distinguish between those who may legitimately proclaim a *massa* and those who may not, but condemns *any* request for or uttering of a *massa*.

According to McKane, the question put to Jeremiah in 23:33, "What is the *massa* of YHWH?" is a satirical reference to Jeremiah's gloomy oracles, which are heavy with disaster. The question is not serious but sarcastic: "What is your latest doom-laden word from Yahweh?"[68] The passage as a whole then vindicates the judgment prophecy of Jeremiah and condemns all those persons who dare mock him and his message by asking, "What is the *massa* of YHWH?" According to McKane the text represents a post-exilic attempt to recapture the significance of the conflict between salvation and judgment prophecy during the time of Jeremiah. "What is intended by vv. 33–40 is an acknowledgment that Jeremiah was vindicated by events: the post-exilic(?) Jewish community must confess that this prophet of doom spoke the word of God and identify themselves with him over against the prophets whose assurances of שׁלוֹם [*shalom*] were proved false by destruction, defeat and exile."[69]

Allen, who suggests that the whole passage reflects the experience of the historical Jeremiah, claims that the issue at stake is heckling.[70] Like McKane, he believes that the initial query about whether there is a *massa* from YHWH is sarcastic, uttered by persons attempting to mock Jeremiah and his burdensome oracles. Jeremiah is instructed to throw the term back at the audience, describing them as a *massa*/burden too heavy for YHWH to tolerate any longer. Part of the apparent confusion in the text results from the weaving together of a question-and-answer format with an announcement of disaster. The gist of the passage is that in an ironic way, those persons who reject an oracle of disaster (*massa*) are confronted with one.

Carroll suggests that the intense emotional tone of the passage reflects some local feud between post-exilic prophets of which we see only a glimpse here. By condemning all references to *massoth* one group was denouncing the characteristic speech of the other. "Prophecy has disintegrated into warring factions, and this echo of battle has survived."[71] A number of scholars see the passage as reflecting a post-exilic attempt to silence the voice of all contemporary prophecy. Overholt maintains

---

68. McKane, *A Critical and Exegetical Commentary*, 1:599.

69. Ibid., 603–4. See also Hill, "The Book of Jeremiah MT and Early Second Temple Conflicts," 40.

70. Allen, *Jeremiah*, 272–74.

71. Carroll, *From Chaos to Covenant*, 180.

that the historical Jeremiah's critique of his prophetic opponents and their role in bringing about YHWH's judgment provided the basis for the later generalization of vv. 34–40 that prophecy itself was dead.[72] The text forbids any more requests for oracles and asserts that what YHWH has answered and spoken in the past is sufficient revelation (vv. 35, 37), and even this has been perverted (v. 36). Similarly, Petersen claims that the purpose of the text is "to prohibit the use of prophetic formulae and thereby to prohibit the prophetic enterprise as we know it from the classical prophets."[73] Recalling earlier prophetic words is permitted (vv. 35, 37), but no new prophetic utterances are to be legitimated by appeals to traditional prophetic formulae. One of the reasons for this blanket prohibition, Petersen claims, is that no adequate test had been devised to determine the validity of contending prophetic claims, and so all such claims were of little value, as implied by v. 36. Armin Lange also reads the text as a denunciation of all new prophetic activity, with the further claim that the addition of 23:34–40 to the end of ch. 23 turns all of 23:9–40 into a condemnation of new prophecy in favor of written prophetic tradition.[74]

Sheppard's explanation for the attempt to silence new prophetic voices is the promulgation of the *Torah* under Ezra as the basis of community life, which made it necessary to rule out fresh prophetic revelation that could potentially conflict with what had been revealed in the *Torah*.[75] Prophetic traditions could be edited and expanded as commentary on the *Torah*, but this *Torah* needed protection from the possibility of future claims to have a new word from God. The term *massa* plays such a key role in 23:33–40 because it had become closely associated with Zechariah and Malachi, the last of the classical prophets, and the text seeks to rule out any further prophetic activity such as represented by these prophets.

When interpreting 23:33–40 in its final form it is important to keep separate the question of the text's origins and original intention, as much as such intentions are recoverable, from the question of what the

---

72. Overholt, *The Threat of Falsehood*, 70–71.

73. Petersen, *Late Israelite Prophecy*, 28. For a discussion of why some post-exilic groups sought to denigrate prophetic claims see pp. 28, 37–38, 99–100.

74. See Lange, *Vom prophetischen Wort*, 287–91; Lange, "Reading the Decline of Prophecy," 184–86. In his commentary Carroll also joins the ranks of scholars who suggest that the text reflects a desire to prohibit all prophetic activity. See *Jeremiah*, 480.

75. Sheppard, "True and False Prophecy," 277–78. For an insightful critique of assertions that post-exilic *Torah*-centered piety stood in tension with belief in fresh revelation through prophets, see Barton, *Oracles of God*, 111–16.

text means now in its new literary context. In its present context (and I suspect also as it was originally written) 23:33–40 does not condemn all prophecy but only prophetic activity associated with *massoth*. For this reason vv. 33–40 follow quite smoothly from vv. 25–32, which also focus on the means whereby the prophets receive and convey their supposed revelations (dreams, stealing YHWH's word, oracling oracles). Therefore, the key to interpreting 23:33–40 is to understand what kind of prophetic activity the term *massa* designates. Long ago already Duhm observed how absurd it is to predict the destruction of the nation just because people use the term *massa*.[76] Duhm's comment is correct, and indicates that there is much more at stake than improper use of prophetic terminology. The extremely harsh punishment (see 23:38–40) suggests that the text is condemning a specific kind of prophetic activity that it regards as particularly virulent. This is in keeping with the rest of 23:9–40, where other types of prophetic activity are denounced for the same reason.

The passage opens by envisioning a scenario where people ask Jeremiah what the *massa* of YHWH is (vv. 33–34). Most translators and commentators follow the LXX, Vulgate, and Old Latin of 23:33, in which the meaning of 23:33 hinges on a clever wordplay on *massa*, which can mean either burden or oracle. The LXX reads, "And if this people or the priest or the prophet should ask, 'What is the burden [λῆμμα] of the Lord?' then you shall say to them, 'You are the burden and I will cast you off [ὑμεῖς ἐστε τὸ λῆμμα καὶ ῥάξω ὑμᾶς], says the Lord.'" These versions reflect the consonantal text אַתֶּם הַמַּשָּׂא (you are the burden), while the MT reads אֶת־מַה־מַשָּׂא (what is the burden?), the difference being division of letters into words. Even some scholars who do not emend the MT still read the Hebrew under the influence of the Greek. For example, the NJPS has, "'What is the *burden*? I will cast you off [וְנָטַשְׁתִּי אֶתְכֶם]'—declares the LORD." If one assumes that there is a pun, then *massa* must be rendered as "burden" and then a verb of throwing off is required, as the LXX has.

The MT, however, reads somewhat differently. "And when this people or the prophet or a priest ask you, 'What is the oracle [מַשָּׂא] of YHWH?' then you shall say to them, 'What is the oracle [אֶת־מַה־מַשָּׂא]? I will abandon you [וְנָטַשְׁתִּי אֶתְכֶם],' declares YHWH."[77] The MT has נטש,

---

76. Duhm, *Das Buch Jeremia*, 196.

77. The Hebrew is awkward here, but I believe it is legitimate to take the אֶת in the difficult phrase אֶת־מַה־מַשָּׂא as marker of the accusative, which in this case introduces what Jeremiah is to say. See the NJPS (compare NIV, ASV, KJV, NKJV, JPS) and Breuer, *The Book of Jeremiah*, 192.

which usually means to leave, abandon, or forsake, but can occasionally mean something like cast off (Ezek 29:5; 32:4).[78] The connection between the two meanings is probably that to throw down or cast something away is equivalent to abandoning it or leaving it behind. The MT contains no explicit statement that *massa* means burden or that the people are YHWH's burden that he will cast off, and so נטש should be translated as "forsake" or "abandon," its normal meaning.

In the LXX the meaning of v. 33 depends on the pun on *massa*, but not so in the MT, where the scenario is that persons come to Jeremiah and ask, "What is the *massa* [oracle] of YHWH?" He is instructed to respond by repeating the question, "What is the *massa* [oracle]?" and then to answer it, "'I will abandon you,' declares YHWH." Jeremiah's answer indicates that there is no other message from YHWH than what he has been proclaiming all along, that disaster is on the way. Although the pun on *massa* lurks in the background in the MT, the meaning of the verse does not depend on it. It is likely that the LXX, Vulgate, and Old Latin witness to an older reading than the MT.[79]

In 23:38-39 the LXX continues the wordplay on *massa* while the MT continues to resist it. In the MT, YHWH declares that because the people have uttered *massoth* even though forbidden to do so, "Therefore, I will utterly *forget* you and abandon you/cast you away . . . from my presence [לָכֵן הִנְנִי וְנָשִׁיתִי אֶתְכֶם נָשֹׁא וְנָטַשְׁתִּי אֶתְכֶם . . . מֵעַל פָּנָי]." The Greek reflects a somewhat different Hebrew *Vorlage*: "Therefore, behold, I will *seize* and throw you down [ἐγὼ λαμβάνω καὶ ῥάσσω ὑμᾶς]." The verb λαμβάνω (to take, grasp, or seize) must reflect the Hebrew root נשא (to take, lift, or carry) instead of נשה (forget), which now stands in the MT.[80] נשא is the root of מַשָּׂא, and thus the LXX reflects a Hebrew text that continues the wordplay on *massa*. Translators and commentators sometimes emend the MT to read, "I will surely *lift you up* and cast you away" (see RSV, NRSV, NAB, NEB, NJB). Such emendation does not do justice to the MT, because the MT reflects a different text that seems to deliberately avoid the wordplay.[81] Except for the artistry of the wordplay, not much

---

78. Holladay, *Jeremiah 1*, 650.

79. Walker's theory is that the difference between the MT and LXX is a result of tampering by the later Masoretes. See Walker, "The Masoretic Pointing of Jeremiah's Pun," 413. Walker provides no explanation for why the Masoretes might have wanted to alter the pun to avoid calling the people YHWH's burden.

80. The Syriac and Vulgate also witness to נשא instead of נשה.

81. This avoidance is illustrated further by the presence of נָשָׁא in the MT of v. 39,

seems to be at stake in the differences between the LXX and MT, because the basic message remains the same: YHWH cannot tolerate the people and decrees disaster upon them, especially upon anyone who dares to speak of a *massa* (v. 34).

The key question, then, is what kind of prophetic speech does *massa* designate? Holladay observes that since *massa* occurs in 23:9–40, where the focus is on castigating false prophets for a variety of offenses, uttering *massoth* must somehow be characteristic of these prophets.[82] If Holladay is correct, then the strict prohibition against *massoth* indicates that a *massa* represents a fundamental contradiction of the basic message of Jeremiah. At the core of Jeremiah's message in 23:9—29:32 and in the book as a whole is the announcement of impending disaster, and the conflict between Jeremiah and other prophets centers on whether YHWH's plans for the immediate future entail disaster or deliverance. Therefore, in 23:33–40 *massa* might designate some type of salvation oracle characteristically delivered by false prophets. This is precisely how the term is used in Lam 2:14.

> Your prophets saw for you
>   delusion and folly,
> and they did not uncover your iniquity
>   so as to restore your fortunes.
> But they saw for you *massoth*
>   of delusion and deception.

Here the deceptive *massoth* of the prophets are cited as one of the primary reasons for the catastrophe of 587. These *massoth* deceived the people and lulled them into an attitude of complacency, when the real calling of the prophets was to expose the nation's sin so that repentance and restoration could occur. These are precisely the points Jer 23:14, 16–17, and 21–22 also make about false prophets. In Lam 2:14 the *massoth* of the prophets

---

a form found nowhere else in the Old Testament. It is pointed as an infinitive absolute, which means that it must be infinitive absolute of the main verb. However, the root of the main verb is נשׂה, not נשׂא. Except for the position of one dot, נשׂא is identical to נשׂא, the root of מַשָּׂא, indicating that originally the text probably contained the wordplay on *massa*. It seems odd that within v. 39 in one instance the MT redaction seems to have replaced נשׂא with נשׂה to avoid the wordplay, but in the next instance it retains נשׂא, even though the pointing avoids the wordplay. Whatever the explanation, the Masoretic tradition must have been aware of the wordplay or potential wordplay on *massa* but deliberately avoided it, perhaps because it wanted *massa* to be understood as "oracle," not "burden."

82. Holladay, *Jeremiah*, 1:650.

must designate their optimistic salvation oracles that led the nation down the road to calamity. It may be just such salvation prophecies that Jer 23:33-40 seeks to forever outlaw. This interpretation explains the emotional intensity of the passage. The language is so harsh because so much is at stake. McKane is correct when he observes that 23:33-40 seeks to recapture the significance of the conflict between judgment and salvation prophecy in the time of Jeremiah, so that the Second Temple community will orient itself toward the word of the true prophet Jeremiah instead of the words of the false prophets of *shalom*.[83]

Perhaps it is possible to be even more precise about what type of prophetic speech *massa* designates. Overholt suggests that in 23:33 *massa* might specify an oracle against a foreign nation, as the term appears to do elsewhere.[84] If this is the case then 23:33-40 may be condemning any desire for a *massa* that predicts destruction for the enemy (i.e., Babylon), thereby implying deliverance for Judah. Outside of Jer 23:33-40 *massa* occurs twenty times in reference to some type of prophetic speech. The most frequent occurrence is in Isaiah, where, with but two exceptions (22:1; 30:6), it always designates an oracle against a foreign nation (13:1; 14:28; 15:1; 17:1; 19:1; 21:1, 11, 13; 23:1). *Massa* probably also designates an oracle or oracles against a foreign nation in Nah 1:1; Zech 9:1; 12:1. In three cases a *massa* is directed at an individual. Ezekiel delivers a *massa* stating that the prince and people of Jerusalem will be exiled (12:10-16). In 2 Kgs 9:25-26 Jehu interprets his assassination of King Joram as fulfillment of Elijah's *massa* predicting disaster on the house of Ahab (see 1 Kgs 21:17-19, 28-29), while 2 Chr 24:27 speaks of *massoth* of judgment directed at King Joash (see 24:17-27).

In all these examples *massa* refers to an oracle predicting doom for someone or some group whom God wishes to punish. Most often the target is a foreign nation, but it can also be an individual, and even Israel (Isa 22:1ff.; 30:6ff.; Ezek 12:10-16). In a number of cases the *massa* that predicts disaster for the enemy also contains a promise of deliverance for the people of God (Isa 14:1-3; 14:32; 16:5; Nah 2:1, 3 [Heb.]; Zech 9:8-17; 12:2-14).[85] There are, however, instances where *massa* seems to

---

83. McKane, *A Critical and Exegetical Commentary*, 1:603-4.

84. Overholt, *The Threat of Falsehood*, 70.

85. Wilson, *Prophecy and Society*, 249, 257-59, speculates that *massa* may have designated a type of prophetic oracle associated with the Jerusalem establishment prophets. He suggests that although *massa* acquired a broader meaning over time, originally it may have referred to an oracle against a foreign nation delivered as part of

refer to prophetic speech in general (Hab 1:1; Mal 1:1), or is part of the heading for a collection of oracles (Zech 9:1; 12:1; Mal 1:1).[86] In several instances *massa* stands as the heading for a non-prophetic poem (Prov 30:1; 31:1), and of course it often refers to a burden of some kind, either literal (Exod 23:5; Jer 17:21) or figurative (Num 11:11, 17).

Massa has a bewildering range of possible meanings that may or may not all be related to each other, but such a situation is not unique. The English word *spike* can mean, among other things, a long nail, a sharp projection of some kind, the long thin heel of a woman's shoe, the act of smashing a volleyball into an opposing team's court, a steep rise in something like interest rates or fever, adding alcohol to a non-alcoholic drink, or even a young mackerel. This wide range of potential meanings is rarely confusing because the context of construction site, volleyball match, shoe store, or party clarifies the meaning. When *massa* is used in a context where false prophets are condemned for proclaiming deliverance, for contradicting Jeremiah's message that punishment is on the way, and for failing to call a sinful nation to repentance, then of all the possible meanings the most likely is an oracle pronouncing destruction of the enemy and thereby implying well-being for Judah. In particular, the close parallels between Lam 2:14 and Jer 23:9–40 suggest this meaning of *massa*.

If this is the meaning of *massa* in 23:33–40, then the text makes relatively good sense despite some difficulties in grammar and syntax. As already indicated, v. 33 reflects a situation where people ask what the *massa* of YHWH is; that is, they are asking what God's oracle of judgment against the enemy might be. Jeremiah is instructed to tell such inquirers, "'What is the *massa*?—I will abandon you,' declares YHWH." The people hope for a *massa* against the enemy (i.e., Babylon) only to have Jeremiah declare that YHWH's *massa* (oracle of judgment) is directed against them[87] (compare Isa 22:1ff.; 30:6ff.; Ezek 12:10–16). Verse 34 follows with a blanket condemnation of any prophet, priest, or layperson who dares utter a *massa* (oracle of judgment against the enemy) in YHWH's name. Verse 35 indicates that instead of requesting a *massa* people may legiti-

---

holy war. See pp. 258, 278.

86. Müller, "מַשָּׂא," 24; Petersen, *Late Israelite Prophecy*, 32; Floyd, "The מַשָּׂא (MAŚŚĀ') as a Type of Prophetic Book," 404–22. For a helpful discussion of how the LXX translates *massa* in prophetic contexts see McKane, "מַשָּׂא in Jeremiah 23:33–40," 36–37.

87. See Overholt, *The Threat of Falsehood*, 70.

mately ask, "What has YHWH answered and what has YHWH spoken?" As discussed earlier, this verse is often read as a prohibition of all future prophecy in favor of seeking guidance from written prophetic traditions that had acquired a certain authority.[88] Such an interpretation is possible only if one extracts the passage from its current literary context and reads it in light of a reputed desire in the Second Temple community to stifle new prophetic activity.[89] In its current context 23:35 legitimates ongoing prophecy by stating that it is still appropriate for people to ask what YHWH has spoken or answered, presumably in response to specific queries put to a prophet as envisioned by v. 33. Only one particular kind of prophetic activity is prohibited—any mention of *massoth*.

Verse 36 gives the reason why a *massa* of YHWH is never to be mentioned again: כִּי הַמַּשָּׂא יִהְיֶה לְאִישׁ דְּבָרוֹ וַהֲפַכְתֶּם אֶת־דִּבְרֵי אֱלֹהִים חַיִּים יְהוָה צְבָאוֹת אֱלֹהֵינוּ. The first clause is difficult but can be rendered something like, "because the *massa* is the word of each." This suggests that the *massa* is the invention of the speaker and not a genuine word from God,[90] which is in keeping with the emphasis in 23:25–32 that the various proclamations of the false prophets represent the deceptions of their own minds. The second clause reads, "you have perverted the words of the living God, YHWH of hosts our God." The implication seems to be that uttering a *massa* is somehow a perversion of YHWH's revelation, perhaps because it contradicts the genuine words of God spoken by Jeremiah. The opening clause of v. 36, "But a *massa* of YHWH you shall *not again/no longer* mention," points to another possible interpretation. Perhaps the text recognizes that some *massoth* delivered in the past were genuine words of YHWH, but in the present historical context a *massa*

---

88. Lange asserts that "What has YHWH answered and what has YHWH spoken?" becomes an exegetical question. *Vom prophetischen Wort*, 289.

89. The text usually marshaled as evidence for a Second Temple rejection of contemporary and future prophecy is Zech 13:2–6. Hill argues that the condemnation of prophecy in Zechariah is the opposite of what occurs in the book of Jeremiah. The prophet Jeremiah is venerated as a way of promoting the credibility of ongoing prophetic ministry, and the book presents prophets and prophecy (even false prophecy) as a normal part of community life. See Hill, "The Book of Jeremiah MT and Early Second Temple Conflicts," especially 41–42; and Hill, "The Book of Jeremiah (MT) and Its Early Second Temple Background," 163–67.

90. McKane comes to a similar conclusion, although he believes it is prophecies of doom that reflect the speaker's mind and not YHWH's word. See McKane, "משא in Jeremiah 23:33–40," 49. That *massa* signifies a message of doom here seems doubtful, because such doom is the dominant note in Jeremiah's prophecy, and the *massa* is depicted in 23:33–40 as standing in opposition to the word of Jeremiah.

can no longer be God's word. Verse 37 provides the same instructions as v. 35 concerning what people may legitimately ask of a prophet instead of a *massa*. The passage then closes with a prediction of brutal punishment for the people and city if they persist in speaking of a *massa* even though God has strictly forbidden any such talk (vv. 38–40).

To many commentators 23:33–40 seems like a peculiar passage that is "un-Jeremianic" and out of place. While the passage is unusual and its difficult grammar and syntax make it a challenge to interpret, the text makes relatively good sense if one understands *massa* as designating an oracle proclaiming destruction of the enemy and deliverance for God's people. The passage fits well into 23:9–40, where the false prophets are condemned for promising deliverance and thereby creating a false sense of security among the people (vv. 14, 16–22). Just as the dreams of the prophets are false, misleading, and ultimately destructive (23:25–32), so are their *massoth*.

SUMMARY

The large concentric unit that reflects on the nature of true and false prophecy (23:9—29:32) opens with a long and blistering attack on the false prophets. By the time the text was written the destruction foretold in 23:9–40 was an all-too-painful reality. By castigating the prophets for a variety of offenses and declaring that they have led the people astray, the text lays much of the blame at their feet. Thus, Jeremiah and his message of doom are vindicated over against the optimistic message of the false prophets. Anything that smacks of false prophecy must be avoided, because such prophecy has already once led the community into the abyss. The text calls the faithful community to learn the painful lessons of the past and heed the ongoing message of Jeremiah.

Despite the ferocity of its attack, the text consistently refers to Jeremiah's opponents as prophets and never questions their status as such.[91] The text seems to recognize both the difficulty of discerning between true and false prophecy and the horrible consequences of failing to do so. Therefore, one of the purposes of the text is to provide criteria for distinguishing between true and false prophecy and to sketch paradigms of each. Prophets who act immorally are by definition false, because the God they claim to speak for is a God who demands righteousness of his

---

91. Hill, "The Book of Jeremiah MT and Early Second Temple Conflicts," 34.

people and spokespersons. Prophets who encourage anything less than total allegiance to YHWH are false. And most important, prophets who promise *shalom* while overlooking the sins of the people are false. They foster complacency and a distorted view of reality that leads to catastrophe. Thus, at the heart of true prophecy stands the ongoing call to moral vigilance and repentance. Characteristic of 23:9–40 is the lack of historical references that link the material to specific events or periods in Jeremiah's life. The text has been shaped in such a way that its paradigms and its critique of false prophecy are not bound to one particular historical context but make ongoing claims upon the community of faith.

4

Section B
A Vision Regarding Exiles and Non-Exiles (24:1–10)

AFTER A LENGTHY PORTRAYAL of the nature of false prophecy in 23:9–40, section B provides a contrast—a sample of true prophecy. Chapter 24 shows no trace of prophetic conflict but depicts the message of the paradigmatic true prophet Jeremiah. The chapter opens very abruptly with no introductory formula, just the simple declaration "YHWH showed me . . . ," emphasizing that Jeremiah's vision comes from God. The rest of the chapter is careful to stress that YHWH speaks directly to the prophet (vv. 3, 4) and that every aspect of his message is the word of YHWH (vv. 5, 8). As a true prophet Jeremiah speaks no dreams or visions of his own mind as the prophets of the previous section do.

The historical note in 24:1b serves a double function. Thematically, its similarity to 29:1–2 links Jeremiah's vision of the figs with his letter to the exiles (29:1–19). Chronologically, the historical note links the vision to a specific time in the ministry of the historical Jeremiah, the period between the first Babylonian deportation of Jews from Jerusalem (598) and the final destruction of the city (587). Some of the punishment pronounced in 23:9–40 and elsewhere in the book has materialized already, but the final fall of the nation still lies in the future. Whereas 23:9–40 portrays how the false prophets have been functioning, ch. 24 indicates what true prophecy has to say in the face of exile and the Babylonian threat.

Concerning the Prophets

YHWH shows Jeremiah two baskets of figs, one filled with high-quality figs and the other with figs so rotten they are inedible, the two types of figs symbolizing two distinct groups of Jews. The state of the figs corresponds not to the moral quality of the two groups but to YHWH's contrasting disposition toward them and the resulting fate that awaits them. Just as the one basket of figs is exceedingly good, so YHWH will treat the Jewish exiles in Babylon in an exceedingly good way (24:5), and just as the other basket of figs is exceedingly rotten, so YHWH will treat King Zedekiah, his officials, the remaining people in Jerusalem and Judah, and those Jews who have fled to Egypt in an exceedingly rotten way that leads to their utter ruin (24:8-10). At the beginning of the book God commissions Jeremiah for a twofold ministry, "to uproot and to pull down, to destroy and to overthrow, to build and to plant" (1:10). Jeremiah's proclamation of both deliverance and punishment in ch. 24 portrays him as fulfilling this mission, and 24:6 even uses vocabulary from his commissioning as YHWH promises to build the exiles and not tear them down, to plant and not uproot them.[1] Jeremiah's twofold ministry in ch. 24 illustrates that while a true prophet does not hesitate to pronounce judgment upon a sinful people, the prophetic role is also to provide comfort and encouragement for a people who have experienced divine punishment, so that the shattered community of exiles can live with hope for a better future and the assurance that God has not forgotten them.

If Jeremiah pronounces a message of well-being to the exiles, then how is his message different from that of the salvation prophets denounced in 23:9-40? To some extent the difference between them and Jeremiah is a matter of timing. "Jeremiah's hope for the future seems always to attach itself to that part of the nation which has passed through the fire of judgment."[2] The false prophets assure the nation that YHWH's saving actions will prevent catastrophe, but Jeremiah envisions salvation only on the other side of catastrophe. Divine judgment is necessary in order to sweep away the sinful realities of the present, but the punishment of exile will change YHWH's attitude toward the people and he will once again show favor to them.

One of the striking features of ch. 24 is the sharp distinction between the exiles of 598 and those persons who were not deported. While

---

1. Other passages in the book that also employ the vocabulary of disaster and deliverance used in 1:10 include 12:14-17; 18:7-10; 31:28, 40; 42:10; 45:4.

2. Skinner, *Prophecy and Religion*, 82. For similar comments see Raitt, *A Theology of Exile*, 113-14.

YHWH promises to restore the exiles to their homeland and once again accept them as his covenant people (vv. 5–7), he decrees in stereotypical language an absolutely horrifying fate for King Zedekiah, his officials, the remnant left in Judah, as well as those Judeans who have fled to Egypt (24:8–10). The intense polemical tone of these verses leads many commentators to see them as self-serving propaganda espousing the political interests of one particular group of Jews involved in some conflict in the exilic or post-exilic period. Nicholson surmises that Deuteronomists living in exile have taken an authentic saying of Jeremiah and developed it in such a way that it asserts "the claims of the Babylonian diaspora to be the true remnant of Israel through whom alone renewal and restoration would be wrought by YHWH."[3] According to Seitz, ch. 24 is a key text in what he calls the "Exilic" or "*Golah* redaction." Seitz contrasts the historical Jeremiah's conviction that hope for the future lay with the community that remained in the land with the "*Golah* redaction's" assertion that the exiles represented the faithful community that would form the nucleus of the restored Israel.[4] Carroll sees the text as a reflection of seniority claims by a specific group of returned exiles during the period of Jerusalem's reconstruction. By claiming that only the exiles of the first deportation would be the beneficiaries of YHWH's saving deeds, Jews who traced their lineage back to this group asserted their claim to superior status in the post-exilic community.[5]

Carolyn J. Sharp argues that the book of Jeremiah contains "the focused and urgent clashing of two titanic ideologies,"[6] in the form of two major Deuteronomistic redactions that "struggle for theological authority

---

3. Nicholson, *Preaching to the Exiles*, 110.

4. Seitz, *Theology in Conflict*, 5, 211–12, 223–25. See also his article, "The Crisis of Interpretation," especially pp. 83–84. Seitz's work draws significantly from that of Pohlmann, who argues that the book of Jeremiah reflects bitter rivalry between descendants of the 598 exile and those left in Judah. See Pohlmann, *Studien zum Jeremiabuch*.

5. Carroll, *Jeremiah*, 482–83, 487–88. Smith does not discuss Jer 24 but provides a sociological analysis of post-exilic conflict triggered by the return of Babylonian exiles, who found that their land and positions of power and influence had been filled by other Jews during their absence. See Smith, *The Religion of the Landless*, 193–97. It is quite possible that Jer 24 has its origins in such a conflict between a *golah* group and those Jews who never left the land. Elsewhere Smith observes how situations of exile and mass social upheaval often lead to conflict within the affected community over physical resources and power. See Smith-Christopher, *A Biblical Theology of Exile*, 81–82.

6. Sharp, *Prophecy and Ideology in Jeremiah*, xvi.

via their portrayals of traditions about Jeremiah and prophets generally in the Deutero-Jeremianic prose."[7] One of these redactions is the product of a political group based in Babylon after the deportations of 598 that sought to claim political and cultic authority. The other Deuteronomistic group was based in Judah and sought to counter the assertions of divine favor and privilege claimed by this *golah* group. The Judah-based traditionists stressed the total destruction of the nation as a result of the persistent unfaithfulness of the people. This group was totally opposed to pro-Babylonian sentiment and rejected the possibility of living in the assimilationist environment of exile. In contrast, the *golah* traditionists, who were responsible for 24:1–10, stressed submission to Babylon both before and after the destruction of Jerusalem. They held out the possibility of future restoration for the Babylonian diaspora, but used hyperbolic rhetoric stressing the severity of God's punishment of the non-exiles as a way to close off any possibility of deliverance for the post-598 community in Judah. These two groups of Deuteronomistic traditionists "grapple in prose and poetic texts in Jeremiah for interpretive control over Jeremianic traditions and for political authority by means of those traditions."[8]

According to Sharp, the indissoluble tension in the book of Jeremiah between the two conflicting Deuteronomistic redactions means that "no synchronic reading that harmonizes the significant ideological tensions within the book will be able to illuminate its meanings without drastic skewing of at least some of the texts under consideration."[9] Instead of listening only for the "first" meaning of the text as historical criticism traditionally seeks to do, or only for the "last" meaning as final-form readers do, or only for the dominant voice in the text, Sharp encourages interpreters to highlight the many theological perspectives that engage each other in the unfinished theological dialogue of the book. While I agree that multiple voices have made their contribution to the book of Jeremiah, I believe that the editorial process has incorporated these diverse voices into a whole that is now far less discordant than Sharp claims, similar to

---

7. Ibid., xiii. For a list of the key texts belonging to each supposed redaction and a more detailed summary of Sharp's conclusions see pp. 157–59. For a critique of theories contrasting homeland versus *golah* redactions or sources, see Leuchter, *The Polemics of Exile*, 5–8, 11–12; and Plant, *Good Figs, Bad Figs*, 32–40.

8. Sharp, *Prophecy and Ideology in Jeremiah*, 124. Because both redactions grapple so intensely with issues related to the exile, Sharp dates them to the exilic period, thereby challenging the theories of McKane, Carroll, and others regarding the post-exilic provenance of most of the Jeremianic prose. See ibid., 161.

9. Ibid., 167.

how a recipe may incorporate the contrasting tastes of sweet and sour spices. As one eats such a dish one may be aware of both the sweet taste of the sugar and the sour taste of the vinegar, but the final effect is quite different than either flavor by itself. Even if one grants Sharp's assertion that a synchronic reading cannot adequately deal with the tensions in the book of Jeremiah, one might still ask the diachronic question of what the editors were seeking to communicate by including the two clashing redactions. If the conflict between the *golah* and Judean groups was as intense as Sharp makes it out to be, then if either one had been in control of the Jeremiah traditions they surely would not have featured their competitor's voice in such a powerful way. This suggests that a different group of tradents was responsible for incorporating and adjudicating between the conflicting redactions, and it is worth asking what these tradents accomplished (or sought to accomplish) by including such tensions in the book. The meaning of the text then no longer depends only on what the original political interest group intended with its own redaction, but also on the effect created by the inclusion of conflicting voices.

It is widely recognized that 1 Samuel 8–12, which describes the origins of Israelite kingship, incorporates narratives that were originally anti-kingship and others that were pro-kingship. The original ideological biases of these contrasting traditions are still evident, but to interpret the text only in light of the original meaning of these traditions would be to miss how they have been skillfully combined so as to create an effect that is quite different than either perspective by itself (much the way a sweet and sour recipe uses sugar and vinegar to create a new flavor). The negative perspective on kingship serves to warn that kingship may encourage trust in a human king rather than in YHWH (1 Sam 8:7, 20; 10:19; 12:6–12), it may lead to becoming like other nations (8:5, 20), and it may introduce oppressive social practices (8:11–18). The positive perspective indicates that kingship is not necessarily in complete tension with the plans and purposes of God. The cumulative effect of the interwoven traditions is to claim that YHWH can accept kingship, but because it presents inherent dangers the king and community must be vigilant in remaining faithful to YHWH (12:23–24), and the king must refrain from oppressing his people and must rule according to God's guidelines (10:25; 12:14).[10]

The tensions in 1 Samuel 8–12 are every bit as great as the tensions in the book of Jeremiah that Sharp claims a synchronic reading cannot

---

10. For a more detailed analysis along similar lines see McCarthy, "The Inauguration of Monarchy in Israel," 401–12.

adequately handle. The brief synchronic discussion of 1 Samuel 8–12 above takes the tensions seriously and illustrates how they play a key role in the meaning of the whole. Sharp's analysis of the book of Jeremiah and ch. 24 is helpful in identifying the tensions that may lie *behind* the text and that in some cases are not fully resolved by the text. However, her approach is less helpful in exploring the contours and meaning of the completed text, which may use the polyphonic voices as ingredients for a dish that tastes quite different than any one of its ingredients.[11]

While the origins of ch. 24 may lie in some partisan struggle over privilege and power, in its present form the text has acquired a broader meaning as a result of having been incorporated into 23:9—29:32. Chapter 24 is paired in the concentric structure with 29:1–19, which contains promises of restoration for the exiles (29:10–14) and destruction for the non-exiles (29:16–19) that are very similar in content and vocabulary to those found in ch. 24. The corresponding panels in a chiasm or concentric structure often complement or comment on each other in such a way that the two create a composite meaning.[12] The close parallels between 24:1–10 and 29:1–19, especially the statement in 29:17 that YHWH will treat the non-exiles like rotten figs that cannot be eaten, signal that sections B and B' should be read in tandem with each other. While ch. 24 and 29:1–19 emphasize basically the same points, a significant new element appears in 29:1–19. The exiles are admonished to accept their situation and make the most of their life in exile because they can expect to be there for a long time (29:4–10). The basic perspective of the book of Jeremiah, and one of the major points stressed by the portrayal of true and false prophecy in 23:9—29:32, is that the exile and the destruction of the nation are divine punishment for Judah's unfaithfulness (see especially 25:1–10; 26:4–6, 12–15) and therefore survivors must embrace the catastrophe as they wait for YHWH's new saving actions in the future, a point stressed by both 24:1–10 and 29:1–19.

Because of the nation's sinfulness YHWH is determined to make a clean sweep, not as a way to annihilate the people but as a way to make possible a re-constitution of the people on a new basis. Exile is an essential element in God's plan because the land must be emptied of its inhabitants, Judah's corrupt institutions (kingship, temple, priesthood) dismantled, and its false ideologies (Royal and Zion theologies)

---

11. For another discussion of how a synchronic reading can sometimes take tensions more seriously than diachronic analyses see Hill, *Friend or Foe?*, 200.

12. See Man, "The Value of Chiasm," 148.

discredited.[13] Therefore, to survive the people must let go of their old worldview and systems of security, and accept exile as an essential element in God's plan for them. However, YHWH remains committed to his people and will in the future restore their fortunes, but this hope is offered only to those willing to embrace the suffering of exile. Thus, the exile represents both judgment and promise at the same time.[14]

The true prophet Jeremiah plays a key role in YHWH's plan because he foretells the catastrophe ahead of time, thereby providing an interpretation that can help a devastated community understand and navigate the bewildering and traumatic course of events. This stands in contrast to the false prophets who promote a distorted picture of both present and future reality, and thereby contribute to the community's ruin and offer no resources to cope with the trauma of the Babylonian onslaught. Chapter 24 and 29:1-19 make it clear that Jeremiah is not just a prophet of doom, but that part of his calling as a true prophet is to exercise pastoral care by pointing to a future hope that can give exiles strength and courage to survive their difficult situation.[15]

Jeremiah's insistence on embracing exile is related to two other developments in Second Temple Judaism that made it possible for all Jews, not just descendants of the 598 deportation, to claim the promises of restoration in 24:5-7 and 29:10-14. One of these developments is the embrace of exile and return as the normative story of all faithful Jews, and the other is the notion that despite restoration in the Persian period, the exile was an ongoing reality that all Jews, even those in the land, still experienced.

Ackroyd observes how in Second Temple literature exile frequently functions "as experience and not merely as historic fact."[16] This is certainly true of the book of Jeremiah, where exile functions as a metaphor for YHWH's destruction of the nation. Thus, when ch. 24 decrees that only a portion of the nation will survive, the point is not so much that only one small group of diaspora Jews will be the objects of divine grace. Because the exile is such a central part of God's plan, remaining in Judah

---

13. This is one of the key points repeated in Stulman's commentary *Jeremiah*, e.g., xix, 1, 22-23, 219-20, 230, 283. For a discussion of how acceptance of exile is typical of the biblical response to 587, see Ackroyd, *Exile and Restoration*, 233-34; and Albertz, *Israel in Exile*, 234-35.

14. Ackroyd, *Exile and Restoration*, 244.

15. Brueggemann, *A Commentary on Jeremiah*, 255.

16. Ackroyd, *Exile and Restoration*, 244.

or fleeing to Egypt symbolizes resistance to accepting God's plan and therefore merits the most severe consequences.[17] Ackroyd points out that Second Temple Judaism came to believe that the experience of judgment and exile could be appropriated not just by living through it but also by accepting its significance and abandoning the sinfulness that caused it.[18] Some scholars see the positive portrayal of potential community reconstruction in the land after 587 (40:1–12; 42:10–12) as standing in tension with Jeremiah's condemnation of those who remain in the land after the first deportation (24:8–10; 29:16–19). Clearly there is some conflict between these two perspectives and they probably belong to what were originally different redactional layers, but read together the contrasting perspectives suggest that the real issue in the completed book is not that God will only favor those Jews who have been dragged off to Babylon. The crux of the matter is whether or not the community is willing to accept the judgment of 587 and heed the instructions of the true prophet Jeremiah for how to live in light of this judgment. After the Babylonians wipe the slate clean in 587 then YHWH's will is to begin the process of reconstructing a faithful community in the land, whether it be with the remnant that remains in the land or with the exiles who will eventually return from Babylon.

Because destruction and exile represent an essential break from Judah's sinful past, the suffering of exile is the context in which God's message of hope for a new future is most powerfully at work.[19] This accounts for the paradoxical role of Babylon in 24:1–10 and 29:1–19. As the place of exile it represents punishment, but since it is also the place from which the exiles will return to the land, it becomes a metaphor of future hope (see also 23:7–8).[20] Chapter 24 reverses expectations with respect to who stands under the grace and wrath of God. If exile represents divine punishment then it must appear that those Jews who have been carted off to Babylon in 598 are the objects of divine wrath while the non-exiles are favored (compare Ezek 11:15; 33:24). But contrary to appearances, those persons who will survive the Babylonian threat are the ones who at present suffer most under it. True prophecy proclaims that only persons

---

17. Brueggemann, *To Pluck Up*, 211; Brueggemann, *A Commentary on Jeremiah*, 219.

18. Ackroyd, *Exile and Restoration*, 243–44.

19. Brueggemann, *A Commentary on Jeremiah*, 256; Stulman, "Jeremiah as a Messenger of Hope," 16–17.

20. Hill, *Friend or Foe?*, 87.

who have embraced God's judgment may receive the word of hope that provides courage to survive that judgment.

This portrayal is similar to the depiction of restoration in Ezra–Nehemiah, where the exile serves as a pool from which different waves of Jews return to participate in the restoration project. These returnees are portrayed not so much as the punished ones trudging home after a long absence but as the saved ones whom God has preserved to carry out the restoration, which they do on their own without cooperation from Jews living in the land. Ironically, those Jews who never left the land and therefore had great opportunity to preserve the Jewish faith and heritage are excluded from participating in the restoration precisely because they never participated in the exile. "The exile is presented as the *prerequisite rite of passage* on or through which claims to be legitimate representative of Israel must be based."[21] Jacob Neusner points out that even though only a minority of Jews ever experienced exile and then a return to the land, this pattern of exile and return became the definitive pattern of meaning for all forms of Judaism ever since.[22] In light of this pattern, texts like Jer 24:5–7 and 29:10–14 invite all Jews to identify with the exile story.

The second development related to Jeremiah's insistence on accepting exile that also facilitated embracing the exile–return story as normative is the conviction that the Jewish people lived in a state of continuing exile. While some Jews of the early post-exilic period believed that the exile had ended with the rise of the Persian empire (see 2 Chr 36:20–23), a number of texts indicate that eventually even the Palestinian Jewish community came to see itself as continuing to live in exile despite the fact that it resided in the land.[23] There is a striking lack of references in Second Temple literature to fulfillment of the promises of restoration found in Isaiah, Jeremiah, and Ezekiel.[24] Because the return to the land and the restoration did not measure up to the glorious hopes expressed in so many prophetic texts, and because a foreign empire continued to rule over Israel, the community viewed these prophetic promises as still

---

21. Fuller, *The Restoration of Israel*, 22. For a more detailed discussion of Ezra–Nehemiah, see ibid., 16–23.

22. Neusner, *Self-Fulfilling Prophecy*, 1–6.

23. Hill, *Friend or Foe?*, 212.

24. Wright, *The New Testament and the People of God*, 269. For a discussion of the Second Temple perception of continuing exile, including some of the biblical and extra-biblical texts that express this outlook, see ibid., 268–72. For a much more detailed analysis see the excellent study by Fuller, *The Restoration of Israel*, 1–101.

unfulfilled. And so paradoxically, the community understood itself to be in exile even while it lived in the promised land,[25] waiting for such divine interventions as God's defeat of enemy nations, the restoration of the Davidic dynasty, and the full and final ingathering of the exiles. Fuller describes exile as an ideological construct through which Jews interpreted their contemporary experience.[26] Exile and return became highly symbolic, with exile representing everything that the Jews found to be wrong with their life and return symbolizing what was necessary to set matters right. Thus, the suffering of the Jewish people in the Second Temple period represented the continuation of exile, and exile became a paradigm by which to speak of new disasters.[27]

When Ezra prays he expresses gratitude for the opportunities afforded by God for restoration under the Persians (Ezra 9:8–9), but he visualizes his community as still mired in the sin of the pre-587 generations and still suffering the consequences (9:6–7), and he describes himself and his contemporaries as slaves (9:8–9). The community has not yet experienced deliverance from the conditions of exile. The same perspective is evident in the book of Nehemiah when Ezra leads the community in a long prayer of confession that repeatedly stresses YHWH's graciousness to Israel and Israel's consistent disobedience (Neh 9:6–37). Conspicuously lacking in Ezra's long list of God's saving actions is any mention of restoration after exile. Instead Ezra speaks of the hardship rightly inflicted on the community, "from the days of the kings of Assyria *until this day*" (Neh 9:32). In addition, he describes his people as ongoing slaves in the land God gave to their ancestors (9:36–37). Ezra visualizes his community as still laboring under the conditions of exile that began already with the Assyrian destruction of the northern kingdom. The book of Daniel, reflecting concerns of the Maccabean era, is set in the period of Babylonian Exile, and uses the exile as a "fiction" in order to portray the sufferings of a much later era as a continuation

---

25. Hill, "'Your Exile Will Be Long,'" 160. Werline's insightful study of penitential prayer in Second Temple Judaism documents how the community experienced itself as living under the weight of its own sin and the resulting divine wrath, longing for restoration from the conditions of exile that still persisted. See Werline, *Penitential Prayer in Second Temple Judaism*, 31–32, 45–47, 51–59, 65–108.

26. Fuller, *The Restoration of Israel*, 8.

27. See Gowan, *Theology of the Prophetic Books*, 196–97. Fuller discusses how even inter-Jewish conflicts were sometimes framed in terms of exile and return. See Fuller, *The Restoration of Israel*, 48–60.

of the Babylonian exile.[28] Jerusalem and the temple still languish under God's wrath (Dan 9:16–17), and Daniel struggles to understand when the seventy-year period of Jerusalem's devastation predicted by Jeremiah will end (9:2). God's response is to reinterpret and re-affirm Jeremiah's prophecy of deliverance as a promise that still remains in effect (9:24–27). In Daniel, "the exile is no longer an historic event to be dated in one period; it is much nearer to being a condition from which only the final age will being release."[29]

Hill observes that even though the book of Jeremiah reached its final form in the Second Temple period after the community experienced some degree of restoration in the land, a number of features of the book create the "fiction" that the exile has not yet ended and that the reader belongs to this world of unended exile.[30] The introduction to the book states that the ministry of Jeremiah extended up to the eleventh year of Zedekiah's reign when Jerusalem was captured (1:3), even though this is inaccurate, since Jeremiah prophesied during the rule of Gedaliah and even later in Egypt (chs. 40–44). The introduction indicates that the intended reader has already experienced the events of 587 and that the historical setting for the book is the time when Jerusalem has been destroyed and the people scattered.[31] However much the editors have used Jeremiah materials to address post-exilic issues, there is no mention of the restoration period, and according to the book's perspective the read-

---

28. Hill, *Friend or Foe?*, 211–12.

29. Ackroyd, *Exile and Restoration*, 242. Other Second Temple texts that portray the exile as still ongoing include Tob 14:4–7; Bar 2:13–14, 30–35; 3:7–8; 2 Macc 1:27–29. For a discussion of these and other texts, see Wright, *The New Testament and the People of God*, 270; Hill, "'Your Exile Will Be Long,'" 159; Hill, "The Construction of Time in Jeremiah 25 (MT)," 158–59; Fuller, *The Restoration of Israel*, 26–48. Tobit 14:5–7 acknowledges the restoration during the Persian period but asserts that it will take a much greater divine intervention to return the exiles, rebuild Jerusalem in splendor, and convert the Gentiles, all in fulfillment of the prophetic promises of restoration. The book of Baruch, probably dating from the Hasmonean period, is set during the Babylonian exile (1:1–2) and portrays the Jewish people as still living in exile and longing for God's deliverance (2:13–14, 30–35; 3:7–8). Jewish apocalyptic literature frequently envisions God's end-time intervention finally bringing a definitive end to exile. See Fuller, *The Restoration of Israel*, 60–84.

30. Hill, *Friend or Foe?*, 27, 94; Hill, "'Your Exile Will Be Long,'" 149–61; Hill, "The Construction of Time in Jeremiah 25 (MT)," 158–59.

31. Fretheim, *Jeremiah*, 4. Fretheim observes how the book's introduction implicitly acknowledges that the audience of the book is not the same as the audience of the historical Jeremiah.

ing community is still living in the immediate shadow of 587. Hill notes how the book closes with the story of Jerusalem's fall even though this event has already been narrated in ch. 39. Thus, the book is deliberately enclosed in an "exilic envelope" and addresses an audience that is encouraged to experience itself as being in exile, even though historically and geographically the return from Babylon has already occurred.[32] Another feature of the book that creates the impression of unended exile is the portrayal of Babylon and Nebuchadnezzar. While both had long disappeared by the time the book reached its final form, they are portrayed as contemporary threats, signifying that the events of exile that began in 587 have not yet come to a close.[33] While the book of Jeremiah portrays the exile as unended, the numerous promises of deliverance as well as the oracles foretelling Babylon's destruction indicate that exile will not be endless.

In linking the construct of unended exile and the grand narrative of exile–return to Jer 24:1–10 and 29:1–19, I depart somewhat from a largely synchronic interpretation. I understand the completed book of Jeremiah to be a Second Temple creation that employs Jeremiah traditions to speak to the issues and needs of a community still struggling with the aftermath of the Babylonian cataclysm. As discussed in more detail in the introduction, the book of Jeremiah does not float in thin air but is closely linked to a particular physical, emotional, and spiritual crisis in the life of a community, and one of its major purposes is to help that community navigate the crisis and reconstitute itself as the renewed people of God. Therefore, exploring how the community experienced the crisis, how it may have understood and appropriated the words of Jeremiah, and how the book connects with the issues and concerns of the original reading community can deepen our insight into the book, even though it need not entirely determine our interpretation. While a text only acquires meaning as a reader or a reading community engages it, we moderns are not free to ascribe any meaning we wish to the words, concepts, and themes found in the book of Jeremiah, because the meaning of words and concepts depends at least to some extent on how these were understood in the original reading community. Therefore, a purely synchronic reading is both inadequate and impossible, and it is helpful to

---

32. Hill, *Friend or Foe?*, 34–35, 194; Hill, "'Your Exile Will Be Long,'" 157.

33. Hill, "'Your Exile Will Be Long,'" 156. For other features of the book that contribute to the image of an unended exile, see the rest of the article.

pay at least some attention to how the early reading community may have understood Jeremiah's message about exile and restoration.

In their final or near-final form, Jer 24:1–10 and 29:1–19 belong to a theological context in which exile had become a governing metaphor shaping the identity of Second Temple Judaism. The community saw itself as continuing to labor under the divinely imposed consequences of past sin, living under a foreign power, with many of its members scattered among the nations, and with a Jerusalem that was a mere reflection of its intended glory. Jeremiah 24:1–10 and 29:1–19 stress two key points. The first is that the community must embrace this situation as divine punishment and live through it on the basis of the true prophet Jeremiah's instructions. The second point is that this situation of exile is not permanent, because ultimately God will intervene to reverse the community's fortunes. Because exile is an essential part of God's plan for Israel, exile represents judgment at the same time as it also becomes the mark of membership in God's elect community.[34] As Neusner points out, Second Temple Judaisms told the story of exile and return, even if this return was still in the future, in such a way that the entire community was invited to identify with this story, despite the fact that only a minority of Jews were ever exiled to Babylon and even a smaller minority ever returned. Texts like Jer 24:1–10 and 29:1–19 invite the entire community to claim and identify with the minority story of the *golah*.[35] This development is similar to how the Exodus story came to function within Judaism, both ancient and contemporary. Only a small number of Israelite ancestors ever experienced anything like an exodus from Egypt (or none at all experienced an exodus if one believes the minimalist historians). Yet the story of the Exodus became the defining story of Judaism and all future members of the community are exhorted to confess, "YHWH brought *us* out of Egypt, from the house of slavery" (Exod 13:14; see also 12:26–27; Deut 5:3).[36]

Jeremiah 24:1–10 and 29:1–19 assume that because the exile is YHWH's means of dealing with the overwhelming sin of Judah, no part of the nation can escape the divine wrath. The exile must be appropriated

---

34. Gowan, *Theology of the Prophetic Books*, 196.

35. See Albertz, *Israel in Exile*, 323.

36. Niebuhr comments on the effect of such foundational stories, whether these be the stories of a religious community or a nation: "When we become members of such a community of selves we adopt its past as our own and thereby are changed in our present existence" (Niebuhr, *The Meaning of Revelation*, 52).

by living through it and/or by accepting its significance as divine judgment. Hence, the text heaps up a multitude of stereotypical terms for destruction and humiliation in order to decree a most bitter fate for those persons who remain in the land or flee to Egypt (24:8–10; 29:17–18). In contrast, the exiles (understood as all those Jews who readily identify with the exile experience) receive a glorious message of salvation. The text never cites the virtues of the exiles as a reason for their favorable treatment over against the non-exiles. Instead of describing the exiles as good (טוֹב), the text declares that God will set his eyes upon them for good and treat them "good" (vv. 6, 5). Divine grace converts the punishment of exile into a new beginning as the exile becomes God's means of starting over to create a faithful people.[37] YHWH will look favorably upon the exiles, restore them to the land, and, borrowing language from Jeremiah's call and other passages, God promises to build and plant them and not overthrow or uproot them (24:6; cf. 1:10; 12:14–17; 18:7–10; 31:28, 40; 42:10; 45:4).

A central feature of the restoration is spiritual renewal. "I will give them a heart to know me, that I am YHWH; and they will be my people and I will be their God, for they will turn to me with their whole heart" (24:7). The book of Jeremiah frequently cites the rebellious heart (meaning the mind, intellect, inclination, will, and character) of the people as a fundamental problem and cause of punishment.[38] In order to live in relationship with God and thrive in the land, the people must have a heart oriented toward YHWH and his ways. Chapter 24 is one of several deliverance passages that assume even judgment does not change the moral condition of a people who lacks the inner capacity to change. Thus, if there is to be restoration God will have to be the one to transform the inward condition of the people (31:33; 32:40; 33:8).[39] It is not the people's spiritual renewal that makes restoration possible, but God's restoration that leads to spiritual renewal (24:7). The positive future is an act of pure divine grace.[40] This emphasis on the grace of God does not function in

---

37. Nicholson, *The Book of the Prophet Jeremiah*, 1:205.

38. See 3:10, 17; 4:14; 5:21, 23–24; 7:24; 9:13 (Heb.), 25 (Heb.); 11:8; 13:10; 16:12; 17:1, 5, 9; 18:12; 22:17.

39. This point is highlighted by Raitt, *A Theology of Exile*, 132–33, 176–78.

40. Craigie et al., *Jeremiah 1–25*, 360–61, read 24:7 differently. They take the כִּי that introduces the final clause as conditional rather than causal—"*if* they turn to me with all their heart"—a translation that makes the new covenant relationship dependent on the people's repentance. The problem with this interpretation is that it stands in

the book as a justification for human indifference or passivity. Rather, it stands in a paradoxical relationship with the consistent call for thoroughgoing repentance and moral vigilance. The overarching message of the book is that survival of the community depends on such repentance and on living a *Torah* way of life, both of which require considerable human effort and initiative.

The call of Jeremiah assigns to him the task of proclaiming both judgment and salvation (1:10). When Jeremiah does so in ch. 24, borrowing language directly from his call (24:6; cf. 1:10), the text presents him as a true prophet faithful to his divine commission. Jeremiah is depicted as knowing when and to whom to deliver a message of judgment and when and to whom a message of salvation. Von Rad, Buber, and Sanders are correct in calling attention to the crucial role of timing and context for discerning whether a prophetic message is true or false. The prophets of salvation condemned in 23:9–40 are false not because their message of deliverance is wrong in and of itself. The book of Jeremiah reckons them as false because they proclaim this message at the wrong time, to the wrong group of people, and with the wrong impact. Jeremiah is portrayed as a true prophet who is attuned to YHWH's changing plans for the people as historical circumstances change. The book of Jeremiah devotes much more space to disaster than deliverance, but the book stubbornly affirms that a significant feature of the ministry of a true prophet like Jeremiah is to announce God's future salvation, as a way to provide a hope capable of sustaining people through the struggles of unended exile.

---

tension with the first part of the verse, which states that God will grant the people a heart to know that he is YHWH, thereby portraying the transformation as dependent on divine and not human initiative.

Raitt points out how Jeremiah's oracles of judgment list many different shortcomings of the people, which then function as justification for divine punishment. In contrast, the oracles of deliverance do not provide grounds for God's saving actions, indicating that this deliverance is rooted in the sheer grace of YHWH. See *A Theology of Exile*, 142–46.

5

Section C

The Symbolic Cup—Destruction of the Nations by Nebuchadnezzar (25:1-38)

SECTION C CONTAINS WHAT may seem like a rather odd combination of themes. Chapter 25 begins by summarizing Jeremiah's prophetic ministry up until the fourth year of Jehoiakim, stressing the nation's refusal to heed Jeremiah and YHWH's line of true prophets. The second part of the chapter describes YHWH's punishment of the nations, including Judah. The effect of linking these two themes is to stress that Judah's refusal to heed the true prophets sets in motion a cataclysmic judgment that engulfs not just Judah but all the other nations of the earth as well. This same connection between the fate of Judah and the fate of the nations is also found in the corresponding section C' (27:1—28:17).

THE REJECTION OF TRUE PROPHECY (25:1-14)

The first part of ch. 25 summarizes the first twenty-three years of Jeremiah's ministry by bringing together the major themes of his message. The highly reflective nature of the passage and its reference to a "book" of Jeremiah prophecies (25:13) indicate that originally it was probably an editorial composition designed to assist in the interpretation of a collection of Jeremiah prophecies.¹ Martin Kessler's assessment of the function of ch. 25 in its present context is remarkably similar to mine, even though he does not observe the concentric structure of 23:9—29:32. "The true/false prophecy conflict which surfaces in Jer 21-24, looms in the background in chapter 25 and continues in the chapters that follow, may provide us with a lens through which to view Jer 25. If that should be the case, then this chapter is *a succinct and emphatic assertion of the contours of true prophecy in the book of Jeremiah*."² The role of ch. 25 in the larger editorial unit is to summarize what true prophecy proclaims in the face of the Babylonian threat, building on what has already been revealed about true prophecy in ch. 24 and spelling out the consequences of disregarding such true prophecy. The true prophecy portrayed in chs. 24 and 25 stands in contrast to the false prophecy described elsewhere in 23:9—29:32 and prepares for ch. 26, which focuses on how the community should respond to true prophecy.

Chapter 25 portrays Jeremiah as the quintessential true prophet. The opening verses stress that "the word which happened [was revealed] to Jeremiah" (25:1) is the same word that the prophet has spoken to the entire community (25:2). For twenty-three years the word of YHWH has been "happening" to Jeremiah and he has persistently proclaimed it (25:3). This stands in contrast to the false prophets of 23:9-40 to whom YHWH has not spoken. Kessler observes how the following scheme serves to summarize Jeremiah's ministry and to emphasize that Jeremiah spoke exactly what was revealed to him.³

---

1. Clements, *Jeremiah*, 148; McKane, *A Critical and Exegetical Commentary*, 1:630. Aejmelaeus, "Jeremiah at the Turning-Point of History," 468-69, points out that except for the chronological reference in v. 3, 25:3-7 contains no phrase that is not found elsewhere in the book. As discussed in chapter 2, the retrospective character of 25:1-14 and the connections to chs. 1 and 36 lead some scholars to suggest that 25:1-14 represents the original conclusion to the rewritten scroll mentioned in 36:32 that supposedly formed the original core of the book of Jeremiah. Other scholars are somewhat more modest in their claims and assert only that 25:1-14 marks a major break in the completed book, without linking this conclusion to theories about the book's editorial history. Thiel claims that the correlation of dates in 25:1-3 and 36:1-2 represents an *editorial* attempt to connect the contents of 1:1—25:14 with the scroll and give the impression that 25:3-14 summarizes the scroll. See Thiel, *Die deuteronomistische Redaktion*, 270. Lundbom is somewhat unique in maintaining that 25:1-14 is not a conclusion of any sort and that there is no major break in the book at ch. 25. See *Jeremiah 21-36*, 238-39.

2. Kessler, "Jeremiah 25,1–29," 47.

3. Ibid., 52.

Concerning the Prophets

1a	הַדָּבָר אֲשֶׁר־הָיָה עַל־יִרְמְיָהוּ עַל־כָּל־עָם	(third person)	REVELATION
	The word which happened to Jeremiah concerning all the people		
2a	אֲשֶׁר דִּבֶּר יִרְמְיָהוּ הַנָּבִיא עַל־כָּל־עָם	(third person)	PROCLAMATION
	which Jeremiah the prophet spoke to all the people		
3a	הָיָה דְבַר־יְהוָה אֵלָי	(first person)	REVELATION
	the word of YHWH happened to me		
3b	וָאֲדַבֵּר אֲלֵיכֶם אַשְׁכֵּים וְדַבֵּר	(first person)	PROCLAMATION
	and I spoke to you persistently		

Another way in which the text highlights Jeremiah's authority is by portraying him as prophesying to both Judah and the nations, and thereby fulfilling the mandate he received at his call (1:5,10).

The first year of Nebuchadnezzar (25:1) corresponds to 605, the year in which Babylon's victory over Egypt and Assyria at the Battle of Carchemish paved the way for Babylonian hegemony over the Fertile Crescent. This reference to the first year of Nebuchadnezzar's rule signals that he will be the agent whom YHWH uses to enact the horrible desolation of Judah and the nations that most of the chapter describes. Judah's pre-exilic world is ending and Nebuchadnezzar's reign of terror is about to begin.[4] In ch. 25 the true prophet Jeremiah offers an explanation for the horrendous destruction Nebuchadnezzar will set in motion. It is striking that the LXX lacks all specific references in 25:1–14 to Babylon or Nebuchadnezzar. It appears that the MT has transformed a general threat of an enemy from the north into a specific threat of defeat by Nebuchadnezzar.[5] One of the effects of the frequent references to Babylon in the MT of ch. 25 is to make sections C and C' (27:1—28:17) correspond more closely.

Given that the book of Jeremiah was compiled in the Second Temple period, another effect of emphasizing God's use of Babylon as agent of divine judgment is to characterize the message of true prophecy as a call to accept the catastrophic destruction of the nation as deserved punishment and as an admonishment to learn crucial lessons. In 25:18 God promises to make the nation an object of hissing and cursing "like this day." The text collapses the time between the first year of Nebuchadnezzar's reign, also called "this day" (v. 3), and the fall of Jerusalem in 587, and speaks as

---

4. Stulman, *Jeremiah*, 226. See also Hill, *Friend or Foe?*, 104–5.
5. Overholt, "King Nebuchadnezzar in the Jeremiah Tradition," 42.

if disaster has already befallen the nation. The expression "like this day" in 25:18 also makes the events portrayed in the chapter contemporaneous with the time of the reader, and since the nation is described as being in ruins, it contributes to the picture of the unended exile.[6] Readers of the book are invited to see themselves as belonging to a time when the conditions of exile still prevail. Thus, ch. 25 is prediction, description, and explanation of catastrophe all rolled into one. The chapter then also becomes a prophetic word about how to live in the time of exile and how to avoid a similar disaster in the future.

Chapter 25 is also dated to the fourth year of Jehoiakim. Linking a prophetic message to a specific year of a king's reign is not unusual, but here the date is particularly significant because the passage summarizes a long phase of Jeremiah's ministry and stresses that from the thirteenth year of Josiah until this day, the fourth year of Jehoiakim, a total of twenty-three years, Jeremiah has persistently proclaimed YHWH's word (25:3). This dating establishes the credentials of Jeremiah as a true prophet who has been faithful and conscientious throughout a long ministry. With one brief statement, "but you have not listened/obeyed," the conclusion to v. 3 introduces the focus of the following verses and characterizes the history of Jeremiah's prophetic proclamation as the history of the people's rejection of that proclamation. The nation has already had twenty-three years to heed the message of Jeremiah but it has totally squandered this opportunity, and so Jeremiah can only declare the consequences of such stubbornness.

The MT emphasizes somewhat more than the LXX the people's rejection of Jeremiah the true prophet. In 25:2 the MT has "Jeremiah the prophet" speaking while the LXX has only "Jeremiah." A more significant difference is that the LXX lacks the reference in 25:3 to the people's consistent refusal to listen to Jeremiah over the last twenty-three years. Another difference is that in the MT 25:3-5 is a speech by Jeremiah while in the LXX the speaker is YHWH, and so in the LXX the people reject the words of YHWH while in the MT they reject the words of Jeremiah. This is not a significant difference, because the book of Jeremiah repeatedly stresses that the words of Jeremiah are the words of YHWH. However, the MT increases the authority of Jeremiah as a prophet whose words should be heeded, and heightens somewhat the emphasis on the people's rejection of true prophecy.

---

6. Hill, *Friend or Foe?*, 93–94, 102.

Concerning the Prophets

A new feature comes to the fore in 25:4–7 that is important for understanding the portrayal of true and false prophecy in all of 23:9—29:32. "YHWH has persistently sent to you all his servants the prophets" (25:4a). This is the first explicit reference in the larger editorial unit to any true prophets other than Jeremiah; until now all other prophets have been condemned as false. Three times 23:9—29:32 asserts that Jeremiah's ministry stands in the tradition of a long line of other faithful prophets who mediate the divine word (25:4; 26:5; 29:19), and three similar references appear elsewhere in the book (7:25; 35:15; 44:4). All of these passages assert that YHWH has *persistently* sent (הַשְׁכֵּם וְשָׁלֹחַ) the prophets (7:25; 25:4; 26:5; 29:19; 35:15; 44:4),[7] implying that he always provides prophetic guidance that the community had better heed. This guidance does not cease with the death of the prophet(s). In 26:17–19 elders cite the words of Micah, asserting that these words provide very specific and crucial guidance for the people of Jeremiah's day. This conviction that God speaks in an ongoing way through his servants the prophets motivated the complex and lengthy process whereby prophetic speech became canonical Scripture.

Because the expression "my servants the prophets" appears primarily in 2 Kings (9:7; 17:13, 23; 21:10; 24:2) and in the Deuteronomistic prose of Jeremiah (7:25; 25:4; 26:5; 29:19; 35:15; 44:4), numerous scholars see the phrase as reflecting a Deuteronomistic view of prophecy.[8] Because this "Deuteronomistic" view is so deeply embedded in the portrayal of true prophecy in the book of Jeremiah, I will explore its origins and content as a way of highlighting its contribution. I do so recognizing that the Deuteronomistic movement did not hold a monopoly on its views about prophecy, and that the movement was not monolithic but encompassed a range of interest groups and theological perspectives[9] that may reflect considerable variation in their understanding of prophecy.[10] Despite

---

7. There are also several passages that portray YHWH as having spoken persistently, some implying more strongly than others that this speaking occurred through prophets (7:13; 11:7; 32:33; 35:14).

8. Other texts that mention YHWH's servants the prophets include Amos 3:7 (often considered to belong to the Deuteronomistic redaction of Amos); Ezek 38:17; Zech 1:6; Ezra 9:11; Dan 9:6, 10. Texts that speak of an individual prophet as servant of YHWH include 1 Kgs 14:18; 15:29; 18:36; 2 Kgs 9:36; 10:10; 14:25; Isa 20:3.

9. On this point see Albertz, *A History of Israelite Religion*, 382.

10. Sharp points out some of the significant differences between the understanding of prophecy in the book of Kings, in Deut 18, and in the Deuteronomistic prose of Jeremiah, and concludes that there is no single Deuteronomistic view of prophecy. See

these qualifiers, the frequent references to a long line of faithful prophets in Deuteronomistic contexts makes some talk of a Deuteronomistic understanding of prophecy unavoidable when exploring the portrayal of true and false prophecy in Jer 23:9—29:32.

Deuteronomy 18:15-22 envisions that YHWH will raise up a succession of prophets as his spokespersons whom Israel must therefore heed. Twice it is explicitly stated that these prophets will be like Moses (18:15, 18), indicating that prophecy has its beginnings in the figure of Moses and is called to carry on his ministry.[11] Since Moses is the great mediator of the covenant and *Torah*, Deuteronomistic tradition frequently portrays the prophets as preachers of *Torah* and Israelite covenant traditions.[12] Deuteronomistic references to a book or collection of *Torah* (Deut 1:5; 28:61; Josh 1:7; 8:31; 1 Sam 10:25; 1 Kgs 2:3; 2 Kgs 22:8) illustrate the development of a conviction that previously revealed truth can be codified in an authoritative "book" of *Torah* that takes precedence over other claims to provide guidance for the community.[13] Because the role of prophecy is to undergird *Torah*, some of the later Deuteronomists reduced the multifaceted prophetic movement to a single succession of prophets who all warn Israel of the dire consequences of failure to repent and obey the *Torah*.[14] This Deuteronomistic reduction of the multifaceted prophetic movement should not be overstated, because the Deuteronomistic History preserves stories of a diversity of prophetic figures who are not portrayed as one single succession of prophets all admonishing the nation to repent and obey the *Torah*.[15]

The Deuteronomistic explanation for the fall of Samaria illustrates the "reduced" conception of prophecy. "YHWH warned Israel and Judah by the hand of every prophet and seer saying, 'Turn from your evil ways and observe my commandments and my statutes in accordance with all the *Torah* which I commanded your fathers, and which I sent to you by the hand of my servants the prophets'" (2 Kgs 17:13).[16] This

---

Sharp, *Prophecy and Ideology in Jeremiah*, 125-56, especially pp. 125-26, 155.

11. See Nicholson, *Preaching to the Exiles*, 46, 48; Seitz, "The Prophet Moses," 5.

12. Nicholson, *Preaching to the Exiles*, 48; Blenkinsopp, *Prophecy and Canon*, 41, 44-45.

13. Blenkinsopp, *Prophecy and Canon*, 36.

14. For an insightful discussion of this process see Clements, *Prophecy and Tradition*, 49-52.

15. See Sharp, *Prophecy and Ideology in Jeremiah*, 128-29.

16. Sharp argues that this passage is an exception to the portrayal of prophecy in

passage portrays the prophets as all having a unified message that the people should repent and obey the *Torah*, and also depicts them as the vehicle by which this *Torah* is actually communicated to Israel. The larger passage stresses that failure to heed the prophets, particularly the refusal to cease worshipping other gods, resulted in the downfall of the northern kingdom (17:14–18). As a consequence of making the prophets out to be preachers of repentance and *Torah*, the original particularity of the prophetic condemnations as seen in the books of Amos, Hosea, and much of Jeremiah was broadened, and these threats lost their close connection to specific historical events and situations.[17] This process was also at work outside Deuteronomistic circles. The message of Amos was originally intended for Northern Israel, but as a way of applying it also to Judah later editors added the very general Judah oracle in 2:4–5, which does not single out any specific sin as do all the other oracles in Amos 1–2, but condemns Judah for rejecting YHWH's *Torah*. This "reduced" conception sums up prophecy as a call to repentance and faithfulness to *Torah*. Thus, even when the catastrophe which the prophets foretold had passed, the need to repent endured.[18]

From the eighth century onward the faith community invested certain prophets and their message with a kind of canonical authority.[19] The projection of a long line of prophets all serving YHWH by calling for repentance and adherence to *Torah*, and the portrayal of Jeremiah as the quintessential true prophet whose message has ongoing relevance were both part of this larger process of ascribing more and more authority to past prophets and the written traditions that reflected their ministry. The catastrophe of 587 and reflections on it contributed enormously to

---

the Deuteronomistic History but characteristic of the portrayal of true prophecy in the prose of Jeremiah. She claims it should be considered Deutero-Jeremianic and not Deuteronomistic. See Sharp, *Prophecy and Ideology in Jeremiah*, 143–47, especially p. 145. Sharp concludes that two quite different traditions developed regarding the function of YHWH's servants the prophets, one Deutero-Jeremianic and the other Deuteronomistic.

17. Clements, *Prophecy and Tradition*, 51–52; Blenkinsopp, *Prophecy and Canon*, 44.

18. Clements, *Prophecy and Tradition*, 44, 52. The interpretation of prophecy as a call to repentance is not arbitrary. Prophets like Amos, Hosea, Micah, and Isaiah named the specific sins they believed were responsible for impending disaster. If human sin occasioned the divine wrath, then it made sense to believe that repentance might forestall it.

19. Ibid., 54.

the authority of those prophets who had foretold disaster. Much of the attempt to understand and come to terms with the Babylonian crisis took the form of interpreting, editing, supplementing, and appropriating the literary heritage of pre-exilic prophets of judgment like Amos, Hosea, Micah, Jeremiah, and Zephaniah.[20] One of the most important interpretations of the disaster was that the nation had refused to heed the long line of true prophets whom YHWH had persistently sent. If rejection of the divine word mediated by the line of true prophets had brought disaster, then in the Second Temple period it was essential to learn the painful lessons of the past by repenting and heeding the prophetic summons to a *Torah* way of life.[21]

The understanding of prophecy sketched above is deeply embedded in the book of Jeremiah, especially in 23:9—29:32, and it comes to the fore particularly in passages that speak of YHWH's servants the prophets (7:25; 25:4; 26:5; 29:19; 35:15; 44:4). According to 7:25-26 this line of YHWH's servants the prophets extends from the time the Israelites left Egypt until the present (i.e., from Moses to Jeremiah).[22] The text is not

---

20. Nissenen, "How Prophecy Became Literature," 156-57, speaks of scribes as "the fathers of the prophetic books." According to Nissenen, various crises related to the destruction and rebuilding of Jerusalem provided the impetus for reusing, reinterpreting, and writing down older prophecies, thereby extending the prophetic process of communication.

21. Clements, *Prophecy and Tradition*, 54, points out that because the community thought of these prophets as being like Moses in that they called for adherence to *Torah*, the vesting of authority in the prophets laid the groundwork for "a canonically conceived work of 'the Law and the Prophets.'" This development was also a major step toward the later view that the prophetic books were commentary on the *Torah*. Mal 3:22 (Eng. 4:4) is a revealing text in that at the conclusion of the book the prophet Malachi specifically calls for adherence to the *Torah* of Moses that YHWH had revealed at Horeb for all Israel. Sheppard believes that the prophetic literature was given its final canonical shape by editors who sought to encourage obedience to the *Torah* of Moses as promulgated by Ezra and who believed that prophecy could in no way challenge the sufficiency of *Torah* as the revealed will of God. See Sheppard, "True and False Prophecy," 278-80.

22. Seitz, "The Prophet Moses," 12, claims that the shapers of the book of Jeremiah viewed him as the last Mosaic prophet. The call of Jeremiah already portrays him as a new Mosaic prophet. Jeremiah is commissioned to proclaim whatever YHWH commands him (1:7), and YHWH promises to place the divine words in his mouth (1:9), just as God promises for the Mosaic prophet of Deut 18:18. Brueggemann argues that the conjunction of the law and the prophets that Moses models comes to fruition in Jeremiah, and that the book as a whole portrays him as a prophet like Moses. See *The Theology of the Book of Jeremiah*, 74-75. In contrast to Seitz and Brueggemann, Sharp argues that there is no redactional attempt in the book to portray Jeremiah as a

specific about what these prophets have persistently been proclaiming, but since ch. 7 spells out particular ways in which Judah has been unfaithful and has thereby consistently refused to heed YHWH's servants the prophets, the text implies that these prophets, just like Jeremiah, must have been warning of impending disaster (7:12–15, 20, 29, 32–34), calling for wholesale repentance (7:3–7), condemning false assurances of well-being (7:4, 8, 10, 14), encouraging obedience to God's ways (7:23), and demanding an end to social injustice (7:5–9), the worship of other gods (7:6, 9, 18–19, 30–31), and the defilement of YHWH's temple (7:10–11, 30).

In ch. 35 Jeremiah contrasts the Rechabites, who have remained obedient to the command of their ancestor, with the rest of the nation, which has utterly refused to heed the long line of prophets YHWH has persistently sent with the message, "Turn now each of you from your evil way and amend your actions, and do not go after other gods to serve them, so that you might dwell in the land which I gave to you and your ancestors" (35:15). Just as in ch. 7, living in the land is conditional upon heeding the prophetic call to forsake other gods and live in obedience to the way of YHWH. In 44:2–10 Jeremiah explains to the Egyptian *golah* why Jerusalem was destroyed. He condemns the wickedness of the nation, focusing particularly on the worship of other gods, and concludes by highlighting disobedience of God's statutes and *Torah*. The nation persisted in its worship of false gods despite YHWH's repeatedly sending his servants the prophets to plead, "Please do not do this abominable thing which I hate" (44:4).

The depiction of YHWH's servants the prophets in 25:4–7 is consistent with other passages in the book that highlight their role, although the term *Torah* does not appear here. In addition to persistently revealing the divine word to Jeremiah for twenty-three years, YHWH has repeatedly sent all his other servants the prophets (vv. 3–4), but as in other texts, the history of true prophecy is also the history of the rejection of true prophecy (v. 4). Allen observes that the ultimate sin in the book of Jeremiah is refusal to heed the true prophetic word and embrace the *Torah* way of life.[23] Chapter 25:1–14 highlights how Jeremiah belongs to a venerable tradition of true prophecy in which he functions as an imposing figure. All these prophets are portrayed as preachers of the first commandment

---

prophet like Moses. See *Prophecy and Ideology in Jeremiah*, 147–55.

23. Allen, *Jeremiah*, 285.

(25:6) who summon the people to forsake their evil ways so that they might remain in the land YHWH promised to them and their ancestors (25:5; cf. 7:3–7). The purpose of true prophecy is to spell out the conditions for God's fulfillment of the promise of land to the patriarchs (cf. 7:7).[24] The true prophets of 25:4–7 stand in sharp contrast to the false prophets of 23:9–40. Instead of assurances of well-being they proclaim words of rebuke and summon the nation to change direction. Instead of promoting immorality (23:11, 14, 15, 17, 22) and apostasy (23:13, 25–27, 32) they call for worship of YHWH alone and obedience to his word.

Who exactly are these anonymous servants the prophets to whose company Jeremiah belongs? Answering this question requires some attention to diachronic issues. If one assumes that the purpose of the book is to record the ministry of the historical Jeremiah, then these prophets must be contemporaries like Uriah (26:20–23) and predecessors like Micah (26:17–19) and others of whom the historical Jeremiah was aware. For the Second Temple community that looked to Jeremiah traditions for guidance, YHWH's servants the prophets must have designated those prophets whose words and deeds were preserved in prophetic traditions, oral and written, that were still in the process of being shaped and amplified but were acquiring increasing authority. Jeremiah's references to a line of true prophets would have provided incentive for accelerating this "canonization" process. For yet later readers who already possessed a "canon" of prophetic literature, YHWH's servants the prophets must have been those prophets whose words and deeds the canon preserved.

Jeremiah's references to a line of YHWH's servants the prophets serve a variety of functions. First of all they represent a claim to authority for what the reader conceives of as "canonical" prophecy, whether that prophecy consists of living individuals, oral prophetic traditions, or completed prophetic books. True prophets, however defined, speak for God and are disregarded at enormous cost. Second, references to YHWH's servants the prophets always stress the persistence with which YHWH sends them, thereby asserting that God always makes prophetic guidance available to the community. At one point in time this would have been through living individuals like Jeremiah, but in a later era the prophetic literature replaces living prophets as the source of divine revelation. A third function of these references is to simplify prophecy into both a call to repent of all forms of evil, especially the worship of other gods, and a

---

24. This point is underscored by a wordplay in 25:5. The people must שׁוּבוּ (repent) so that they might וִישְׁבוּ (dwell) perpetually in the land.

summons to obey the will of God as revealed in *Torah*. A fourth function is to provide a theodicy for the events of 587.[25] Failure to heed the words of Jeremiah and the other true prophets led to Jerusalem's destruction. Jeremiah 25, for example, never issues a call to repentance but merely announces that the people's refusal to heed the prophetic pleas will lead to YHWH's summoning the Babylonians (25:8–11) and to a desolation that prevails until "this day" (25:18).

Chapter 25 is one of many passages in the book that assumes judgment is unavoidable. Some scholars note how the book vacillates between declaring that disaster is inevitable and calling the nation to repentance so that it might yet avert catastrophe.[26] Sharp explains this tension by linking these emphases diachronically to different redactional layers. Perhaps they do originate in different redactional layers, but synchronically the tension between these two emphases serves a fundamental purpose. The book of Jeremiah cannot rewrite history but can only account for it, and so it stresses that the sinfulness of the nation reached a point of no return and judgment became inevitable. However, a major lesson the book seeks to teach is that history can repeat itself, and so the reading community must heed the message of Jeremiah and the other true prophets by repenting and obeying God's will. Therefore, numerous passages stress that despite the late hour, God still holds out through the voice of true prophecy the possibility of repentance and averting disaster (7:5–7; 18:1–11; 26:3, 13; 36:3), even though such a possibility is a fiction from the perspective of the completed book. Clements observes how the call to repentance in Jeremiah, which he claims outweighs the inevitability of disaster, counteracts the fatalism and despair engendered by the fall of the nation.[27] True prophecy assures the faithful that turning toward YHWH always remains a live possibility and will ensure a positive future. Stulman and Kim describe the prophetic books, including Jeremiah, as "meaning-making literature for communities under siege," siege referring to the challenging conditions of life under succeeding empires in the post-587 era.[28] One significant feature of this meaning-making was to create within the community a sense of agency and empowerment even

---

25. For a more detailed discussion of theodicy as it relates to the book of Jeremiah, see Raitt, *A Theology of Exile*, 83–105; Stulman, *Jeremiah*, 32–34.

26. Sharp, *Prophecy and Ideology in Jeremiah*, 41–42; Moberly, *Prophecy and Discernment*, 95–99.

27. Clements, "Prophecy Interpreted," 40–44.

28. Stulman and Kim, *You Are My People*, 9–23.

while it lived under the restrictions of empire. Although the fate of Jeremiah's original audience had been sealed, written prophecy "re-presents" to future generations "the missed opportunities as new opportunities: divine mandates once rejected are now viable options for the reading or listening community. In this way victims of disaster and their children are empowered to take back their lives and carve out a future when none seems possible."[29]

Other Second Temple texts use the motif of YHWH's servants the prophets in a way similar to that of the book of Jeremiah. Zech 1:2-6 exhorts its readers not to be like their ancestors, who rejected the call to repent issued by YHWH's servants the prophets. Because this refusal resulted in the catastrophe of 587, the lesson to be learned is that the community must constantly obey the summons to repent, which is the essence of true prophecy. As Clements has observed, the disaster predicted by YHWH's servants the prophets came and went, but the summons and opportunity to repent and obey the *Torah* remained in effect.[30] Ezra is portrayed as having learned this lesson. After he hears that some Jews have married foreigners (Ezra 9:1-2), he utters a prayer in which he confesses how the people have refused to heed God's commandments that were spoken to Israel through YHWH's servants the prophets before Israel even entered the land (9:10-12). Ezra must be thinking of Moses and a succession of Mosaic prophets who are proclaimers of *Torah*. Ezra then specifically refers to the exile and destruction of the nation, stressing the grave danger of repeating the mistakes of the past and suffering the same consequences (9:13-14). The catastrophe has passed but the need to heed the true prophets and repent continues. Daniel puzzles over the delay in the fulfillment of Jeremiah's prophecy that Jerusalem's devastation will last only seventy years, and then he utters a long prayer confessing the sins of his people. Twice he mentions how the kings, officials, and ancestors, *as well as his own generation*, have refused to heed the message of YHWH's servants the prophets (Dan 9:6, 8-10). He understands this message to entail a call to repent and heed YHWH's laws (9:5, 10). These passages illustrate how the Jeremiah tradition's presentation of the essence of true prophecy as being a summons to repent and obey the *Torah* belongs to a larger biblical portrayal of the nature of true prophecy.

---

29. Ibid., 17.
30. Clements, *Prophecy and Tradition*, 44, 52.

Concerning the Prophets

The emphasis on acknowledging the sinfulness of the community and on repentance, which is so central to 23:9—29:32 and to texts that speak of YHWH's servants the prophets, is part of a larger development in Second Temple Judaism. A central feature of Jewish piety in this period was penitential prayer, illustrating the community's deep sense of having forsaken the ways of God and thereby bringing upon itself the catastrophe of 587.[31] Despite the partial restoration under the Persians, the community still languished under foreign domination and the material and spiritual conditions of its life were a far cry from what was envisioned by the prophetic promises of restoration. Therefore, the community still saw itself as suffering under the divine wrath brought on by both past and present unfaithfulness (see for example Ezra 9–10; Neh 1:4–11; 9:1–38; Dan 9; Bar 1:15—3:8). A pervasive theme in Second Temple literature is the call for penitence, repentance, and determination to follow God's will, all as part of the hopeful message that the community is not powerless in the face of the ongoing conditions of exile. Human faithfulness will hopefully move YHWH to intervene and fulfill the promises of restoration (see, for example, Deut 4:25–31; 30:1–10; 1 Kgs 8:33–34, 46–53; Isa 59:1–20; 65:1–2; Bar 2:13–18; 3:2–5; 4:1—5:9).

Sheppard observes that the biblical portrayal of true and false prophecy is not primarily interested in providing criteria for distinguishing between the two, even though some of the prophetic conflict texts reflect situations where this was a very live issue. Rather, the texts as we now have them are more interested in offering "guides to the interpretation of the words and deeds of the true 'biblical' prophets in contrast to their adversaries."[32] This is certainly true of ch. 25 and most of 23:9—29:32, where there is much less concern with providing specific criteria than with spelling out how the faithful community is to appropriate the message of Jeremiah and the other true prophets.

At 25:8 there is a minor break in the text. The larger passage is in the form of an invective-threat oracle, in which the people's persistent refusal to heed the voice of true prophecy (25:3–7) constitutes the basis for the punishment announced in 25:8–11. YHWH will summon the clans of the north and Nebuchadnezzar to wreak utter devastation upon the land of Judah and all the surrounding nations (25:9–11). The refusal of

---

31. See the insightful book by Werline, *Penitential Prayer in Second Temple Judaism*, and the shorter discussion in Smith-Christopher, *A Biblical Theology of Exile*, 111–23.

32. Sheppard, "True and False Prophecy," 271.

Judah to heed Jeremiah and YHWH's servants the prophets unleashes a cataclysm that engulfs the surrounding nations as well. As mentioned at the beginning of this chapter, herein lies the connection between the first part of ch. 25 (vv. 1-14), focusing on Judah's response to true prophecy, and the bulk of the chapter, which deals with YHWH's devastation of the broader world (vv. 15-38). The entire chapter contains only one reference to any sin on the part of the nations (v. 31). Their destruction is the collateral damage of YHWH's punishment of Judah. The welfare of the world is to some extent dependent upon God's people heeding the voice of true prophecy.

Two wordplays highlight the irony of the situation. Judah has refused to heed the *servants* (prophets) whom YHWH has *sent* (25:4), therefore he will now *send* a very different *servant* in the form of Nebuchadnezzar, whom the people will not be able to ignore (25:9). The expression "Nebuchadnezzar my servant" is shocking because normally the title "servant of YHWH" signifies endearment and special status, and nowhere outside the book of Jeremiah does the Old Testament call a foreigner YHWH's servant.[33] Ascribing this title to Nebuchadnezzar is a highly provocative move emphasizing how YHWH's judgment is mediated through an enemy king, and that YHWH's and Nebuchadnezzar's actions coalesce.[34] However, both here and in 27:6, where Nebuchadnezzar is also called YHWH's servant, the text portrays Nebuchadnezzar as passive despite his massive power, and YHWH as responsible for all the action.[35]

According to royal traditions the Davidic king is the "servant of YHWH," and so ascribing the title to Nebuchadnezzar signals that God is abandoning the Davidic dynasty and replacing it with a foreign emperor as temporary caretaker of his people.[36] In the Second Temple period this positive portrayal of Nebuchadnezzar would have contributed to a legitimation of Judah's continuing domination by the powerful empires of

---

33. Lundbom, *Jeremiah 21-36*, 247. Jeremiah 27:6 and 43:10 also designate Nebuchadnezzar as YHWH's servant. The presence of the title in 25:9 and 27:6 serves to strengthen the parallels between sections C and C' of the concentric structure. In all three cases the expression is lacking in the LXX.

34. Fretheim, *Jeremiah*, 363.

35. See Osuji, *Where Is the Truth?*, 304.

36. Hill, *Friend or Foe?*, 103, 108-10. Among the many texts that speak of the Davidic king as servant of YHWH are 2 Sam 3:18; 7:5, 8, 19, 20, 21, 25, 26, 27, 28, 29; 1 Kgs 3:6, 7, 8, 9; 8:24, 25, 26, 28-30; 11:13, 32, 34, 38; Ps 78:70; 89:3, 20, 50; 132:10.

the day and allowed the community to interpret its subjugated status as a continuation of the Babylonian exile.[37]

After an initial proclamation of annihilating judgment on Judah and the nations, the text shifts to an announcement of Babylon's punishment that functions as a muted message of deliverance for Babylon's victims (25:12–14). The announcements of judgment and deliverance are held together by the figure of seventy years.[38] In 25:11 the seventy years designates a lengthy period of Babylonian hegemony and underscores the severity of God's punishment, but 25:12–14 stresses that the hated Babylonian domination is limited to a period of seventy years, after which YHWH will initiate a reversal of fortunes and Babylon will be subjugated. Jeremiah's claim that Babylonian domination will last a long time stands in contrast to the message of false prophets in chs. 27 and 28, who maintain that divine intervention will occur in the near future (27:16; 28:2–4, 11). The end of Babylon suggests the possibility of deliverance for Judah, but any hope is muted because the text says nothing about the potential for Judah's future beyond the assurance that the ruthless power of Babylon will come to an end. Hill observes how the book of Jeremiah is unlike the book of Ezekiel, where the movement from judgment to salvation is smooth and salvation has the last word.[39] Jeremiah begins and ends with disaster, and salvation passages stand out like oases of hope in a land of judgment, an apt description of 23:9—29:32, where promises of deliverance are surrounded by powerful announcements of catastrophe (24:5–7; 25:12–14; 27:22; 29:10–14, 32). The effect is to promise that salvation is coming, but it is still some way off for a community that continues to experience the conditions of exile. Whereas the assertion that Nebuchadnezzar is YHWH's servant functions to promote acceptance of foreign domination, the claim that Babylon is ultimately doomed suggests that the community need not submit uncritically nor view such submission as its eternal calling.

---

37. Ibid., 213.

38. Miller, "The Book of Jeremiah," 792. Seventy years may be an ancient convention for a period of divine displeasure. See Applegate, "Jeremiah and the Seventy Years in the Hebrew Bible," 93; Leuchter, *The Polemics of Exile*, 47. For a helpful discussion of the many possible meanings that have been suggested for the seventy years, see Carroll, *Jeremiah*, 493–95. Second Chronicles 36:21, Zech 1:12, and Dan 9:2 all view the exile as lasting seventy years, but in the latter two texts the seventy years is not understood literally, nor has it yet come to an end.

39. Hill, "The Construction of Time in Jeremiah 25 (MT)," 157–58; Hill, *Friend or Foe?*, 30–35.

The punishment of Babylon will occur as a result of YHWH fulfilling "all my words which I have spoken concerning it which are written in *this book* which Jeremiah prophesied concerning all the nations" (25:13). This statement points ahead to the oracles concerning Babylon found at the end of the book in the MT (chs. 50–51), but the mention of a book is also important in terms of the depiction of true prophecy. Stulman documents the significant shift that occurs in the book of Jeremiah from oral to written prophecy. The references to authoritative documents containing YHWH's words (25:13; 29:1–19; 30:2; 36:1–32; 45:1; 51:60–64) indicate that "the scroll, and not the presence of the prophet, becomes a dominant symbol and a primary medium of divine revelation. As such, written prophecy represents an authorized mode by which a community of 'readers' encounters transcendence and grasps the purposes of God."[40] Twice in 23:9—29:32 a document functions as an important symbol of the revelation conveyed by true prophecy, here in 25:13 and especially later when Jeremiah writes a letter to the exiles (29:1–19).

THE CUP OF WRATH (25:15-38)

In 25:15-16 YHWH instructs Jeremiah to perform the symbolic action of making all the nations drink the cup of wrath that will make them retch and go crazy because of the punishing sword that YHWH will unleash against them. Since it is difficult to imagine Jeremiah literally forcing the nations to drink the cup of wrath (cf. 25:17), the text is best understood as a vision or quasi-vision report that portrays YHWH as the host of a banquet who appoints Jeremiah as the server of wine.[41]

The universal scope of the disaster is emphasized by frequent references to all the earth and all nations (25:17, 26, 29, 30–31, 32–33) and the absence of the names of specific nations in the description of overwhelming destruction. Yet the text explicitly states at the outset that Judah is the first to drink the cup of wrath (25:17-18). God's judgment begins with his own people, a point highlighted in 25:28-29, which states that since YHWH's judgment starts with his own city, it is inconceivable that the

---

40. Stulman, *Order amid Chaos*, 108. See the much fuller discussion, 100–108. On the transformation of orality into writing see also Carroll, "Inscribing the Covenant," especially 61–62.

41. Lundbom, *Jeremiah 21-36*, 267; Allen, *Jeremiah*, 289. Other texts that speak of a cup of wrath as divine judgment include Jer 13:12–14; 49:12; 51:7; Isa 51:17, 22; Ezek 23:31–34; Obad 16; Hab 2:16; Ps 75:9 [Heb.]; Lam 4:21.

nations can avoid catastrophe. This is yet another way in which the text intertwines the fates of Judah and the nations.

When describing the destruction of Judah, 25:18 concludes with the phrase "like this day," indicating that the judgment against Judah and its cities has already occurred. The following verses speak of the destruction of Egypt and a host of other peoples (25:19–26). From the perspective of the completed text the judgment of the nations has been partially realized already. However, the universal scope of the predicted devastation, the linking of Babylon's punishment to the punishment of the nations (25:26), and the reference to the judgment occurring "on *that* day" (25:33) all indicate that a worldwide catastrophe is yet to come at some undetermined point in the future. The construction of time in ch. 25 places the reader in an in-between phase, when divine judgment has begun and is still ongoing but apocalyptic-type catastrophe still lies in the future.[42] Hill points out that this construction of time illustrates how the final form of the book addresses an audience that is in exile or should experience itself as such, and should accept this exile as rightly deserved punishment.[43]

In 25:1–14 Babylon appears as a real historical empire through which YHWH enacts judgment on Judah and the nations, a portrayal that continues into the cup of wrath section. However, in 25:26 Babylon is no longer agent of YHWH's judgment but subject of it. Babylon appears at the concluding climax of a long list of nations who must drink the cup of wrath, and is designated by the cipher *Sheshach*.[44] In this way the text clothes Babylon in mystery and makes it the evil and arrogant empire par excellence, whose destruction is the climax of God's judgment of the world.[45] The portrayal of Babylon in ch. 25 is in keeping with the depiction of Babylon in the book as a whole. YHWH chooses Babylon as the means to carry out judgment on Judah and the nations, but Babylon also becomes the symbol of the arrogant empire that must be humbled and destroyed (see especially the lengthy oracles in chs. 50–51).

---

42. For a fuller discussion see Hill, "The Construction of Time in Jeremiah 25 (MT)," 154–57.

43. Ibid., 158–59.

44. *Sheshach* (שֵׁשַׁךְ) is an atbash, a cipher in which each letter represents the letter at the same distance from the opposite end of the alphabet. Thus, שֵׁשַׁךְ corresponds to בָּבֶל, which is Babylon.

45. Hill, *Friend or Foe?*, 122–23; Hill, "The Book of Jeremiah (MT) and Its Early Second Temple Background," 156.

Section C

The overall picture in 25:15–38 is of an international order that is coming unglued.[46] Stulman observes that ch. 25 should be read against the background of the Babylonian devastation of Judah, when the magnitude of death, suffering, and destruction raised serious questions about the power and sovereignty of YHWH,[47] questions that may well have persisted for some time. In ch. 25 the true prophet Jeremiah unambiguously affirms that the chaos unleashed by Babylon and the even greater chaos of a still-to-come cosmic judgment are entirely within the plans and purposes of God, and far from undermining his sovereignty constitute an expression of it. The chapter seeks to assure the community in physical and/or metaphorical exile that despite its present suffering, God is still sovereign and all the nations are subject to his will. Chapter 25 contains no explicit promises of Judah's restoration, but it portrays an all-powerful God who controls the fate of all peoples. Thus, when the reader arrives at promises of deliverance elsewhere in the book, she should have confidence that the God who stands behind these promises has the power to fulfill them.

Within 23:9—29:32 one of the main purposes of ch. 25 is to establish the credibility of Jeremiah as a true prophet belonging to a venerable tradition of true prophecy through which YHWH continues to speak. YHWH grants Jeremiah insight into the divine plan for Judah and the nations and calls him to proclaim that plan. Chapter 25 demonstrates what it means for Jeremiah to act as YHWH's prophet to the nations (cf. 1:5, 10), explaining how the fate of the nations is related to the life of God's people. In contrast to the false prophets, who can only mouth promises of well-being when the world stands on the brink of catastrophe (23:17, 27:9, 14, 16; 28:2–4, 10–11; 29:8–9, 24–28), Jeremiah proclaims God's judgment upon all peoples. The fact that Judah and many other nations have already experienced this judgment lends credibility to Jeremiah's interpretation of events, past and future. Only the divine word revealed through him and the other true prophets, in contrast to the deceptive words of the false prophets, can assist the community in navigating the treacherous waters of unended exile in order to arrive on the other shore a chastened and repentant community.

---

46. Brueggemann, *A Commentary on Jeremiah*, 225.
47. Stulman, *Jeremiah*, 229.

6

Section D

Proper and Improper Responses to True Prophecy (26:1–24)

AFTER OBSERVING THAT JEREMIAH 26 is composed of several redactional layers Carroll comments, "As a result of these diverse interferences the final form of the story mystifies the modern reader as to its meaning."[1] Sharp asserts that ch. 26 contains so many tensions that attempts to interpret it as a relatively coherent literary unit cannot succeed.[2] Comments like this illustrate how recognition of the concentric structure of 23:9—29:32 may significantly change how one reads ch. 26. Awareness of careful organization encourages attention to coherence and overarching purpose within ch. 26 rather than to disjunctions and tensions. If one recognizes that the major focus of the redactional unit is the nature of true and false prophecy, then it becomes clear how ch. 26 strings together anecdotes from the lives of three different prophets—Jeremiah (vv. 1–16), Micah (vv. 17–19), and Uriah (vv. 20–23)—in order to highlight both appropriate and inappropriate responses to the true prophetic word.

Osuji reads the text as a coherent whole, but because he works with Jeremiah 26–29 as the thematic unit and believes that it opens the second

1. Carroll, *Jeremiah*, 515.
2. Sharp, *Prophecy and Ideology in Jeremiah*, 56.

half of the book of Jeremiah, he does not link these chapters closely to what precedes them, and so he concludes that the main purpose of ch. 26 is to legitimate Jeremiah as a true prophet.[3] There can be little doubt that the chapter portrays Jeremiah as a true prophet, but after the preceding material on true and false prophecy, and after all the content of Jeremiah 1–25, there is little further need to legitimate Jeremiah as YHWH's true prophet. Rather, the focus in ch. 26 is squarely on proper and improper responses to the prophetic summons to repentance.

As discussed in chapter 2, the center of a chiasm or concentric structure normally contains the most theologically significant material or marks a major turning point of some kind. At the center of 23:9—29:32 stands a section in which three true prophets confront the community, each with a similar message summoning it to repent. In the first and last incidents the community rejects the message and squanders some of its last opportunities to avoid catastrophe, but in the middle incident Hezekiah and his contemporaries respond appropriately to Micah's pronouncement of disaster and thereby prevent national calamity.

JEREMIAH IS ALMOST KILLED (26:1-16)

Scholars are often puzzled by the fact that the reaction to Jeremiah's temple sermon is found in ch. 26 while the actual sermon is located in ch. 7. The reason for this separation is that ch. 7 focuses on the content of the sermon, whereas ch. 26 is interested in the community's response to YHWH's word, symbolized by how it treats prophets who deliver an unpopular message. While ch. 7 provides no date for Jeremiah's sermon, 26:1 dates it to the first year of King Jehoiakim. In the book of Jeremiah, Jehoiakim is a model of disobedience, highlighted particularly by the oracle of condemnation in 22:13–19 and by his burning of the scroll containing the words of YHWH (36:21–26). His hardheartedness also comes to the fore in 26:20–23 when he executes the prophet Uriah. By dating the events of ch. 26 to the first year of Jehoiakim, the text stresses that from the very outset of his reign Jehoiakim wasted his opportunities to heed the word of YHWH as proclaimed by the true prophets.[4]

YHWH instructs Jeremiah to stand in the court of the temple and proclaim to all the worshippers "all the words that I have commanded

---

3. Osuji, *Where Is the Truth?*, 119, 121.
4. O'Connor, "'Do Not Trim a Word,'" 619; Stulman, *Jeremiah*, 237.

you to speak to them," and then he warns, "Do not omit anything" (26:2). The text stresses that Jeremiah does not act on his own initiative but only because he is commanded. In fact the story is told in YHWH's voice. Instead of a narrator reporting that Jeremiah received instructions and then carried them out, the first part of the story takes the form of YHWH giving instructions to Jeremiah (26:2–6). This narrative technique makes the words of the story the words of YHWH himself, thereby enhancing the text's claim to authority over the reader who, like Jeremiah, hears these words as direct divine address.[5] The commission to speak "*all* the words that I command you" and the warning not to hold back anything both suggest a recapitulation of the entire prophetic message,[6] which heightens the paradigmatic nature of the story, as in one sense it is Jeremiah's prophetic message as a whole that the crowd spurns in the following verses.

Chapter 7 provides no motive for the temple sermon, but in ch. 26 the reason is given even before the summary of its content: "Perhaps they will listen and turn [וְיָשֻׁבוּ] each from his evil way, so that I may renounce the evil I am devising to bring upon them because of their evil deeds" (26:3). This reason is remarkably similar to YHWH's rationale for commanding Jeremiah to write on a scroll all the oracles of his entire prophetic career. "Perhaps the house of Judah will listen to all the evil I am devising to bring upon them so that they might turn [יָשׁוּבוּ] each from his evil way, so that I might forgive their iniquity and their sin" (36:3). The similarity between the reasons given in chs. 26 and 36 enhances the depiction of Jeremiah's ministry as a call to repentance, and strengthens the impression that ch. 26 is also a paradigmatic story like ch. 36, portraying the fate of Jeremiah's entire prophetic message.

The text emphasizes that the future of the people is in their own hands, because YHWH's actions depend on their response to the word of true prophecy. The completed book recognizes that the possibility of averting disaster is a "fiction," as even ch. 7 records YHWH ordering Jeremiah not to pray for the people because their doom is fixed (7:16; cf. 14:11–12; 15:1). The interpretation of the symbolic cup of wrath in 25:15–38 makes it clear that Judah is headed for irrevocable doom, and has already in fact experienced that doom (25:18). However, the "fiction" that it is never too late to repent and thereby avoid disaster is kept alive

---

5. Keown et al., *Jeremiah 26–52*, 5; McEntire, "A Prophetic Chorus of Others," 302.
6. Meyer, *Jeremia und die falschen Propheten*, 19–20.

as an encouragement to the implied reader that future catastrophe can be avoided if the community repents. This message is perhaps most explicit in the story of how Jeremiah watches the potter reshape wet clay that does not conform to his designs. Even though YHWH may decree destruction for a nation, human repentance can always change the divine plan, just like divine plans for well-being can also be revoked if the nation acts wickedly (18:7–10). For members of a faith community living in difficult times, such an assurance can be heartening because it affirms that God ultimately seeks their well-being and that they are not mere victims of historical circumstances but largely control their own destiny. (To what extent such reassurances are realistic is, of course, another matter.) The summons to repent with its possibility of averting disaster is a distinctive feature of the book of Jeremiah. In contrast, for example, Ezekiel's message of judgment, which is also set before the destruction of Jerusalem, does not call for repentance. Ezekiel simply assumes that Judah's fate is sealed and his role is to announce and explain this irrevocable doom.[7]

The first part of ch. 26 is resumptive, abridging the longer sermon of ch. 7 to a mere three verses (vv. 4–6). A lengthy summary would shift the focus to the content of the sermon rather than onto the community's reaction to it. God's command not to omit anything (26:2) coupled with the omniscient narrator's report that Jeremiah proclaimed everything YHWH commanded him (v. 8) indicate that the completeness of the message is not compromised by the narrative abridgment. Given the brevity of the sermon summary, what it chooses to retain is revealing in terms of the purpose and message of ch. 26. "You shall say to them: Thus says YHWH, 'If you do not listen to me by walking in my *Torah* which I have set before you; heeding the words of my servants the prophets whom I have persistently been sending to you—but you have not heeded them—then I will make this house like Shiloh, and this city I will make a curse for all the nations of the earth'" (26:4–6).

The reference to Shiloh is the strongest link between chs. 7 and 26 (cf. 7:12–15), and without this reference it would not be obvious that the events of ch. 26 are a reaction to the sermon of ch. 7. The threat to make the temple and city like Shiloh, the old cultic center presumably destroyed by the Philistines during the era of Samuel (1 Sam 4:12–22), is a direct challenge to Zion theology, the ideological foundation of the nation. Besides being the center of community and religious life, the temple

---

7. See Middlemas, *The Templeless Age*, 83–87.

was also the symbolic and physical guarantee of divine protection and blessing for the nation. Numerous commentators read the prediction of Jerusalem's destruction against this backdrop of Zion theology.[8] There is no doubt that the entire book, including 23:9—29:32, portrays Jeremiah as undercutting the ideological foundations of national existence by claiming that Israel's election traditions are no guarantee of safety. The extreme reaction of the people and the religious leadership to the sermon indicates that Jeremiah has challenged sacred political and religious dogma.

Despite all these factors, ch. 26 is not particularly interested in portraying Jeremiah as opponent of Zion theology. The specific undermining of Zion traditions in 7:4, 8–15 is summarized only in the briefest way in 26:6. In fact, all the accusations of specific sins in ch. 7 are omitted in ch. 26 in favor of characterizing the whole sermon as a straightforward plea to turn away from evil deeds and obey the *Torah* (26:3–4). Not only does the text portray this summons to repent and obey the *Torah* as the essence of Jeremiah's message, v. 5 presents it as the characteristic message of all YHWH's servants the prophets whom he has persistently been sending. The reference to YHWH's servants the prophets in v. 5 fits awkwardly between the first and second parts of the conditional sentence of 26:4b–6, indicating that it is probably a later addition to the text,[9] intended to link Jeremiah with YHWH's line of faithful prophets and characterize all true prophecy as being a call to repent and obey the *Torah*.

The portrayal here of Jeremiah and YHWH's servants the prophets fits the Second Temple understanding of prophecy outlined in the previous chapter. Whereas in ch. 7 Jeremiah castigates the nation for a variety of specific offenses and calls for a number of concrete changes in lifestyle (vv. 4–11, 17–18, 30–31), ch. 26 transforms this specificity into a general call to repent and obey the *Torah*. We see here the Deuteronomistic view that proved so influential in the Second Temple era, that the *Torah* as revealed to Moses is the basis of Israel's life and that true prophets carry on the ministry of Moses by demanding faithfulness to this *Torah*.[10] By portraying Jeremiah and the other true prophets as preachers of the law

---

8. See especially Brueggemann, *To Build, To Plant*, 6–7.

9. Hossfeld and Meyer, "Der Prophet vor dem Tribunal," 35; Meyer, *Jeremia und die falschen Propheten*, 20.

10. For a discussion of how the book of Jeremiah portrays him as a teacher of Torah, see Maier, "Jeremiah as Teacher of Torah." Maier concludes that most references to *Torah* in the book assume a God-given written code of law. See ibid., 24, 31.

of Moses, the final form of the book establishes a close link between the law and the prophets.[11] Sheppard notes how in some of the earlier passages of the book of Isaiah the word *Torah* refers to the teaching of the prophet (8:16, 20; 30:9). However, later editorial levels have introduced another view of the *Torah* of God reminiscent of the Mosaic law (see 2:3; 5:24; 42:4, 21, 24; 51:4, 7), thereby transforming the earlier references to *Torah* as the words of the prophet into references to the Mosaic *Torah* as well.[12] As Sheppard observes, this helps account for why Judaism came to read the book of Isaiah as commentary on the Mosaic *Torah*. The book of Jeremiah contains only one reference to *Torah* as the words of human beings (priests—18:18), and elsewhere it always designates the collective instructions of YHWH (2:8; 6:19; 8:8; 9:12 [Heb.]; 16:11; 26:4; 31:33; 32:23; 44:10, 23). Once the book of Jeremiah came to be read in the context of a larger body of Scripture, this *Torah* was identified with the law of Moses, and Jeremiah and the other prophets all became preachers of this Mosaic *Torah*.

The summary of the temple sermon concludes with God's threat to make the temple and Jerusalem like Shiloh (26:6), expecting the reader to remember YHWH's declaration in 7:12-15 that just as the sin of a previous generation made him destroy Shiloh, where his name used to dwell, so the current generation's sin is driving him to destroy the place where his name currently dwells. The references to Shiloh reinforce a pattern of divine activity. Whether it be in Samuel's time, Jeremiah's time, or in the time of the implied reader, God's people always face the threat of punishment unless they heed the prophetic call to faithful living.

The summary of Jeremiah's temple sermon is in the form of a conditional statement stressing that the fate of the city is not predetermined but depends on the people's response. Fretheim observes the distinction between God's absolute and circumstantial will. God's absolute will is for Israel's blessing and salvation and that is why he calls the people to repent, versus simply pronouncing disaster upon them. However, the current situation of overwhelming unfaithfulness is intolerable and so for a time God's circumstantial will for judgment will take precedence. Yet, God's promises of deliverance elsewhere in the book indicate that ultimately God desires new life and a new divine-human relationship for the

---

11. Childs, *Introduction to the Old Testament*, 353. See also Sheppard, "True and False Prophecy," 277-78.

12. Sheppard, "Isaiah 1-39," 548.

community of faith.¹³ As Stulman notes, God's judgment of the nation is based on "a passionate longing for a relationship with Israel as well as a savage intolerance for evil."¹⁴ The greatest danger to Israel's existence is not loss of nationhood or independence at the hands of the Babylonians, but loss of faithfulness to YHWH and his ways.¹⁵ Hence, the ministry of true prophecy is to diagnose the nation's true illness and call for the healing balm of repentance and obedience to *Torah*.

The immediate response to Jeremiah's sermon is that the priests, prophets, and all the people are so outraged by his threat that the temple and city will become like Shiloh that they seize and threaten to lynch him. The intensity of the crowd's emotions and opposition is illustrated by the first words they speak: "You will surely die [26:8] "![מוֹט תָּמוּת). By calling for Jeremiah's death, the crowd implies that they regard him as one of the false prophets mentioned in Deut 18:20 (cf. 13:6 [Heb.]) who must be executed because he poses a dire threat to the community. In biblical law the death penalty is reserved for the most serious offenses perceived as posing the gravest threat to community welfare.¹⁶ Because Jeremiah contradicts Royal–Zion traditions he is regarded as both a religious heretic and a political traitor, and few communities ancient or modern have much sympathy for either, especially for traitors who are regarded as particularly dangerous.

The opposition to YHWH's word occurs in the temple, the place where that word should be most honored, and it is led by priests and prophets, persons who should be most sensitive to that word. The story depicts a paradigmatic confrontation illustrating how the religious establishment of Jeremiah's day sought to silence true prophecy. The story knows of two kinds of prophets. Jeremiah the true prophet, representing YHWH's servants the prophets, is opposed by prophets of the Jerusalem establishment who call for his death. The fact that they too are called prophets illustrates that Hebrew has no term for "false prophet," although

---

13. Fretheim, *Jeremiah*, 376.

14. Stulman, *Jeremiah*, 22. For a fuller discussion of this point see ibid., 22–23. From a contemporary theological perspective, such a way of envisioning the divine–human relationship is highly problematic. As feminists have pointed out, the image of a powerful male deity punishing his spouse or child Israel in the interests of re-establishing a loving relationship provides a model of marriage, family, and relationships that all too easily legitimizes male violence against women and children.

15. Keown et al., *Jeremiah 26–52*, 59.

16. Stulman, *Order amid Chaos*, 66–67; Stulman, *Jeremiah*, 238–39.

the idea that nothing good can come from prophets who oppose Jeremiah is certainly present here. The LXX's use of *pseudoprophetai* in vv. 7, 8, 11, 16 makes explicit what is implicit in the Hebrew. Despite the role of these prophets as Jeremiah's accusers, the conflict between true and false prophecy is not a central issue in ch. 26. The other prophets are all anonymous and play only a minor role as Jeremiah's accusers, a role they share with the priests and also the people to some extent. The primary concern of the chapter is to sketch different responses to true prophets in the interest of highlighting the proper way to appropriate the message of true prophecy.

The execution or possible execution of a prophet plays a major role in ch. 26. After Jeremiah is almost lynched officials convene a hearing to determine if he deserves to die (vv. 10–16). Some elders of the land cite the precedent of Micah's prediction of Jerusalem's destruction, and then ask if King Hezekiah and his contemporaries responded by killing Micah (v. 19). The unfortunate prophet Uriah does not fare as well as Micah but is threatened (v. 21) and then executed by King Jehoiakim (v. 23). The last verse of the chapter describes how Ahikam rescues Jeremiah from a similar fate at the hands of the people (v. 24). The key issue in ch. 26, the acceptance or rejection of YHWH's word as delivered by the true prophet, is symbolized by how the speaker of that word is treated.

The threat that Jeremiah faces enhances his image and authority as a true prophet. In a context where YHWH's message stands in such tension with what the nation wants to hear, suffering becomes one of the marks of the true prophet. Especially since Jeremiah internalizes YHWH's message and ministry so deeply, it is inevitable that he will suffer at the hands of a people resistant to the ways of YHWH. Jeremiah is warned of opposition in his call already (1:8, 17–19), and he concludes his prophetic ministry in Egypt, where he has been dragged against his will (43:1–7). In between he faces frequent opposition from members of his home community (11:18–23), his own kin (12:6), anonymous persecutors (15:15, 20–21; 17:18; 18:18–20; 20:7, 10–11), Pashhur the priest (20:1–2), King Jehoiakim (36:26), and high-ranking officials (37:11–16; 38:1–6). The execution of Uriah for speaking the same words as Jeremiah (26:20) and the crowd's attempt to lynch Jeremiah illustrate how serious the threat to his life is in ch. 26. Yet Jeremiah faithfully and fearlessly proclaims YHWH's words, and even dares to call his accusers to repentance when he is on trial for his life (v. 13).

Carroll is correct in noting the artificial nature of the scene, because a call to repent and obey the *Torah* such as Jeremiah issues in 26:4–6 would hardly have led to a lynch mob.[17] This artificiality illustrates that the chapter is more interested in making theological points than in telling a story that is realistic in all its details. When the priests, prophets, and crowd initially seize and accuse Jeremiah they omit the conditional element in his prophecy and rephrase it as a straight declaration of disaster: "Why did you prophesy in the name of YHWH saying, 'This house will become like Shiloh and this city will be made desolate, without inhabitant?'" (26:9). The people's distortion of Jeremiah's message portrays them as ignoring YHWH's call to repent and obey the *Torah*, and provides another example of the failure to listen that is so powerfully highlighted in the book as a whole.[18] The text does not suggest that the audience's summary of Jeremiah's prophecy misinterprets the gist of his message. In the second incident of ch. 26 Micah's prediction of Jerusalem's destruction is interpreted as constituting a call to repentance (vv. 17–19). If a prediction of Jerusalem's destruction equals a summons to repent, then the reverse can also be true, a call to repent may equal a proclamation of disaster, especially looking back from the post-587 era when it was obvious that the nation had not repented. The final form of the book knows that the possibility of repentance during Jeremiah's day is a fiction, and so at one level the people's eliminating the conditional element from Jeremiah's prophecy actually represents considerable insight on their part—they recognize that Jeremiah is in effect pronouncing their doom.

Before the crowd can lynch Jeremiah, officials from the royal palace intervene to conduct a proper hearing (26:10). The priests and prophets act as prosecutors, alleging that Jeremiah merits the death penalty because of what he has prophesied against the city (26:11). It is puzzling that the role of the people suddenly changes. Earlier "all the people" were part of the crowd that seized Jeremiah and demanded his death (26:8), but now they join the royal officials as judge and jury whom the prosecutors (priests and prophets) seek to convince (26:11). McKane notes how the proceedings in ch. 26 do not coincide with what was standard legal procedure in ancient Judah.[19] The text is more interested in theological concerns than in portraying a realistic court scene.

17. Carroll, *Jeremiah*, 515.
18. Miller, "The Book of Jeremiah," 773; Keown et al., *Jeremiah 26–52*, 22.
19. McKane, *A Critical and Exegetical Commentary*, 2:676–81. Somewhat in contrast, Osuji describes how the narrator constructs a formal court scene. See Osuji,

After the prosecution has rested its case Jeremiah is given opportunity to defend himself before the jury composed of the officials and all the people (26:12). He concedes that he is guilty as charged of prophesying against the city, and he does not contest the interpretation that his prophecy is an announcement of doom (26:12). Jeremiah makes no attempt to logically explain the truth of his message but begins and ends his defense by claiming that he is only following YHWH's orders to proclaim all these words against the nation (26:12–15). Long maintains that by appealing to his divine commission Jeremiah is disclaiming personal responsibility for his actions.[20] Because he has followed YHWH's orders he is above human law and cannot be held accountable for uttering a message that would legitimately lead to a death sentence for someone else who might speak the same words. At the historical level the claim to have a divine commission might represent disassociation from the message and a plea to be considered immune from prosecution. However, in a highly theological story like Jeremiah 26, Jeremiah's claim to be doing YHWH's bidding serves not to disassociate him from the message but to stress the truth of the message because of its origins. The book of Jeremiah probably more than any other prophetic book emphasizes that the message originates with YHWH, but the book does the opposite of disassociating the prophet from the message. Over and over Jeremiah suffers for his words and actions, and he does not plead immunity on the grounds that he is only following orders. One of the unique characteristics of the Jeremiah tradition is how the prophet is so bound up with the divine word that his life becomes the message.[21]

The first pillar of Jeremiah's defense is the claim to be speaking for YHWH, while the second is repetition of God's plea for repentance. "Now, amend your ways and deeds and listen to the voice of YHWH your God and YHWH will revoke the disaster which he has pronounced concerning you" (26:13). Given that YHWH has already determined to

---

Where Is the Truth?, 137–38.

20. Long, "Prophetic Authority," 6–7.

21. One of the best examples of Jeremiah living the message is YHWH's command that he not marry and have children, because children born during his time will only experience horrible suffering (16:1–4; cf. 16:5–9). Another illustration of Jeremiah's identity with the message comes in his second confession, where he claims to have eaten YHWH's words, which filled him with joy but also indignation, and prevented him from joining others in normal human celebrations (15:16–17). For a fuller discussion of how the life of Jeremiah is the message, see O'Connor, "The Prophet Jeremiah"; Stulman, *Order amid Chaos*, 137–66; Stulman, *Jeremiah*, 43–44.

destroy the nation, Jeremiah's unwelcome word of judgment is actually an offer of rescue.[22] By pointing to the only possible way of averting catastrophe, Jeremiah is portrayed as desiring the well-being of his people. The message of true prophecy is that repentance and averting disaster are ever-present possibilities, and therefore, God's people control their own destiny. As pointed out in previous chapters, 23:9—29:32 repeatedly seeks to overcome temporal and spatial limitations and place the implied readers back in Jeremiah's time, where they hear the voice of true prophecy and must make a decision on which everything rests.

Given that Jeremiah's defense consists of a statement of credentials (YHWH has sent me) and a repetition of God's plea for repentance, it is not really Jeremiah but YHWH's word that is on trial. Jeremiah places himself into the hands of the court, saying that the people can do with him what is good and just in their eyes (26:14), a surrender that "dramatically underscores the decision facing the community which this text places before them anew—to accept or reject the prophetic word."[23] As a way to encourage his audience (readers) to make the right choice, Jeremiah warns that the people better know for sure (יָדֹעַ תֵּדְעוּ) that if they kill him they will bring innocent blood upon themselves and their city, because YHWH has truly sent him (26:15). Since the shedding of innocent blood is a heinous crime that God avenges by bringing disaster upon both the guilty party and the community,[24] Jeremiah underscores that killing him (rejecting his message) will bring dire consequences. By claiming one final time that YHWH has sent him, Jeremiah asserts that he can be executed and silenced but the prophetic message stands and must be engaged because it is from YHWH.[25]

In 26:16 the court renders its verdict that Jeremiah does not deserve death, because he has prophesied in the name of YHWH. Some scholars take this to mean that the officials and the people validate Jeremiah as a true prophet, and consequently that all of 26:1–16 affirms Jeremiah's authenticity as a true prophet, first through his own defense and then also through the legal verdict rendered by a properly constituted court.[26]

22. Brueggemann, *A Commentary on Jeremiah*, 235.
23. O'Connor, "'Do Not Trim a Word,'" 622.
24. See Gen 4:10–12; Deut 19:10, 13; 21:8–9; 1 Sam. 19:5; 1 Kgs 2:31; 2 Kgs 21:16; 24:4; Jer 7:6; 19:4; 22:17; Jonah 1:14; Ps 106:38.
25. Brueggemann, *A Commentary on Jeremiah*, 235.
26. O'Connor, "'Do Not Trim a Word,'" 622. Osuji, *Where Is the Truth?*, 143–44. See also Jones, *Jeremiah*, 340.

There is no doubt that 26:1–16 presents Jeremiah as a true prophet, but legitimating him as a true prophet is not the purpose served by the court's verdict. The text *assumes* and *portrays* Jeremiah's status as a true prophet throughout, a status that depends on his carrying out the divine commission, not on the opinion of a human court composed of people and royal officials known for their insensitivity to the ways of God. The officials and the people only acknowledge that Jeremiah has spoken in the name of YHWH and does not merit death, but no one acknowledges the truth of his words and no one heeds his call to repent, in stark contrast to how Hezekiah embraces the message of Micah (26:17–19). As Allen observes, the "deafening silence" regarding the deeper issue of the truth of Jeremiah's prophecy and the tabling of this critical issue bring their own condemnation.[27]

In rendering the verdict the *officials* and *all the people* declare to the *priests* and *prophets*, "This man is not deserving of death" (26:16), thereby reversing both in content and word order the earlier allegation that the *priests* and *prophets* made to the *officials* and *all the people*, "Deserving of death is this man" (26:11). The text juxtaposes the people and officials who take Jeremiah's side with the priests and prophets who seek his death. The opposition of priests and prophets to Jeremiah is not surprising (cf. 23:9–12), since one of the major assertions of 23:9—29:32 is that the nation's religious leaders, especially the prophets, contradict the message of Jeremiah, lead the people astray, and therefore bear much of the blame for the catastrophe of 587. The role of the people and officials in ch. 26 is more difficult to understand.

McKane observes that the officials are responsible to the king for the political management of the nation, and so in this context their responsibility is to assess if Jeremiah poses a danger to national security.[28] Their verdict indicates that they regard him as merely a religious character who poses little threat, and thus there is no need to execute him. McKane's analysis seems off the mark in that few persons in ancient (or modern) times would have distinguished so sharply between political and religious realms. Jeremiah challenges Royal and Zion traditions and so his "religious" pronouncements have profound political implications and make the political establishment so anxious that it frequently persecutes him. Even in ch. 26 King Jehoiakim feels so threatened by Uriah,

---

27. Allen, *Jeremiah*, 300.
28. McKane, *A Critical and Exegetical Commentary*, 2:680–81.

who prophesies a message like that of Jeremiah, that Jehoiakim is not content to allow Uriah to languish in Egyptian exile, where he presumably poses no further danger, but extradites Uriah and then executes him (26:20–23).

The role of the people is even more difficult to interpret than the role of the officials. Why do they change from calling for Jeremiah's death to acquitting him? Their position as jurors is particularly puzzling. The text explicitly portrays "all the people" as constituting part of the jury (vv. 11, 12, 16), even though realistically the royal officials would probably be the ones to render judgment in such cases, with the people as mere bystanders. Some scholars suggest that "all of the people" really means some of the people, and that the story is dealing with different groups of people.[29] The problem with this reading is that the text gives no indication that different groups are involved. The confusing role of the people is sometimes attributed to different redactional layers in the chapter that have not been completely harmonized.[30] This explanation may account for the origins of the text but does not explain how the final text portrays the role of the people. O'Connor suggests that the changing role of the people is a literary device designed to illustrate that Jeremiah was able to persuade a large number of people of the truth of his words.[31] While this may be somewhat of an over-interpretation, since there is little evidence that Jeremiah's audience actually heeds his message, it probably points in the right direction. Although Jeremiah's prophetic message meets sharp opposition in ch. 26, there are hints that not everyone totally rejects YHWH's word. The religious leadership remains hardened, but the verdict of the people and royal officials indicates that they do not believe that Jeremiah and his message must be eliminated. The elders of the land cite the prophecy of Micah as a way to encourage the nation to heed Jeremiah's message (26:17–19), and the royal official Ahikam saves Jeremiah's life (26:24). Stulman makes much of these "hints" of support, pointing out that ch. 26 is the first time in the book that Jeremiah's message receives anything other than a completely hostile response.[32] After ch. 26 there are other instances when royal officials rescue or assist Jeremiah (36:11–19, 25; 38:7–13). Stulman believes that the positive response of the officials,

29. Thompson, *The Book of Jeremiah*, 521; Holladay, *Jeremiah 2*, 105.
30. Carroll, *From Chaos to Covenant*, 93, 95; Sharp, *Prophecy and Ideology in Jeremiah*, 54–62.
31. O'Connor, "'Do Not Trim a Word,'" 621.
32. Stulman, *Order amid Chaos*, 67–68; Stulman, *Jeremiah*, 240–42.

elders, and people is part of the hope proclaimed by the second half of the book. This positive response signals the possibility of a new beginning for a community whose old world is collapsing. I agree with Stulman's and O'Connor's basic analysis, although I believe that the hope in ch. 26 is significantly more muted than they suggest. There is some level of acceptance for Jeremiah and his message, but the last verse of the chapter still portrays the people as seeking to kill him (26:24). The royal officials prevent Jeremiah's summary execution and declare that he does not deserve death, but royal officials also collude in Jehoiakim's execution of Uriah, who prophesies the same message as Jeremiah (26:20–23).

The ambivalence in the story illustrates the mixed response to true prophecy. A few persons are receptive but the overall reaction is hostility and rejection. The people and religious leadership nearly lynch Jeremiah for issuing a call to repent, and then the prosecution at his trial demands the death penalty. The court's verdict spares Jeremiah and does signal some openness to him and his message, but there is no mention of the people or officials taking Jeremiah's message to heart, and so the overall picture is of a nation ignoring and rejecting the voice of true prophecy. The repentance of King Hezekiah and his generation, reported in the Micah incident that follows immediately, provides a contrast to the response of Jeremiah's contemporaries and illustrates the negative thrust of 26:1–16.

For understanding how ch. 26 functions it is important to recognize that one block of material ends with v. 16. Jeremiah has been tried, the verdict rendered, and the case is in one sense closed. Verse 17 marks a new beginning, a fact not observed by many commentators and obscured by the paragraphing in some translations (RSV, NRSV, NEB, NJB). If one assumes that the chief purpose of ch. 26 is to document reaction to Jeremiah's temple sermon and subsequent trial, then one might not observe the divisions in the chapter. Once one recognizes that the key issue is response to the true prophetic word, then it becomes obvious how the chapter falls into three distinct sections (vv. 1–16, 17–19, 20–24).

MICAH INSPIRES REPENTANCE (26:17–19)

At the center of the central section of the entire concentric unit stands the story of how Micah's prophecy of disaster inspired King Hezekiah to repent, with the result that catastrophe was averted. This paradigmatic story provides the only example in all of 23:9—29:32 of an enthusiastically appropriate response to the words of a true prophet.

The opening verse introduces a new set of characters, indicating that a new story is beginning. Some "men from the elders of the land" arise and remind "the entire assembly of the people [אֶל־כָּל־קְהַל הָעָם]" of the prophet Micah's declaration during the time of Hezekiah. This is the only passage in prophetic literature that quotes another prophetic book by name.

> Zion will be plowed like a field,
>   And Jerusalem will become a pile of ruins,
>   And the temple mount a forested height. (26:18; cf. Mic 3:12)

This prophecy of Jerusalem's destruction establishes a close parallel between Micah and Jeremiah.

All three incidents in ch. 26 are linked by claims that the temple and city will be destroyed (26:6, 9, 12, 18, 20), and in each incident the prophet faces death or the possibility of death.[33] Linking Jeremiah's prophecy to that of Micah who is already acknowledged here as a "canonical" prophet, affirms that Jeremiah's prediction of Jerusalem's end is congruent with true prophetic tradition. This both testifies to and undergirds convictions regarding a tradition of true prophecy whose central themes and characteristics are clearly established.[34] In 26:5 God instructs Jeremiah to admonish the people to heed YHWH's servants the prophets whom he persistently sends to the people. Chapter 26 records incidents involving three such servants, illustrating that YHWH indeed sends such prophets persistently, and that they consistently proclaim divine judgment on the nation with the expectation that such announcements should spur repentance.

Two rhetorical questions and a conclusion follow the quotation of Micah's prophecy. "Did Hezekiah king of Judah and all Judah indeed kill him? Did he not fear YHWH and entreat YHWH's favor, so that YHWH renounced the disaster which he had pronounced concerning them? But we are bringing a great disaster upon ourselves" (26:19). On the basis of this verse some scholars conclude that Jeremiah's life was spared because of the precedent of Micah. If the primary purpose of 26:17–19 were to present legal evidence in Jeremiah's defense, then these verses would

---

33. Hardmeier, "Die Propheten Micha und Jesaja," 178; Holt, "Jeremiah's Temple Sermon," 82–83.

34. See Clements, *Jeremiah*, 156.

come before the court hands down its verdict in v. 16. In its present position the Micah incident is superfluous to the trial, and while it does support Jeremiah's acquittal, its real purpose is to model the appropriate response to true prophecy. The speech of the elders is less a defense of Jeremiah than it is praise of Hezekiah's actions.[35]

In response to the penance of Micah's generation, "YHWH renounced the disaster which he had pronounced concerning them [וַיִּנָּחֶם יְהוָה אֶל־הָרָעָה אֲשֶׁר־דִּבֶּר עֲלֵיהֶם]" (26:19). This is very similar to what YHWH tells Jeremiah he will do if the people of Jeremiah's day repent—"I will revoke the disaster which I am devising to bring upon them [וְנִחַמְתִּי אֶל־הָרָעָה אֲשֶׁר אָנֹכִי חֹשֵׁב לַעֲשׂוֹת לָהֶם]" (26:3)—and is identical to what Jeremiah informs the courtroom YHWH will do if the nation amends its ways (26:13). These similarities establish a pattern of divine activity. Just like YHWH revoked the punishment during Hezekiah's time, he is eager to revoke it during Jeremiah's time, and by implication in any time and place, if there is genuine repentance and obedience. The open-endedness of the rhetorical questions confronts the reader with the same life and death questions that Jeremiah's generation faced.[36] Once again the text collapses the time between the implied reader and Jeremiah's era, and invites the reader to stand in the hour of fateful decision.

The example of Micah illustrates that prophets can be successful, that the community can respond positively to the prophetic message, and that catastrophe can be averted. The elders citing the precedent of Micah in defense of Jeremiah indicates that even during the bleak time leading up to 587, a remnant at least, some of its members even possessing significant social rank, sought to defend Jeremiah and embrace the message of YHWH's servants the prophets. The way in which Micah's prophecy is quoted indicates that a true prophetic word once uttered, does not lose its relevance or authority with the passage of time. If this is the case with a relatively minor prophet like Micah, it must be true of all YHWH's servants the prophets, especially a colossus like Jeremiah.

The Micah incident presents a particular understanding of the nature of true prophecy. Micah's words are a straightforward prediction of the destruction of temple and city (26:18; cf. Mic 3:12), and yet the elders of Jeremiah's time interpret this announcement as a summons to repent, even though the book of Micah never issues such a plea. The

---

35. O'Connor, "'Do Not Trim a Word,'" 623.
36. Keown et al., *Jeremiah 26–52*, 33.

fact that Micah's prediction of Jerusalem's demise was not fulfilled is not interpreted as a failure of prophecy but rather as a success story.[37] The prophetic word achieved its intended goal by inspiring Hezekiah and his contemporaries to change course, allowing YHWH to revoke the judgment. A major purpose of the Micah incident is to yet again present true prophecy as constituting a call to repent, and to underscore the importance of responding properly to such a summons.

The elders follow up their rhetorical questions about the response of Micah's contemporaries with the ominous comment, "but we are bringing a great disaster upon ourselves" (26:19) This statement implies that Jeremiah has not yet been acquitted but that the people are inviting dire consequences by still intending to execute him (v. 19a). The elders' statement also assumes that the people are refusing to heed the message of Jeremiah as delivered in 26:1–16, which confirms the analysis that this initial story portrays the community as rejecting Jeremiah and his message. The elders' concluding remark also highlights the sinfulness of the nation. During Micah's time a prophet could deliver a harsh word without being persecuted and the message was even embraced, but now the nation rejects prophets like Jeremiah and Uriah and threatens them with death, thereby sealing its own doom.[38] The rhetorical questions and concluding statement of the elders leave v. 19 somewhat open-ended, thereby throwing the challenge of how to respond to the true prophet Jeremiah into the lap of the reader.[39]

With respect to the composition of ch. 26, the trial of Jeremiah probably constitutes the original story that has attracted two other incidents.[40] Even though ch. 26 now contains three discrete paradigmatic stories, each focusing on the response to true prophecy, the Micah and

---

37. O'Connor, "'Do Not Trim a Word,'" 623. The understanding of prophecy depicted here is similar to the view underlying the book of Jonah. In response to Jonah's one brief pronouncement of Nineveh's destruction, the entire city repents and YHWH revokes the punishment (Jonah 3:4–10). Hibbard, "True and False Prophecy," argues that in Jeremiah the predictive element of prophecy recedes in favor of the call to repentance as the primary criterion of true prophecy. He claims that the Micah incident challenges the criterion of fulfillment as outlined by Deut 18:15–22, according to which Micah should be regarded as a false prophet because Jerusalem was not destroyed as he predicted. See ibid., 12–19.

38. Holt, "Jeremiah's Temple Sermon," 84.

39. Osuji, *Where Is the Truth?*, 384.

40. Hossfeld and Meyer, "Der Prophet vor dem Tribunal," 48–49; O'Connor, "'Do Not Trim a Word,'" 623.

Uriah incidents are linked to the trial scene in such a way that the whole chapter can be read as one continuous narrative. The example of Micah is exactly the kind of precedent that would speak in Jeremiah's defense. The emphatic question asking if Hezekiah and all Judah killed Micah (26:19) links the Micah incident to the trial scene, where the issue is also whether or not to kill a prophet. The concluding warning of the elders, "but we are bringing a great disaster upon ourselves," assumes that Jeremiah is still in grave danger and that his message should be heeded. The Uriah story illustrates the serious threat Jeremiah still faces even after his acquittal, and the chapter concludes with Ahikam's special intervention that saves Jeremiah from execution (26:24). Thus, when commentators read the whole chapter as a continuous narrative, they are to some extent following the lead of the text. However, to understand the purpose of the chapter within the larger concentric unit, it is also important to observe the contours of the three separate stories and the unique contribution each makes.

URIAH IS KILLED (26:20-24)

The story of the unfortunate prophet Uriah is somewhat more loosely connected to the trial scene than is the incident involving Micah, which can at least be cited as a precedent in support of Jeremiah, whereas the execution of Uriah establishes a precedent that works against him. Still, there are parallels between all three incidents in ch. 26, especially between the Uriah and Micah stories. Both prophets are from outside Jerusalem and announce the doom of the nation, and the stories highlight the contrasting responses of kings Hezekiah and Jehoiakim. The Uriah incident also has links to the first part of the chapter. Verse 20 opens, "There was *also* a man [וְגַם־אִישׁ הָיָה] prophesying," implying that Uriah is in some way similar to Micah, and since Micah is similar to Jeremiah, Uriah must also parallel Jeremiah. The end of v. 20 underscores this parallel by stating that Uriah prophesied concerning the city and land, "just like all the words of Jeremiah." All three prophets announce the destruction of Jerusalem, and Jeremiah and Uriah both face the threat of death. In a sense the Uriah incident undoes Jeremiah's acquittal in v. 16 by implying that Jeremiah's fate is still up in the air and he still faces enormous danger. The closing verse confirms this by indicating that had Ahikam not rescued Jeremiah, he would have suffered the same fate as Uriah.

Despite these connections, the major purpose of 26:20–24 is not to contribute to the trial scene but to provide a model of how *not* to respond to a true prophet, and also to illustrate the nation's total rejection of the true prophetic word. When Jehoiakim, his warriors, and officials hear Uriah prophesy "just like all the words of Jeremiah," the king determines to kill the seditious prophet. The text displays no interest in the specific words of Uriah, only in the nation's response to him. Uriah gets wind of the king's designs and flees to Egypt, but Jehoiakim sends his officers to extradite Uriah so that he can execute him. Jehoiakim is not content to allow Uriah to languish in exile out of harm's way, but goes to enormous lengths to silence the voice of true prophecy, thereby illustrating both how threatened he feels by a message of judgment and how thoroughly he rejects the divine word that holds out the possibility of life.[41] As a last indignity and symbol of his disregard for the prophet and his message, Jehoiakim casts Uriah's body into the grave of the common people. Such mistreatment of a corpse is intended to dishonor a person, symbolize victory over them and their cause, and intimidate their sympathizers.[42]

The juxtaposition of the Micah and Uriah incidents provides contrasting paradigms for responding to the message of true prophecy, and portrays Jehoiakim's actions as all the more vile in contrast to Hezekiah's embrace of Micah's message. The account of the otherwise unknown Uriah is extremely sparse, and except for his name and place of origin the other details about him all link him to Jeremiah. He prophesies in the name of YHWH against the city and land, "just like all the words of Jeremiah" (26:20), a statement not made about Micah. Uriah represents Jeremiah and through him Jeremiah is executed in effigy, symbolizing the king and nation's utter rejection of true prophecy.

Both the Uriah and Micah incidents highlight the crucial role played by the king, who is assumed to be responsible for the well-being of the nation by ensuring his own and the people's faithfulness.[43] Jehoiakim's failure in this regard, already from the very beginning of his reign (26:1), indicates that ch. 26 lays much of the blame for the catastrophe of 587 upon his shoulders. The first incident in ch. 26 highlights how the religious establishment (prophets and priests) rejects Jeremiah by seeking

---

41. For a discussion of why ancient kings felt threatened by prophetic voices that challenged royal policies, see Roberts, "Prophets and Kings," 352–54.

42. Kegler, "The Prophetic Discourse and Political Praxis of Jeremiah," 50.

43. Nicholson, *The Book of the Prophet Jeremiah* 2:25–26. This notion of the king's responsibility is also the Deuteronomistic view underlying the book of Kings.

his death, while the last incident highlights how the royal establishment (king, soldiers, and officials) rejects Uriah/Jeremiah. The people are an uncertain group caught in the middle, but their first and last reaction to Jeremiah is to seek his life (26:8, 24).

Despite highlighting the role of the nation's religious and political leadership, the chapter does not overlook the importance of faithful response on the part of the people. While the text portrays only Hezekiah as repenting,[44] and it is Jehoiakim who is responsible for executing Uriah, Nicholson is probably correct in pointing out that in ch. 26 the king personifies the nation,[45] and thus the king's response to the prophetic word symbolizes the response of the nation as a whole. The chapter clearly indicates that the prophetic word is addressed to the entire community. Jeremiah delivers his sermon in the temple so that he can address all the cities of Judah and summon them to obedience (26:2-6), and during his trial he calls the entire audience to repent (26:12-13). The elders' defense of Jeremiah is addressed to "the whole assembly of the people" (26:17), and Micah is described as speaking to all the people of Judah (26:18). The following verse asks if Hezekiah and all of Judah killed Micah. The statement of the elders that concludes the Micah incident also emphasizes the responsibility of the people: "but *we* are bringing a great disaster upon *our*selves" (v. 19). The story of Uriah focuses more narrowly on the responsibility of Jehoiakim and his court, but the last verse of the chapter states that the people still intend to kill Jeremiah, and only Ahikam's timely intervention saves him.

In the curious concluding verse it is the people and not the king or religious leadership who are out to get Jeremiah. The verse acts as if no verdict has yet been rendered in the court scene, or as if the people are refusing to accept their own verdict. The tensions in the chapter around the role of the people may be due to the combination of different sources, but in the completed text the people's inconsistency characterizes them as fickle and ultimately hostile to true prophecy. From the perspective

---

44. The LXX, Syriac, and Vulgate all have plural verbs in 26:19, thereby portraying both Hezekiah and the people as repenting. These versions probably witness to a Hebrew text that also had the plural. My suspicion is that the MT's singular is original and that the plural represents an attempt to make explicit what is implied in the original, that both king and people respond positively to Micah. It is more difficult to explain why the Masoretic redaction would downplay the repentance of the people, since such repentance serves as a positive example for the later reading audience.

45. Nicholson, *Preaching to the Exiles*, 17; Nicholson, *The Book of the Prophet Jeremiah*, 2:26.

of both v. 24 and the Uriah incident, the threat of death hangs over Jeremiah's head throughout the chapter, until Ahikam finally rescues him. Verse 24 binds all three incidents of the chapter together into a "single" narrative by alluding back to the original trial scene and finally bringing closure to the two key questions raised there: will Jeremiah escape with his life, and will the community heed his message?

Another effect of v. 24 and the Uriah incident is to enhance the personage and authority of Jeremiah by demonstrating his courage and faithfulness in the face of persecution. His message is the kind that can get a prophet killed, yet he fearlessly proclaims it anyway in the temple and during his trial. This is in keeping with numerous other passages that portray Jeremiah as harassed and persecuted but still faithful in the face of danger (11:18–19; 12:5–6; 15:10–11, 15, 20–21; 17:18; 18:18–20, 23; 20:1–2, 10–12; 32:1–2; 36:26; 37:13–16; 38:4–6). The rescue of Jeremiah is a "quiet reminder" of the divine promise at his call and in response to his confessions, that God will deliver him from his enemies (1:8, 18–19; 15:20–21).[46] Because Jeremiah is a true prophet speaking for God, human opposition cannot silence him.

While most of the nation spurns Jeremiah and his message, two exceptions emerge in ch. 26. Some elders come to Jeremiah's defense by citing the prophecy of Micah, and Ahikam rescues Jeremiah from death. This is the first time in the book that supporters of the prophet appear, and the following chapters will tell of other islands of support in a sea of almost overwhelming opposition (29:3; 36:4–8, 19, 25, 32; 38:7–13). These supporters function as paradigms of faithfulness who have heard and accepted the prophetic message.[47] Their positive example speaks hopefully about the possibilities of faithfulness in the future, and encourages later readers to embrace and defend the message of true prophecy as found in the Jeremiah tradition.

Chapter 26 opens by expressing hope that the nation might yet heed the word of YHWH proclaimed by Jeremiah and the other true prophets, and repent and obey the *Torah* so as to avert catastrophe (vv. 3–6), but the

---

46. Lundbom, *Jeremiah 21–36*, 285. O'Connor observes that despite the people's opposition to Jeremiah, in a variety of ways his survival actually embodies their fate. His surviving both the events of 587 and the numerous threats to his life is a symbol of possibility in the face of disaster, and a sign that the people may also have a future. See O'Connor, "Surviving Disaster," 372–77; O'Connor, "The Prophet Jeremiah," 137–40.

47. O'Connor, "'Do Not Trim a Word,'" 630; Stulman, *Jeremiah*, 242; Seitz, "The Place of the Reader," 73.

chapter closes by asserting that this word has been rejected by all but a very few, and so the opportunity to change the course of history has been lost. Thus, the chapter functions as a theodicy, explaining how the nation careened into disaster by refusing to heed YHWH's servants the prophets. The chapter also emphasizes that canonical prophets like Jeremiah, Micah, and Uriah confront the community of faith in every generation with a message that is a matter of life and death. The persistent call of true prophecy is to choose the way of life.

7

Section C'

The Symbolic Yoke—All Nations Must Serve Nebuchadnezzar (27:1—28:17)

DESPITE CONTAINING MATERIAL FROM originally diverse sources, at some point Jeremiah 27-29 probably constituted an independent cycle of material,[1] and in chapter 2 I propose that these chapters formed the foundation upon which the rest of 23:9—29:32 was constructed. Chapters 27-29 are dominated by the theme of Jeremiah's conflict with false prophets over the issue of how long Babylonian hegemony will last and how the nation(s) should respond to it.[2] These chapters are set between the first deportation of 598 and the final destruction of the nation,

---

1. The major evidence for the unity of chs. 27-29 is their unique spelling of the names Jeremiah, Nebuchadnezzar, and Zedekiah. For additional evidence pointing to the unity of chs. 27-29 see Volz, *Der Prophet Jeremia*, 255; Rudolph, *Jeremia*, 157-58; Overholt, "Jeremiah 27-29," 242; Carroll, *Jeremiah*, 523-24; Miller, "The Book of Jeremiah," 768; Plant, *Good Figs, Bad Figs*, 96-100.

2. If one reads the text historically, then these chapters can be viewed against the backdrop of the conflict between pro-Egyptian and pro-Babylonian parties among the leaders of Judah after the first Babylonian invasion. See for example Overholt, *The Threat of Falsehood*, 30-33. While such a reading makes good sense, the text never presents the advice of Jeremiah the true prophet as *Realpolitik* but as good theology, because he speaks for YHWH. Lange, *Vom prophetischen Wort*, 241-43, 258-60, claims that the major purpose of chs. 27-29 is to contradict the salvation hopes of Haggai and Zechariah.

and they grapple with the theological and political implications of Babylonian domination. The material repeatedly stresses that the false prophets have terribly misled the nation by predicting a quick end to the exile and Babylonian power, whereas Jeremiah has consistently proclaimed that the people must submit to Babylon because Nebuchadnezzar is YHWH's agent to punish both Judah and the nations. The major purpose of chs. 27–29 is to emphasize that the community can only survive if it rejects the naive hopes propagated by false prophets and instead embraces exile and judgment as God's short-term plan for the nation.

The two halves of section C' seem to have been combined secondarily.[3] Chapter 27 is a first-person narrative while ch. 28 is told in the third person. Both chapters focus on symbolic actions of Jeremiah involving a yoke, but the actions are different. In ch. 27 Jeremiah makes yokes and sends them to the leaders of nations with the message that they must submit to the yoke of Babylon, while in ch. 28 Jeremiah himself wears the yoke, symbolizing that Judah must also submit. Whatever their origins, the stories in section C' are now closely linked. The dispute between Jeremiah and Hananiah in ch. 28 is sparked by Jeremiah's prophecy in ch. 27, and the report of Hananiah breaking the yoke off Jeremiah's neck (28:10) depends on 27:2, which is the only verse indicating that Jeremiah is wearing a yoke. When Hananiah refutes Jeremiah's prophecy in 28:2–4 he responds to the two main symbols that dominate Jeremiah's prophecy in ch. 27, the yoke and the temple utensils.[4]

In ch. 26, the central section of the concentric structure, YHWH offers the nation an opportunity to repent and avert catastrophe, but the execution of Uriah and the attempt on Jeremiah's life indicate that the offer is spurned. Section C' spells out the dire consequences of such rejection of true prophecy. YHWH has raised up the mighty Nebuchadnezzar as agent of judgment who has already once smitten the people. An even harsher punishment awaits both Judah and the nations unless they heed the true prophetic word and submit to YHWH's will by accepting the yoke of Babylonian domination. Sections C (ch. 25) and C' (chs. 27–28) are similar in that Judah's refusal to repent in response to the admonitions of Jeremiah and YHWH's servants the prophets leads YHWH to summon Nebuchadnezzar. Both sections portray Jeremiah as a prophet to the nations, in both the nations are sucked into the earth-shattering

---

3. Bright, *Jeremiah*, 201; Carroll, *Jeremiah*, 540–41.

4. Overholt, *The Threat of Falsehood*, 27. For additional links between chs. 27 and 28, see Jones, *Jeremiah*, 354.

events by which YHWH punishes Judah, and in both the fate of Judah is inextricably linked to the fate of the nations. One significant difference between the two sections is that in C Jeremiah simply announces the devastation of the nations, whereas in C' he offers them a course of action to avoid further disaster.

THE YOKE OF BABYLON (27:1–22)

The story of chs. 27–28 is clearly set during the reign of Zedekiah, between the first deportation and the final defeat of the nation (27:3, 12, 16–22; 28:1, 3–4), yet ch. 27 opens with the historical note, "In the beginning of the reign of King Jehoiakim," which is almost identical to the opening of ch. 26. Perhaps this is not merely a scribal error, as is frequently surmised, but a technique to suggest that Zedekiah and the people of his time share the failings of Jehoiakim in terms of how they respond to true prophecy.[5] In 27:2–3 YHWH instructs Jeremiah to make thongs and yoke bars for himself and wear them upon his neck, and then send yokes to the kings of the nations via the envoys who have traveled to Jerusalem to confer with King Zedekiah.[6] Such a meeting of foreign ambassadors combined with Jeremiah's using the occasion to announce that all these nations must serve Nebuchadnezzar creates the impression that Zedekiah and other vassal states are plotting revolt against their Babylonian overlords. The rest of ch. 27 contains three speeches in which Jeremiah explains the meaning of his symbolic action. Each oracle has a different audience but is similar in content and vocabulary. The first addresses five foreign kings (27:5–11), the second King Zedekiah of Judah (27:12–15), and the third the priests and people (27:16–22).[7] Each oracle makes four essential points: 1) serve Nebuchadnezzar king of Babylon (vv. 5–8, 12–13, 17); 2) do not listen to your false prophets (and diviners) who prophesy *sheqer*

---

5. See Leuchter, *The Polemics of Exile*, 40. The LXX lacks all of 27:1.

6. There is some awkwardness here because Jeremiah's wearing the yoke makes sense for the events of ch. 28 but not for ch. 27, and the instruction to send yokes to the kings of five different nations fits the message of ch. 27 but not ch. 28. The confusion is compounded because the text is not clear about whether Jeremiah is to make only one yoke or a series of them (27:2–3). These tensions probably result from combining once-independent stories, but they do not significantly affect the meaning of chs. 27–28.

7. This last speech focusing on the temple utensils may be a later addition because it depends less on the symbolic action involving the yoke than on the story of ch. 28.

(vv. 9–10, 14–15, 16); 3) if you disobey you will be punished (vv. 8, 13, 17); and 4) if you obey by submitting to Nebuchadnezzar you will survive (vv. 11, 12, 17).

To the Nations (27:5–11)

The first oracle is addressed to the foreign kings and begins by establishing the theological basis for all that follows in chs. 27–28. By his great might YHWH has created the earth and the humans and beasts that populate it, and therefore he may give the earth to whomever he deems appropriate (27:5). In the current historical era YHWH has given "all these nations" and even the wild animals to Nebuchadnezzar his servant (27:6). Therefore, any nation that resists placing its neck under the Babylonian yoke is in rebellion against the creator of the universe and will be utterly destroyed (27:8). Rhetorically, the message of chs. 27–28 is addressed to the small Second Temple community of YHWH worshippers, but these chapters deliberately situate God's actions against Judah in the context of God's sovereignty over the nations and even all of creation. True prophets like Jeremiah "consider the whole world to be the arena in which the word of God holds sway."[8]

The text boldly claims a convergence between the divine will and the emergence of the feared Babylonian empire,[9] and in an astounding move God designates Nebuchadnezzar as his own servant (27:6), just as in the corresponding section C (25:9).[10] As YHWH's servant, Nebuchadnezzar will establish a rule so extensive that it will encompass the nations and even the wild animals normally beyond human control (27:6). Despite Nebuchadnezzar's might, he is entirely passive in the text, as it is the power of YHWH that props him up.[11] On the basis of this positive

---

8. O'Connor, "The Prophet Jeremiah," 130. See ibid., 132–34 for a discussion of how Jeremiah's prophetic vocation is concerned not only with Judah but with the broad sweep of international politics and even the created order.

9. Brueggemann, *A Commentary on Jeremiah*, 243.

10. The only other passage in Jeremiah or the entire Old Testament that calls Nebuchadnezzar YHWH's servant is 43:10. Calling Nebuchadnezzar YHWH's servant is not to claim that he worships YHWH, but that he carries out (unknowingly) the divine will. For a fuller discussion of how the text portrays Nebuchadnezzar positively see Hill, *Friend or Foe?*, 127–39. Aejmelaeus argues that calling Nebuchadnezzar servant of YHWH could have occurred only at a time when the bitter memories of the historical Nebuchadnezzar had faded. See Aejmelaeus, "'Nebuchadnezzar, My Servant,'" 13.

11. Osuji, *Where Is the Truth?*, 308.

depiction of Babylon some scholars claim that Jeremiah is portrayed as pro-Babylonian.[12] The text offers a somewhat more nuanced picture, as it never suggests that Jeremiah harbors any positive sentiments toward Babylon, and 27:7 specifically states that Babylonian domination will last only as long as Nebuchadnezzar, his son, and grandson rule; then Babylon will suffer a reversal of fortune and experience the same kind of servitude that it imposed on others.[13] Several times in 23:9—29:32 Jeremiah explicitly foretells the destruction of Babylon (25:12–14, 26; 27:7; 29:10; cf. chs. 50–51), which would be the precondition for the deliverance he envisions (24:5–7; 27:22; 29:10–14, 32). These predictions of Babylon's downfall amid some of the harshest descriptions of YHWH's punishment of Judah illustrate that true prophecy is more than just a message of disaster, but is called, "To destroy and to overthrow, To build and to plant" (1:10). The strikingly positive depiction of Babylon is less an apology for the Babylonian empire than a rhetorical call to accept the exile and destruction of the nation as merited judgment from the hand of YHWH.

After promising annihilation for any nation unwilling to accept servitude to Babylon, Jeremiah exhorts the nations, "Do not listen to your *prophets*, augurs, dreamers, diviners, and sorcerers who tell you, 'you shall not serve the king of Babylon'" (27:9). This warning is intensified by the switch from third-person conditional statements in vv. 8 and 10 to second-person plural imperative verbs here.[14] The matter of false prophecy is quite artificial in the present context and has probably been introduced secondarily,[15] which illustrates how the chapter deliberately highlights the topic of false prophecy. One of the major purposes of 23:9—29:32 is to establish contrasting paradigms of true and false prophecy. The text recognizes that the nations have a variety of intermediaries, but because all exhibit the well-defined characteristics of Judah's false prophets, some of them are called prophets (v. 9) and all are described as prophesying (v. 10).[16] The text portrays these pagan intermediaries as

---

12. See for example Carroll, *Jeremiah*, 524, 532.

13. The LXX lacks 27:7, indicating that the verse has probably been added in the Masoretic redaction to correspond to a similar but more detailed prediction of Babylon's downfall in 25:12–14 of section C.

14. Osuji, *Where Is the Truth?*, 181.

15. See McKane, *A Critical and Exegetical Commentary*, 2:cxxxv, 696, 701–2, 708.

16. In 27:9 the LXX calls the foreign intermediaries *pseudoprophetai*. It is not clear whether this is because they are pagan or because they have a false message. The prophets of Judah in 27:12–22 are not called *pseudoprophetai* even though their

exact counterparts of Judah's false prophets, since Jeremiah warns the nations not to heed their prophets and intermediaries just as he warns Zedekiah (v. 14) and the people of Judah (v. 16) not to heed their prophets. Both Judah's prophets and the foreign prophets instruct their people not to serve Babylon, a message Jeremiah labels *sheqer* (vv. 9-10, 14, 16-17). Jeremiah informs the nations that if they heed their prophets then YHWH will banish them from their homeland and destroy them (v. 10), a fate similar to what awaits Judah if it listens to its false prophets (vv. 13, 15, 17). Just as in 23:9-40 and chs. 28 and 29, false prophets lead their communities astray with an optimistic message of *sheqer* that has an absolutely destructive quality because it obscures the reality of YHWH's will and the historical situation, and thereby raises false hopes that lead to suicidal policies of resistance to Babylon.[17]

Jeremiah's oracle to the foreign kings closes by laying out a positive option for the nations. "The nation which brings its neck under the yoke of the king of Babylon and serves him [וַעֲבָדוֹ] I will leave upon its land, declares YHWH, and they will till it [וַעֲבָדָהּ] and dwell upon it" (27:11). Serving (עבד) Babylon will allow the nations to continue tilling (עבד) their land. "Serve" is a leitmotif in ch. 27 (occurring eight times in vv. 5-11), stressing that there is no escape from servitude to Babylon. Even for pagan nations, heeding the voice of true prophecy is a matter of life and death. In the other two oracles Jeremiah offers Zedekiah and the people of Judah life if they will serve the king of Babylon (vv. 12, 17). The true prophet may utter harsh words, but ultimately only such a message of judgment has the potential to open people's eyes to reality and outline a course of action that leads to life.

To Zedekiah (27:12-15)

In the second oracle of ch. 27 Jeremiah delivers the same message to Zedekiah as he has just sent to the nations, illustrating the consistency of true prophecy. The repeated use of plural imperatives indicates that both Zedekiah and the nation are addressed. Judah, like the nations, is ordered

---

message is just as false.

17. Overholt, *The Threat of Falsehood*, 76. The paradigm of false prophecy evident in chs. 27-28 is also illustrated by 20:6, where Jeremiah accuses the "priest" Pashhur of "prophesying" *sheqer*, even though there is no other hint that Pashhur is a prophet or has uttered prophetic oracles. His opposition to Jeremiah's prediction of destruction by the Babylonians (20:1-6) means that he has "prophesied" *sheqer*.

Concerning the Prophets

to bring its neck under the yoke of the king of Babylon and serve him so that it might live (v. 12; cf. v. 8). Just like the nations, Judah is threatened with the triad of sword, famine, and pestilence if it refuses (v. 13; cf. v. 8). Just like the nations, Judah must not listen to the prophets who are prophesying *sheqer*, "you shall not serve the king of Babylon" (v. 14; cf. vv. 9–10). In both cases the prophets mislead their communities with the result that YHWH will banish (נדח) the people and they will perish (אבד) (vv. 10, 15), with v. 15 stressing that Judah's prophets in particular will share in this fate. These similarities between Judah's prophets and foreign intermediaries characterize the former as little better than pagan diviners.[18] The Zedekiah oracle expands somewhat on the critique of the prophets by declaring that YHWH did not send them yet they prophesy *sheqer* in his name (v. 15), an accusation that would not make sense for foreign intermediaries who make no claim to prophesy for YHWH.

To the Priests and People (27:16–22)

Jeremiah's third oracle is addressed to the priests and all the people, suggesting that the common people share responsibility with the nation's kings and priests for the catastrophe that resulted from heeding the false prophets. Jeremiah warns his audience not to listen to prophetic assurances that the temple utensils, looted during the first Babylonian invasion, will soon be returned (27:16). This message does not quite follow from Jeremiah's symbolic action of sending yokes to various kings but fits with ch. 28, where the fate of the temple utensils is central and symbolizes the fate of Jerusalem and the nation. This artificiality indicates how 27:16–22 seeks to set up a contrast between true and false prophecy that focuses on the fate of the temple, city, and nation. The false prophets in this third oracle have a somewhat different message than that of their counterparts in the other two speeches, but the implications of their message are similar: Babylonian domination is temporary and therefore the people should resist it. Jeremiah calls this message *sheqer* (v. 16) and exhorts the people to serve the king of Babylon so that they might live (v. 17). Following the pattern of the second oracle, this possibility of choosing life is followed by a question (cf. 27:12–13), "Why should this city be ruined?" (27:17). In all three speeches of ch. 27 Jeremiah places before the people a positive alternative (27:11, 12, 17), emphasizing that to some

---

18. Lange, *Vom prophetischen Wort*, 239.

extent the people's fate is in their own hands and depends on how they respond to the message of true prophecy.

In 27:18 Jeremiah challenges the false prophets to demonstrate their power by interceding with YHWH to prevent the remaining utensils in the temple, royal palace, and city from being carted off to Babylon. Intercession was one of the major roles of a prophet,[19] and Israelite tradition portrays Moses as the intercessory prophet par excellence.[20] On three occasions YHWH forbids Jeremiah to intercede on behalf of the people because their advanced stage of unfaithfulness renders such intercession inappropriate (7:16; 11:14; 14:11–12; cf. 15:1; 18:20; 37:3), which illustrates that under normal circumstances intercession was expected of a prophet like Jeremiah. Given the significance of intercession, the Jerusalem prophets' failure to intercede effectively demonstrates their powerlessness and lack of connectedness to YHWH. The text is retrospective, addressing an audience who already knows that nothing prevented the Babylonians from completing their destruction and looting of the temple and city. Challenging the prophets to a task that has no possibility of success is a rhetorical device to discredit any prophets who have announced the well-being of the nation. In vv. 19–22 Jeremiah in essence retracts his challenge to intercede by announcing that instead of restoring the plundered temple utensils from exile, YHWH will ensure that whatever utensils still remain will also be carted off. Ironically, false prophecy accomplishes the opposite of what it intends, because it encourages the nation to resist Babylon and adopt a course of action that leads to the final destruction of the temple and the exile of its utensils.[21]

Nebuchadnezzar's looting of the temple is an affront to Zion traditions and illustrates the impotence of the cultic system based in the temple. For the other prophets the temple utensils function as a symbol of hope that YHWH will soon reverse the nation's fortunes and restore the political and religious system disrupted by the Babylonians.[22] Jere-

19. See von Rad, "Falschen Propheten," 114–15; Kraus, *Prophetie in der Krisis*, 80; and Rhodes, "Israel's Prophets as Intercessors," 107–28.

20. See Seitz, "The Prophet Moses," 6–7.

21. Lange, *Vom prophetishen Wort*, 243.

22. Ackroyd, "The Temple Vessels," 175. Ackroyd points out how the temple utensils became an important symbol for many Second Temple Jews, signifying the continuity of later worship with the pre-exilic temple cult. Ackroyd's observations may explain why the MT of 27:19–22 is much longer than the LXX version and displays much more interest in these utensils. For a discussion of why conquering kings carried off cultic objects and how subject peoples experienced such despoiling, see Osuji,

miah transforms this symbol of hope into a symbol of disaster, declaring that the judgment that YHWH initiated with the first deportation and the looting of the temple will be completed, symbolized by the taking to Babylon of all remaining treasures from the temple and city.[23] However, for Jeremiah these utensils also function as a symbol of hope, albeit a subdued or delayed hope. The MT of 27:22, in contrast to the LXX which lacks the last half of the verse, states that the utensils will remain in Babylon until YHWH takes note of them and restores them "to this place." This assurance implies a restoration of both the people and their worship life, and indicates yet again that deliverance and not disaster is YHWH's final will for the people. Jeremiah agrees with his prophetic opponents about the ultimate fate of the temple utensils and what they symbolize for the community, but he disagrees on the matter of timing, and in this case timing is everything because it determines the nature of the community's response to Babylonian domination. While Jeremiah affirms hope in the saving nature of YHWH, he does not base this hope on Zion traditions as his opponents do. Restoration will come only after the punishment of exile has been embraced and lived through. In contrast to the false prophets, Jeremiah is portrayed as knowing when and to whom to sound the note of judgment, and when and to whom to sound the note of deliverance.[24]

The portrayal of false prophets in ch. 27 is quite artificial in that none of these prophets is ever named and they do not come alive as real adversaries.[25] The purpose of the chapter is not historical verisimilitude but theological reflection on two conflicting understandings of the community's life, refracted through the lens of false versus true prophecy.

JEREMIAH VERSUS HANANIAH (28:1–17)

Chapter 27 contrasts the message of Jeremiah with that of the false prophets but the conflict is indirect, unlike ch. 28, which focuses on a direct confrontation between Hananiah and Jeremiah. Hananiah serves as a specific example of those prophets who are condemned as a group in ch. 27 for minimizing the Babylonian threat, and he acts as a foil for the

---

Where Is the Truth?, 187.
23. Jones, *Jeremiah*, 352.
24. Brueggemann, *To Build, to Plant*, 35.
25. Hossfeld and Meyer, *Prophet gegen Prophet*, 103.

presentation of Jeremiah as true prophet. Chapter 28 breaks neatly into four sections, as the two prophets take turns speaking and acting—Hananiah in vv. 1–4, Jeremiah in vv. 5–9, Hananiah in vv. 10–11, and Jeremiah in vv. 12–17.[26]

One of the means 23:9—29:32 uses to establish the truthfulness and consistency of the message of Jeremiah and YHWH's servants the prophets is to create paradigms of both true and false prophecy. Thus, when Hananiah appears on the scene in ch. 28 and contradicts the word of the quintessential true prophet Jeremiah, there is no suspense about who is the true or false prophet or about what the message of true prophecy is, nor does the text depict Jeremiah as listening to Hananiah and taking his message seriously. The LXX is attuned to these dynamics and labels Hananiah a *pseudoprophetes* already in the first verse of the chapter. Interpretations of ch. 28 that focus on Jeremiah's uncertainty as to the divine plan for this hour in history or that deal with YHWH's prerogative to change his mind are not attuned to the actual biblical portrayal.[27] The point of the story in its present form and context is that no matter what an impressive prophet like Hananiah might say or do, neither is YHWH about to revise his plans concerning Babylonian domination nor will the consistent message of Jeremiah the true prophet change from what he proclaims in ch. 27, or in the rest of 23:9—29:32, or since the beginning of the book.

Hananiah Contradicts Jeremiah (28:1–4)

Chapter 28 stresses that the confrontation between Hananiah and Jeremiah is public, taking place in the temple with the priests (vv. 1, 5) and all the people (vv. 1, 5, 7, 11) as witnesses. The four references to the people as observers suggests that the conflict between true and false prophecy is not just a matter for religious professionals to adjudicate but is something that ordinary people witness and must take sides on. The LXX labels Hananiah a "false prophet" once (v. 1), and after that does not refer to either Jeremiah or Hananiah as a prophet. The MT calls Jeremiah (vv. 5, 6, 10, 11, 12, 15) and Hananiah (vv. 1, 5, 10, 12, 15, 17) a "prophet" six times

26. Holladay, *Jeremiah 2*, 126. For a somewhat different outline of the structure that involves dividing the chapter into two acts, see Osuji, *Where Is the Truth?*, 198.

27. See also Moberly, *Prophecy and Discernment*, 106–7. For interpretations focusing on Jeremiah's uncertainty or YHWH's prerogative to change the divine plan, see the discussion in chapter 1 of the works of Buber, Childs, and Osuji.

each, and four times both are called "prophet" in the same sentence (vv. 5, 10, 12, 15). The MT of ch. 28 presents a case of prophet against prophet,[28] as it describes one of the Bible's most dramatic encounters between true and false prophecy.

The opening speech of Hananiah represents a direct response to Jeremiah's oracles of ch. 27 and sets him up as the antithesis of Jeremiah.[29] Hananiah speaks before the same audience of people and priests addressed by Jeremiah's previous oracles (27:16; 28:1), and both prophets begin by using the classic messenger formula, "Thus says YHWH" (27:16, 19, 21; 28:2). However, the lack of any notice by the narrator that YHWH speaks to or commissions Hananiah is more than a little telling. In a chiastic oracle,[30] Hananiah directly contradicts Jeremiah by declaring that YHWH has broken the yoke of the king of Babylon and within two years will bring the temple utensils and also the exiles back from Babylon:[31]

---

28. Hill documents that throughout much of the book the MT, in comparison to the LXX, displays a heightened interest in the figure of the prophet: Hill, "The Book of Jeremiah MT and Early Second Temple Conflicts." He concludes that this interest reflects late Persian or early Greek period conflicts about the role of prophecy in the community. In contrast to a text like Zech 13:2–6, the MT of Jeremiah is much more tolerant of prophecy and envisions both true and false prophecy as ongoing features of community life. The evenhanded designation of both Hananiah and Jeremiah as prophets indicates that in the MT, "the issue is not the office of prophecy itself, but rather the question of a conflict between people who ... are exercising a ministry that was regarded as a normal part of the community's life" (p. 34).

29. Osuji, *Where Is the Truth?*, 200.

30. See Keown et al., *Jeremiah 26–52*, 54; Osuji, *Where Is the Truth?*, 201–2.

31. Wilson, *Sociological Approaches*, 77–80, analyzes the confrontation between Jeremiah and Hananiah in terms of the two prophets acting as representatives of different support groups that had conflicting social, political, and religious interests. This analysis is helpful for understanding the historical incident that may underlie Jer 28, but the biblical portrayal suppresses the political and sociological dimensions in favor of painting the issue primarily in theological terms. Sharp also seeks to reconstruct the historical situation behind the text and concludes that the prediction of YHWH's exile of the remaining temple utensils represents an attempt by the pro-*golah* redaction to reject the possibility of any legitimate cultic or community life in Palestine. See Sharp, *Prophecy and Ideology*, 92. If the faithful community and its cult will continue it must be in Babylon under the authority of the already exiled priests and leaders. Jeremiah's offer of "submit to Babylon and live" does not mean that those who submit can continue to live in the land, but that they too will be exiled and then live under the authority of the *golah* community. Sharp's interpretation cannot be the meaning of the text in its final form, and I doubt it was the meaning even of earlier versions. The whole point of ch. 27 is that heeding the call of true prophecy to serve Babylon offers (or did offer) both Judah and the nations a way to avoid total defeat. Jeremiah informs the nations that if they submit to Nebuchadnezzar, then YHWH will allow them to

Section C'

> YHWH has broken the yoke of the king of Babylon (28:2b)
> YHWH will return the exiled temple utensils to this place (28:3)
> YHWH will return the exiled people to this place (28:4a)
> YHWH will break the yoke of the king of Babylon (28:4b)

It is fitting that the conflict between true and false prophecy is illustrated by a specific prophet whose name, Hananiah, means "YHWH is gracious." Hananiah is portrayed as being rooted in Israel's election traditions that stressed divine protection of the nation, and so he imagines that the nation's institutions and life can remain virtually unscathed by exile and dislocation.[32]

Hananiah attaches the specific time frame of two years to his proclamation of deliverance. Jeremiah also announces the return of the exiled temple utensils (27:22), but according to him deliverance lies a long way in the future (seventy years—25:11; 29:10). Much more is at stake here than just timing. A two-year waiting period encourages impatient endurance of Babylonian domination and perhaps even revolt, and denies any massive break in national life. A seventy-year period encourages acceptance of the profound reality of exile, a recognition that an entire era and way of life are over, a deep soul-searching about the causes of the catastrophe, and creative thinking about new foundations for communal life in the midst of and beyond exile.

While Hananiah is depicted as a false prophet he is not portrayed as a prophetic impostor, for he exhibits all the outward signs of a genuine prophet capable of a rather impressive prophetic performance. The text repeatedly calls him a prophet (28:1, 5, 10, 12, 15, 17), he speaks in the name of YHWH, and he uses the proper forms of prophetic speech: "Thus says YHWH of hosts the God of Israel" (v. 2); "declares YHWH [נְאֻם יְהוָה]" (v. 4); "thus says YHWH" (v. 11). By breaking Jeremiah's yoke, Hananiah performs a symbolic action and then offers an interpretation, just as a true prophet would do (vv. 10–11). His message is rooted in traditional theology and there is no mention of immorality or personal

---

continue living in their land (27:11). When Jeremiah then places a similar offer before Judah, "serve the king of Babylon and live" (27:12, 17), this can hardly mean that such submission will still result in exile, especially since 27:17 indicates that the destruction of Jerusalem can be avoided by serving Babylon.

32. Stulman, *Order amid Chaos*, 74; Stulman, "Conflicting Paths to Hope in Jeremiah," 50–51.

shortcomings that would disqualify him from being a genuine prophet.³³ The text does lack any reference to a divine commission for Hananiah, in contrast to Jeremiah, who receives two direct commands from YHWH (27:1–4; 28:12–13). The only criterion that comes into play for judging Hananiah false is the content of his message. For the implied reader history has demonstrated how false Hananiah was in his predictions, and the larger editorial context makes it clear from the moment Hananiah speaks that he is a false prophet. Still, the text seems to acknowledge that in real-life situations it can be difficult to distinguish between true and false prophecy, because prophetic speech and actions can be mimicked and so there are no outward forms that provide adequate criteria for discernment. Prophets can only be judged true or false on the basis of their message, and so one of the purposes of ch. 28 is to contribute to the paradigms of true and false prophecy and thereby assist readers in the essential task of such discernment.

Jeremiah Responds (28:5–9)

Osuji depicts an assertive and confident Hananiah taking control of the stage in the first part of ch. 28, while the quiet, humble, and defensive Jeremiah goes his way in order to avoid confrontation.³⁴ I suggest that the text portrays the situation somewhat differently. Hananiah is assertive but Jeremiah interrupts his prophetic performance and seizes the spotlight from him before he can perform the symbolic action of breaking the yoke. By challenging Hananiah and introducing the genre of dispute into the scenario, Jeremiah downgrades Hananiah's "word of YHWH" to but one opinion in a contested debate.³⁵ In these two ways Jeremiah demonstrates from the outset that Hananiah's message is false.

The text highlights that Jeremiah's response to Hananiah takes place publicly in the temple before the same audience of priests and "all the people" who witness Hananiah's initial prophesy (v. 5; cf. v. 1). Jeremiah responds to Hananiah in two distinct ways. First, he expresses his personal wish that Hananiah's prophecy may be fulfilled (v. 6), but then the longer part of his response consists of reservations about the truth of this prophecy (vv. 7–9). These reservations are based on two different criteria

---

33. For a similar discussion, see Osuji, *Where Is the Truth?*, 215–16, 317, 385.
34. Ibid., 213, 312.
35. Allen, *Jeremiah*, 316.

for judging the truth of a prophetic word: its agreement with a tradition of judgment prophecy (v. 8), and its fulfillment (v. 9).

Carroll is correct in highlighting how Jeremiah's response to Hananiah is somewhat surprising and uncharacteristic of a prophet normally so sure of his message.[36] In ch. 27 Jeremiah prophecies three times that all nations must submit to Babylon, and three times he warns against listening to false prophets who urge resistance. Then in ch. 28, when confronted by a specific example of such a prophet, instead of denouncing Hananiah for leading the nation astray, he utters a wish that Hananiah's false prophecy might come to pass. "Amen, may YHWH do so, may YHWH fulfill your words which you prophesied and return the utensils of the temple and all the exiles from Babylon to this place" (v. 6). Jeremiah's response does not affirm the truthfulness of the prophecy, but rather expresses his personal wish that Hananiah's word might be true, thereby indicating that he does not personally desire the doom of the nation.[37] True prophets actually seek the welfare of their people, as illustrated by Jeremiah's impassioned plea for repentance in ch. 26 and his exhortations in ch. 27 to serve Babylon and live. Jeremiah's response also signifies that in theory, YHWH can commission prophets to announce words of salvation and can bring such predictions to fulfillment. In theory this is possible, but the reader knows that in the case of Hananiah such has not been the case.

After expressing his wish that Hananiah's prophecy might come true, Jeremiah invites Hananiah and the audience (and the implied reader) to consider an argument that speaks against his opponent's prophecy and provides criteria for discerning between true and false prophecy. Jeremiah introduces his reservations in such a way as to emphasize their gravity. "But listen now to this word which I am speaking in your hearing and in the hearing of all the people" (v. 7). The first reservation consists of an appeal to a canonical tradition of judgment prophecy. "The prophets who were before me and before you from of old prophesied against many

---

36. Carroll, *Jeremiah*, 540–41. See also Childs, "True and False Prophets," 135–36. The conclusion Carroll draws from the surprising nature of Jeremiah's response is that ch. 28 is an independent story that can only be properly understood if read as independent of its context. To do otherwise only exposes the contradictions between ch. 28 and the material surrounding it. In contrast, I suggest that while ch. 28 may at one time have been independent, it is now so closely integrated with ch. 27 that Carroll's approach misses the meaning and purpose of the story in its present form.

37. Weiser, *Jeremia*, 246; Kraus, *Prophetie in der Krisis*, 92; Wolff, "How Can We Recognize False Prophets?" 68; Fretheim, *Jeremiah*, 393; Miller, "The Book of Jeremiah," 785.

nations and great kingdoms, war, disaster, and pestilence" (v. 8). The text both assumes and supports the authority of a canonical line of true prophets, and so a crucial criterion for the validity of specific prophecies is consistency with divine revelation already embodied in established prophetic tradition.[38] Jeremiah's appeal to this tradition implies that even though future generations may not always be privileged to have prophets of his own stature in their midst, they can still draw on prophetic tradition as their guide.

Jeremiah depicts the history of true prophecy as a history of judgment prophecy. Earlier passages in 23:9—29:32 speak of YHWH's servants the prophets who have consistently warned the people to repent and obey the *Torah* (25:4-6; 26:4-5), and the incidents in ch. 26 provide examples of three specific prophets who all have a message of disaster. In all these cases the text portrays the prophets as having a unified message. The incident involving Micah (26:17-19) demonstrates how a proclamation of judgment doubles as a call to repentance, while Jeremiah's pleas for repentance in essence constitute announcements of judgment, because the nation did not repent and therefore experienced the punishment he warned of (see the discussion in the previous chapter of 26:3-6, 9, 13). Thus, prophets who announce judgment are at the same time summoning the community to repentance, and vice versa. This means that the judgment prophets referred to in 28:8 must be identical with prophets like Micah and Uriah, as well as YHWH's servants the prophets who call for repentance and obedience.

The way Jeremiah speaks to Hananiah about the prophets "who were before me and before you" (v. 8) indicates that he considers Hananiah a prophetic peer. Hananiah is not a false prophet in any ontological sense but a prophet who claims to speak a word of YHWH that must be tested.[39] The first way Jeremiah discredits Hananiah's message is on the basis of deviation from canonical prophetic tradition. Jeremiah's second reservation focuses on fulfillment: "Concerning the prophet who prophesies *shalom*, when the word of the prophet comes to pass then it will be known that YHWH really sent him" (28:9). Fulfillment is one of the major Old Testament criteria for judging the truth of a prophecy,[40] but

38. See Clements, *Jeremiah*, 168.

39. Sharp, "The Call of Jeremiah and Diaspora Politics," 430.

40. For a discussion and list of key texts see Long, "Prophetic Authority," 13–14; and De Vries, *Prophet against Prophet*, 142–44. Deuteronomy 18:21–22 sets forth the criterion of fulfillment in its most explicit form.

Section C'

what is unique here is that the criterion is applied only to prophecies of well-being. In real-life situations the criterion of fulfillment is not particularly useful because a prophetic message, especially that of Jeremiah, normally calls for an immediate response, not a delayed one that waits until the outcome of events is known. The criterion of fulfillment is useful only in hindsight and was probably the most important criterion for determining which prophets were eventually reckoned as canonical and which not.[41] The implied reader knows that Hananiah's prophecy was not fulfilled and so he is discredited, but the reader also knows that Jeremiah's predictions of doom were all too horribly fulfilled, and so he is vindicated as the paradigmatic true prophet whose message carries ongoing power and authority.

The book of Jeremiah and even 23:9—29:32 contain numerous promises of deliverance, and so 28:9 should not be read as precluding the truthfulness of any prophecies of *shalom*. However, according to 23:9—29:32 and especially 28:8-9, the dominant note in true prophecy is judgment, and so the burden of proof lies with the prophet who announces a message of salvation. This raises the question of what to make of Jeremiah's unfulfilled prophesies of deliverance. There never was a restoration of northern Israel (cf. 31:1-9, 15-22), nor did YHWH make a new covenant with a reunited Israel and place the *Torah* into their hearts (cf. 31:31-34). Childs points out that already within the book of Jeremiah such promises have been detached from their original historical moorings and their fulfillment projected into the eschatological future, while in the meantime they serve as promises of YHWH's faithfulness.[42] Such reinterpretation was part of the Second Temple community's self-perception of living in an unended exile, even though it had experienced some restoration and a return to the land (see the discussion in chapter 4). As texts like Dan 9:2 and Zech 7:5 illustrate, in a much later era Jeremiah's promises of restoration were still viewed as true prophecies waiting to be fulfilled. Because the majority of Jeremiah's predictions came to pass, especially those foretelling disaster, he was regarded as possessing such authority that any prophecies attributed to him were by definition true. Most of the canonical prophetic books contain unfulfilled predictions, but the determining factor in their canonization was that their message as a whole was

---

41. De Vries, *Prophet against Prophet*, 144.
42. Childs, *Introduction to the Old Testament*, 351.

considered reliable.[43] Once these writings acquired authoritative status, then the onus was on the reading community to discern the ongoing truth and relevance of their content, even their "unfulfilled" promises. Despite the book of Jeremiah's deep-rooted hope, it remains so wary of *shalom* prophets who have brought catastrophe upon the nation that 28:9 burdens them with the onus of fulfillment, as a way to ensure that they never again dupe the community with their *sheqer*.

Hananiah Breaks the Yoke (28:10–11)

After Jeremiah voices his reservations, Hananiah carries on with his prophetic performance that Jeremiah has interrupted, and he removes the yoke from Jeremiah's neck, breaks it, and announces in YHWH's name, "Just like this I will break the yoke of Nebuchadnezzar King of Babylon from upon the neck of all the nations, within two years" (28:11). By using the vocabulary of 27:8–15 Hananiah condemns himself, as he directly contradicts YHWH's word proclaimed by Jeremiah. Hananiah voices the convictions of the Royal–Zion traditions that God will not allow the nation and city to be destroyed, but the issue goes far beyond just the fate of Judah. Jeremiah's initial prophecy in ch. 27 stresses that as creator of the earth YHWH has placed *all the nations* (v. 7) under Nebuchadnezzar's temporary authority. Jeremiah's reservation about Hananiah's optimistic prophecy mentions a line of prophets who announced calamity against "*many nations and great kingdoms*" (28:8), and Hananiah claims that YHWH will break the Babylonian yoke from the neck of "*all the nations*" (28:11). The issue in both sections C (ch. 25) and C' (chs. 27–28) is YHWH's plan for the nations, and in both Judah's destiny is bound up with the destiny of the nations and Jeremiah functions as a prophet to the nations.

By publicly contradicting Jeremiah and neutralizing his symbolic action, Hananiah is in essence claiming that Jeremiah is a false prophet.[44] Jeremiah says nothing and simply goes his way (28:11). The confident and assertive Jeremiah of ch. 27, who has just prophesied three times that all the nations must not listen to their misleading prophets, simply slinks away when confronted by a specific example of such a false prophet. Jeremiah's "surprising" silence and retreat in the face of opposition

---

43. De Vries, *Prophet against Prophet*, 144.
44. Quell, *Wahre und falsche Propheten*, 47.

have spawned several explanations, most of which assume that Jeremiah leaves the scene because of some uncertainty.

Overholt notes that the characteristic form of prophetic speech is the invective-threat oracle. The threat is the word of YHWH, which the prophet is obliged to deliver verbatim, but he has considerable freedom in composing the invective analyzing why YHWH is planning judgment. Perhaps Jeremiah is silent because he needs to withdraw in order to rethink his analysis of the political and social condition of the people.[45] Buber, Kraus, Childs, and Osuji all link Jeremiah's supposed uncertainty to his recognition that the divine will for history is dynamic.[46] Jeremiah is open to the possibility that God's will may change, and so he must withdraw in order to listen again for the word of YHWH. If one reads the text historically then it is possible that Jeremiah's departure is due to some type of uncertainty, although the reservations he raises about Hananiah's message make this somewhat doubtful.

As Childs observes, at the historical level there must have been considerable confusion at times in ancient Israel regarding who was a true and who was a false prophet.[47] However, as Childs has also observed, the canonical process has shaped the material in such a way as to eliminate this confusion, so that later readers will know what is true and what is false prophecy. Childs offers keen insights into the purpose of the biblical portrayal of true and false prophecy, but in the case of Jer 28 he misreads somewhat the biblical portrayal. From the very outset of the story Hananiah is depicted as precisely the kind of false prophet Jeremiah has just warned about in ch. 27, and so there is no need for Jeremiah to be uncertain about anything. The book of Jeremiah as a whole, and especially 23:9—29:32, stresses that the true prophet Jeremiah has persistently proclaimed YHWH's plan to send disaster unless the nation repents. The issue in ch. 28 can hardly be that as a result of the words of a false prophet, Jeremiah now has to wait for a new divine word because YHWH might be changing his mind.

---

45. Overholt, *The Threat of Falsehood*, 97.

46. Buber, "False Prophets," 166–67; Kraus, *Prophetie in der Krisis*, 94, 98–99; Childs, "True and False Prophets," 139; Osuji, *Where Is the Truth?*, 214–15, 387–89.

47. Childs, "True and False Prophets," 140–42. Sheppard observes that while there may have been confusion for Israelite society at large, the prophetic support groups operated with certain sets of criteria that they believed validated their prophets as true; Sheppard, "True and False Prophecy," 267.

Jeremiah's departure from the scene does not signal uncertainty but has to do with how true prophecy functions. Jeremiah cannot retort immediately with an oracle from YHWH because that would make him like the false prophets who speak what arises from their own minds (cf. 23:16, 26), or who prophesy without having been sent (cf. 23:21, 32; 28:15; 29:9, 31), or who act on their own in a variety of other ways (23:25, 27–28, 31; 29:8, 21, 23, 25). One of the central features of the portrayal of true and false prophecy in 23:9—29:32 is that false prophets act on their own volition, in contrast to true prophets, who only speak or act when commissioned by YHWH. Therefore, the true prophet is not a debater who can toss out words of YHWH at will, but must wait for such a word to come.[48] In 42:7 it takes ten days before Jeremiah receives an answer to a specific question he has put before YHWH. Given that Jeremiah cannot rebuke Hananiah immediately with a word from YHWH, it is all the more significant that he demonstrates Hananiah false through the reservations he voices in 28:7–9.

Jeremiah Responds (28:12–17)

After Jeremiah's retreat in the face of Hananiah's oracle, 28:12 stresses that YHWH commands Jeremiah to speak a new word, illustrating how much the ministry of a true prophet depends on the word of YHWH.[49] Three times the response to Hananiah uses the messenger formula "thus says YHWH" (vv. 13, 14, 16), in contrast to Jeremiah's initial response to Hananiah representing his own opinion, where there is no such claim to divine revelation (vv. 7–9). The first part of the message for Hananiah, which focuses on the fate of the nations, is communicated via a narration of what YHWH commands Jeremiah to speak (vv. 13–14), but the text does not report Jeremiah actually delivering these words. Conversely,

---

48. This interpretation applies only to the MT, because 28:7 in the LXX designates Jeremiah's reservations as "the word of the Lord." Rudolph is an exception among commentators in that he correctly observes that Jeremiah is silent and leaves the scene because YHWH's word does not come whenever one might wish it to; Rudolph, *Jeremia*, 165. Second Samuel 7:1–17 is probably a composite text, but in its final form the prophet Nathan initially responds favorably to David's desire to build a temple, a response not designated as a word of YHWH (vv. 1–3). Later Nathan receives a contradictory word from YHWH, and he must retract his initial response (vv. 4–7). A prophet who does not first listen for the divine message may be forced to take back his words.

49. Kraus, *Prophetie in der Krisis*, 99.

Section C'

when Jeremiah confronts Hananiah he speaks for YHWH and foretells Hananiah's impending death (vv. 15-16), which the text does not record YHWH as saying anything about. Because Jeremiah is consistently faithful in his prophetic responsibilities, the text implies that he does deliver the message YHWH reveals to him, and because Jeremiah does not speak on his own behalf, the text also implies that the prediction of Hananiah's death is part of YHWH's message. The text uses a narrative technique that avoids unnecessary repetition but at the same time emphasizes that Jeremiah receives his message from YHWH and then faithfully delivers it.[50]

YHWH instructs Jeremiah to tell Hananiah, "You have broken wooden yoke-bars, only to make iron ones in their place" (v. 13).[51] Not only has Hananiah's symbolic action been powerless to break the yoke of Babylonian domination, it has actually intensified the judgment. In ch. 27 YHWH holds out to Judah and the nations the possibility of voluntary submission to the wooden Babylonian yoke, but Hananiah's actions have precluded this option and now Judah and the nations will labor as draft animals under a harsher unbreakable iron yoke (v. 14). Jeremiah's prophecy in 28:13-16 makes the same points as do his three oracles in ch. 27.[52] YHWH has placed a yoke upon the nations and so they must serve Babylon (28:14), whose domination is so comprehensive that it even includes the wild animals (28:14). Hananiah has spoken *sheqer* (28:15) just like the prophets of ch. 27, and so he will be banished and perish (28:16) just like the rebellious people of ch. 27. These parallels illustrate the close connections between chs. 27 and 28, highlight the unchanging nature of true prophecy, stress that YHWH's plans are not about to change, and portray Hananiah as an example of the false prophets who were condemned in a general way in ch. 27.

The first part of Jeremiah's response to Hananiah concerns the fate of the nations, and hence the wrongness of Hananiah's message. The second part concerns the fate of Hananiah himself and takes the form of an

---

50. Osuji, *Where Is the Truth?*, 222.

51. This is Bright's translation; see Bright, *Jeremiah*, 198. Many translators and commentators follow the LXX, which reads, "You broke yokes of wood but *I will make* instead of them yokes of iron." The difference between the two readings is very minor in Hebrew, וְעָשִׂיתָ versus וְעָשִׂיתִי. The LXX reading where YHWH, not Hananiah, fashions the iron yoke makes more sense, but the meaning of both versions is essentially the same.

52. Childs, "True and False Prophets," 138.

invective-threat oracle. The first part of the invective asserts that YHWH did not send Hananiah. Ultimately, the conflict is not between Jeremiah and Hananiah, but between YHWH and Hananiah.[53] Jeremiah also accuses Hananiah of making the people trust in *sheqer* (28:15). Elsewhere 23:9—29:32 accuses the false prophets of prophesying without being sent (23:21, 32; 27:15; 29:9, 31) and prophesying *sheqer* (23:14, 25, 26, 32; 27:10, 14, 15, 16; 29:9, 21, 23, 31), which indicates how Hananiah is depicted here as the quintessential false prophet. As mentioned earlier in this chapter, the *sheqer* that Hananiah and other prophets proclaim refers to the distorted worldview and false sense of security, fostering religious and political choices that lead to catastrophe.[54]

There is irony in the sentence YHWH decrees for Hananiah. Hananiah prophesied even though YHWH did not *send him* (28:15), therefore YHWH will *send him* from the face of the earth (28:16). The oracle concludes by predicting that within the year Hananiah will die (28:16) and then summarizes why he deserves such a fate: "because you have urged disloyalty/apostasy against YHWH [כִּי־סָרָה דִבַּרְתָּ אֶל־יְהוָה]." סָרָה occurs eight times in the Old Testament, three times in contexts dealing with prophecy. One is Deut 13:6 (Heb.) and the other two are Jer 28:16 and 29:32, which are virtually identical. In both Jeremiah passages the LXX lacks the accusation that the false prophet has urged disloyalty, perhaps indicating that the clause has been added to the MT on the basis of Deut 13:6. In Deut 13:2–6 Moses instructs the Israelites that they must not heed a prophet or dreamer who urges them to follow other gods, even if he can wow them with impressive signs and wonders. Instead, such a prophet must be killed, "because he has urged disloyalty/apostasy against YHWH your God [כִּי דִבֶּר־סָרָה עַל־יְהוָה אֱלֹהֵיכֶם]." Hananiah is portrayed as one of the dangerous prophets Deut 13:2–6 warns about. He is associated with paganism, as his false assurances of divine protection are depicted as equivalent to encouraging the worship of other gods. In contrast, by quoting Moses Jeremiah appears as a prophet like Moses whose ministry is a continuation of the ministry of Moses, the fountainhead of Israelite prophecy (cf. Deut. 18:15–19).[55]

The conclusion to ch. 28 states that Hananiah died that same year in the seventh month (v. 17), and thus Jeremiah's prediction is fulfilled

---

53. Osuji, *Where Is the Truth?*, 221.
54. Overholt, *The Threat of Falsehood*, 103.
55. Blenkinsopp, *Prophecy and Canon*, 52.

within a mere two months (cf. 28:1). Given that both Deut 13:6 and 18:20 prescribe death as punishment for false prophecy, Hananiah's fate discredits his message and demonstrates that he is such a false prophet. His death is a foretaste of the disaster that ch. 27 decrees for the nations and their false prophets, and symbolizes the death of his vision.[56]

The first three sections of ch. 28 indicate that the confrontation between Jeremiah and Hananiah takes place before a public audience (vv. 1, 5, 11), but the same is not said of Jeremiah's vindication in the final scene. The text emphasizes that the community is called to discern between prophets, but it is not concerned with the conclusions reached by the original audience. Rather, its goal is to instruct the reading community how to identify false prophecy and how to appropriate the message of the true prophet Jeremiah. Any prophecy that minimizes the impact of exile and the divine judgment that it represents leads to death. The way of life requires embracing disaster and learning to live faithfully amidst its pain and dislocation, as the next section (29:1–19) will spell out in more detail.

---

56. Lange, *Vom prophetischen Wort*, 243–44, 258; Allen, *Jeremiah*, 318. As Allen points out, elsewhere in the book the punitive death of an individual or a group is linked to the disaster that will befall the nation (11:23; 14:15–16; 20:6; 22:18–19; 36:30–31).

8

Section B'
A Letter Regarding Exiles and Non-Exiles (29:1-19)

CHAPTER 29 CONTINUES THE dispute at the heart of chs. 27-28, Jeremiah's conflict with false prophets over the length of Babylonian domination and exile.[1] Chapter 29 consists of three incidents (vv. 1-19, 20-23, 24-32) in which Jeremiah addresses persons consigned to exile in Babylon, confronts prophets who claim the exile will be short, and labels such false prophecy *sheqer*. Despite numerous rough spots, some perhaps a result of incorporating material from different letters (see 29:1, 25, 31), and some resulting from additions and redactional activity, the entire chapter forms a continuous narrative. However, a significant break occurs at v. 20, where the first letter has ended and Jeremiah begins to address a new message to the exiles. Thus, the chapter falls into two sections, B' (29:1-19) and A' (29:20-32), which correspond in the larger concentric unit to sections B (24:1-10) and A (23:9-40).

Section B' begins with Jeremiah writing a letter to the exiles of 598, telling them to prepare for a long stay and instructing them how to adapt to life in Babylon. This section builds on the previous one by explaining what it means to embrace the exile as YHWH's judgment. The use of a letter or written document represents an expansion of the authority of the true prophetic word. The word is portable, able to travel where

---

1. Brueggemann, *To Build, to Plant*, 38.

the prophet cannot.² If the word can travel geographically and address an audience that has never seen Jeremiah, then it must also be portable chronologically, able to address later generations of the faithful who hear the prophet through the written rather than spoken word.

Section B' opens with a long introduction describing how Jeremiah sends a letter to the elders of the exile, and to the priests, prophets, and all the people whom Nebuchadnezzar has exiled to Babylon (29:1-2). The similar chronology and persons mentioned in 29:1-2 and 24:1 signal that 29:1-19 should be read in light of Jeremiah's vision of the good and bad figs.³ The inclusion of prophets in the list of recipients both recalls the conflict of chs. 27-28 and points ahead to Jeremiah's fourfold critique of the *golah* prophets (29:8-9, 15, 21-23, 31-32). The LXX prepares the reader for this condemnation by already labeling them *pseudoprophetai* in 29:1. Jeremiah sends the letter via Elasah, son of Shaphan, and Gemariah, son of Hilkiah, who are Zedekiah's emissaries to Babylon (29:3), another example of how some members of the ruling elite are depicted as at least somewhat sympathetic to Jeremiah and the message of true prophecy. Jeremiah's letter has two main thrusts: the exile will be long and so the exiles must adapt to it, and there will be a time of YHWH's deliverance beyond the present calamity.

The first part of the letter emphasizes that the exiles must settle down for a long stay in Babylon by building houses and planting gardens (29:5), presumably in order to procure the material necessities of life. Jeremiah instructs them to marry and bear children to ensure that their numbers do not diminish (29:6). These exhortations cut in two opposing directions. On the one hand, they hold out the possibility of meaningful life in exile revolving around home, family, and economic productivity, and thereby encourage the exiles to seize the opportunities of their new setting to create healthy community.⁴ The exile can become more than just an experience of punishment. On the other hand, such advice to

---

2. Keown et al., *Jeremiah 26-52*, 69. See Stulman, *Jeremiah*, 28-29, for a helpful discussion of how the written word of Jeremiah acquires even greater authority than the spoken word.

3. Keown et al., *Jeremiah 26-52*, 69.

4. Hill demonstrates how 29:5-6 uses vocabulary employed elsewhere in the Old Testament to speak of the blessings of life in the promised land. This blurs the distinction between Babylon and Judah and suggests that living in exile can be like living in the homeland. Conversely, in the Second Temple period, when the community viewed itself as living in an unended exile, life in Judah could also be experienced as life in exile. See Hill, "'Your Exile Will Be Long,'" 150-52; Hill, *Friend or Foe?*, 147-50.

persons yearning for YHWH's intervention and a quick return to their homeland constitutes a message of judgment. Other prophets were predicting that Babylonian domination would be short-lived (27:16), and Hananiah even projects a period of two years (28:3, 11), implying that there is no need for the exiles to unpack their suitcases.[5]

Jeremiah's most remarkable exhortation is, "Seek the *shalom* of the city to which I have exiled you, and pray to YHWH on its behalf, for in its *shalom* is your *shalom*" (29:7). Jeremiah contradicts the root assumptions of the false prophets that the welfare of the exiles depends on Babylon's demise, in contrast calling the exiles to envision their own welfare as so closely linked to the welfare of Babylon that they actively seek the well-being of the enemy who has inflicted such enormous suffering on them. The people who are not worthy of Jeremiah's prayers (7:16; 11:14; 14:11) are now commanded to pray for their brutal oppressor. The radical nature of true prophecy shines through as Jeremiah undercuts central features of Israelite piety and faith, such as possession of the land and YHWH's defense of the sacred city and the nation. Traditionally, Jerusalem was the city associated with *shalom* (Gen. 14:18; Ps 76:3 [Heb.]; 122:6-8; 147:14; Isa 26:3; 52:7; 54:13; 66:12), the Hebrew consonants שׁלם even forming part of the city's name, יְרוּשָׁלַם, but Jeremiah insists that the exiles must find *shalom* by seeking the *shalom* of the enemy who will destroy Jerusalem. This admonition also constitutes a critique of the false prophets who are elsewhere associated with proclamation of *shalom* (23:17; 6:14; 8:11; 14:13; cf. Ezek 13:10, 16; Mic 3:5).[6]

Jeremiah's assertion that Babylon replaces Jerusalem as the place where the exiles may experience security and well-being blurs the distinction between the land of Judah and the land of exile, and calls the exiles to perceive Babylon as home.[7] Until this point Jeremiah has stressed YHWH's withdrawal of *shalom* from the community (4:10; 8:15; 12:12; 14:19; 15:5; 16:5), and so the offer of *shalom* in 29:7 marks the beginning

---

5. Smith points out how the issue in all of chs. 27–29 is how to be faithful and survive under foreign political domination. He claims that while other prophets counseled violent resistance to Babylon, Jeremiah's political strategy constituted a form of nonviolent social resistance. See Smith, *Religion of the Landless*, 135–37; and Smith, "Jeremiah as Prophet of Nonviolent Resistance," 104.

6. For a discussion of how the prophets were rooted in the *shalom* theology of the Jerusalem cult, see Sisson, "Jeremiah and the Jerusalem Conception of Peace."

7. For a more detailed discussion see Hill, *Friend or Foe?*, 147–52.

Section B'

of a new era[8] when embrace of exile can turn the tide from divine judgment to blessing. Because exile is at the heart of YHWH's plan for dealing with a faithless people, the community must accept the massive physical and spiritual dislocation of exile, but just such letting go of old realities makes possible new forms of community life that already stand under divine blessing.

Jeremiah's admonitions in chs. 27–29 to accept Babylonian domination may sound like passivity in the face of foreign oppression, but Jeremiah's stance is quite different than passive resignation. Babylon may be YHWH's agent of judgment, but exile and Babylonian domination will be temporary (24:5–7; 25:12–14; 27:7; 29:10–14), emphasized especially by the oracles in chs. 50–51 depicting Babylon's destruction. Babylon is ultimately a cruel and arrogant empire that will some day receive its just desserts. Jeremiah relativizes allegiance to Babylon and attachment to life there by encouraging the exiles to live in anticipation of the day when YHWH will destroy Babylon and restore them to their homeland. The advice in the letter to the exiles represents a particular strategy for community survival.[9] Prophets like Hananiah link the community's survival to survival of the nation, and so Judah as a nation-state must be rigorously defended. Jeremiah undercuts such nationalism and relativizes the significance of land, monarchy, temple, and political independence, and asserts that in the new post-587 world the community must learn to live in diaspora. Jeremiah counsels acceptance of Babylonian domination but he does not promote assimilation or passivity. He advises the exiles to build homes and plant gardens, presumably so that the community will thrive materially and economically. He counsels them to raise families so that the community will not die out. By stressing YHWH's future restoration of the exiles to their homeland, Jeremiah encourages them to maintain their unique identity as people of YHWH with a future not linked to Babylon. Jeremiah has repeatedly called for repentance, worshipping only YHWH and obeying *Torah*, which are all counter-cultural actions in the context of exile, intended to make possible the renewal and survival of a diasporic faith community that will maintain its distinctive identity in the challenging post-587 world.[10]

---

8. Plant, *Good Figs, Bad Figs*, 121, 127.

9. See the discussion by Smith, *The Religion of the Landless*, 132–37, who labels Jeremiah's strategy "nonviolent resistance."

10. Domeris, "When Metaphor Becomes Myth," 250–60, analyzes the use of "antilanguage" in the book of Jeremiah and the role it plays in creating an alternative

Concerning the Prophets

After instructing the exiles to seek the *shalom* of Babylon, Jeremiah admonishes them not to be deceived by the prophets and diviners in their midst who have not been sent by YHWH but are prophesying *sheqer* in his name (29:8-9). Numerous scholars observe that these verses are somewhat intrusive and have probably been added in order to introduce the conflict between true and false prophecy into the letter.[11] The position of the warning about false prophets immediately after Jeremiah has counseled the exiles to prepare for a long stay in Babylon characterizes these prophets as deceiving the community with assurances that Babylonian domination will be short-lived. Jeremiah accuses these exilic prophets of speaking *sheqer*, the same accusation he levels in chs. 27–28 at prophets who are encouraging resistance to Babylon (27:10, 15, 16; 28:15). The vocabulary in 29:8 of *prophets*, *diviners*, and *dreams* echoes the similar terms in 27:9 used to designate foreign intermediaries, and thereby smears the Jewish prophets in exile with the brush of paganism.[12] Warning the exiles not to heed false prophets portrays even the community in Babylon as tempted by the voice of false prophecy to minimize the massive break from pre-exilic life that exile represents.

In the first oracle of the letter Jeremiah counsels the exiles how to adapt to their situation (vv. 4–7), in the second he warns them about their prophets (vv. 8–9), and in the third he promises deliverance (vv. 10–14). However, this message of hope is not like that of the false prophets in that it accepts the judgment of exile, as is illustrated by how it begins: "When Babylon's seventy years are completed" (29:10). Seventy years is probably a symbolic expression for the fullness of time that divine judgment will last, and as such it holds together both judgment and hope.[13] On the one hand seventy years affirms that there will be a definite end to Babylonian oppression, while on the other hand it indicates that none of the current generation will experience that end. Against popular hopes that divine punishment can be avoided, Jeremiah asserts that exile represents an unavoidable and massive religious, social, and political dislocation that must be embraced. Against voices of despair, Jeremiah affirms that YHWH's gracious nature will ultimately ensure the restoration of a

---

religious and social "antisociety" that has clear boundaries and resists assimilation into the dominant society.

11. See for example Seidl, *Texte und Einheiten in Jeremia 27–29*, 139–40; Nicholson, *Preaching to the Exiles*, 98; Carroll, *Jeremiah*, 556.

12. Lange, *Vom prophetischen Wort*, 259.

13. Miller, "The Book of Jeremiah," 792.

chastised people. "'True prophecy' is the capacity to say the right thing at the right time, a capacity not exercised by the prophets of optimism nor by the voices of despair."[14]

Carroll claims that Jeremiah's promise of deliverance in 29:10–14 looks suspiciously like the message of Hananiah and the other false prophets so thoroughly condemned in the previous chapters, the only difference being timing.[15] Carroll is correct in observing this similarity but he minimizes the crucial significance of timing. The conflict between Jeremiah and the false prophets is not over YHWH's ultimate will for the people. In the end there will be *shalom*, but the issue is what will happen in the interim and how should the community live in this interim.

Israel's positive future is set in motion by YHWH's promise, "I will visit you and fulfill my word of good [אֶת־דְּבָרִי הַטּוֹב] concerning you to return you to this place" (29:10). The term *visit* (פקד) normally describes how YHWH "visits" punishment on someone, but in the future the community will experience a visitation of grace. God's promise to fulfill his "word of good" points outside the chapter to promises of restoration elsewhere in 23:9—29:32 and in the book as a whole, particularly 25:12–14, which foretells the defeat of Babylon after seventy years, and 24:6 (of the corresponding section B), which also describes God's restoration of the exiles as the "good" that he will do. The restoration promised in both ch. 24 and Jeremiah's letter has physical and spiritual dimensions. YHWH promises to return the exiles to their homeland, grant them *shalom* instead of disaster, give them a hopeful future (29:10–11), restore their fortunes, and gather them from all the places to which he has driven them (29:14). This physical restoration lies seventy years in the future, but the spiritual renewal is offered as a present possibility. "[When] you will call upon me and come and pray to me, I will heed you. [When] you will search for me you will find [me], if you seek me with all your heart. I will let you find me, declares YHWH, and I will restore your fortunes" (29:12–14).[16] YHWH's promise to heed the people when they pray stands in sharp contrast to earlier prohibitions that Jeremiah is not to pray for

14. Brueggemann, *A Commentary on Jeremiah*, 260.
15. Carroll, *Jeremiah*, 557.
16. Some translations preface 29:12 with the adverb "then," thereby suggesting that the spiritual renewal is conditional upon the physical restoration and will only occur after the seventy years (NRSV, RSV, NIV, KJV, NKJ). Since the Hebrew lacks the adverb, I prefer to follow other translations and commentators and read the succession of imperfect verbs as implying ongoing or habitual action.

the nation because it is destined for destruction (7:16; 11:14; 14:11). The renewed effectiveness of prayer indicates that the divine wrath has begun to lift and that the exiles can already experience a foretaste of the coming salvation.[17] YHWH's availability in exile is an act of grace that makes possible new forms of piety. Genuine faithfulness and meaningful relationship with God are possible even though the community is cut off from temple, cult, sacrifice, city, and land—the focus of piety and the expected channels of divine presence prior to 587.[18]

Jeremiah's announcement of salvation encourages a community coping with the challenging conditions of exile, but it also functions as a call to repentance. The faithful life in exile (as well as non-exile) relies on a paradoxical mixture of grace and human effort, passivity and action.[19] The new beginning in Israel's life only becomes possible as a result of God's merciful forgiveness and intervention. However, the invitation to seek YHWH and to pray summons the community to grasp the opportunity God offers for a new beginning in the divine–human relationship.[20] The invitation to wholeheartedly seek YHWH (vv. 12–13) actually constitutes a call to repentance and total reorientation, because seeking YHWH with all their hearts is precisely what the people of pre-exilic times failed to do as they worshipped other gods and refused to obey the *Torah*. Even when true prophecy announces salvation, in a roundabout way it still calls for repentance.

The promise of future deliverance is followed by a prediction of the terrible destruction of the community remaining in the land (29:16–19). This passage is lacking in the LXX, and many commentators recognize it as an addition to the MT based on 24:8–10. In chapter 2 of this book I argue that 29:16–19 was added in order to make section B' (29:1–19) parallel section B (24:1–10) more closely. As in 24:8–10, YHWH promises horrible punishment for the non-exiled king and people of Jerusalem that seems truly excessive. YHWH will afflict them with sword, famine, and pestilence, treat them like loathsome figs too rotten to be eaten, and make them a curse, reproach, and object of horror among all the nations. The existence of the community in the land indicates that divine

17. Macholz, "Jeremia in der Kontinuität der Prophetie," 318.

18. Numerous commentators emphasize Jeremiah's vision of a new way of maintaining the divine–human relationship. See Volz, *Jeremia*, 272–74; Weiser, *Jeremia*, 254–55; Jones, *Jeremiah*, 361, 365; Clements, *Jeremiah*, 173.

19. Miller, "The Book of Jeremiah," 759.

20. Albertz, *Israel in Exile*, 337, 438.

punishment of the nation is not yet complete, and so the effect of vv. 16–19 is to stress how thoroughly YHWH will complete this punishment and that the promised salvation will not arrive until judgment has run its course.[21]

Numerous scholars argue that 29:16–19 is a propaganda piece asserting the claims of the exilic community to represent the future of YHWH's people, in contrast to the non-exiles whom he utterly rejects.[22] Carroll sees the passage as a politically partisan document from the period of reconstruction promoting the interests of Jews who could trace their ancestry to the deportation of 598 over those who were never exiled or who were exiled later.[23] The origins of 29:16–19 may well lie in some ideological and sociological conflict, but this fact does not explain the meaning of these verses in their present literary context.

Jeremiah's letter is addressed to the deportees of 598 living in Babylon, but in 29:14 YHWH declares, "I will gather you from *all the peoples* and from *all the places to which I have banished you.*"[24] The recipients of God's deliverance are a much larger diaspora than just the first group of exiles to Babylon. The reason YHWH gives for the horrible punishment of the non-exiles is that he has persistently sent his servants the prophets, "but *you* did not listen" (29:19). The "you" being indicted here must designate the exiles since the letter is addressed to them. The mention of YHWH's servants the prophets recalls earlier indictments of the entire nation for not heeding the true prophets whom YHWH has persistently sent (25:4; 26:5). The *golah* also is included in the unfaithful community meriting punishment, illustrating that the completed text does not delineate as sharply between the exiles and non-exiles as might appear at first glance.

The current position of vv. 16–19 also blurs the line between the two groups. The larger passage would read more smoothly if vv. 16–19 had been inserted before and not after v. 15, which reads, "Because *you* have said, 'YHWH has raised up for us prophets in Babylon.'" This verse has experienced several changes in meaning and function. Originally,

---

21. Thompson, *Jeremiah*, 548.

22. Nicholson, *Jeremiah* 2:46–47; Seitz, *Theology in Conflict*, 212; Sharp, *Prophecy and Ideology in Jeremiah*, 109–10.

23. Carroll, *Jeremiah*, 562–63.

24. The LXX lacks 29:14, indicating that the MT emphasizes the future hope more than does the LXX, and gives greater attention to the broader diaspora and not just the *golah* in Babylon.

it probably followed Jeremiah's exhortation to the exiles not to listen to their prophets (29:8–9) and served to introduce his specific condemnation of three such prophets (29:21–32).[25] When editors added the promise of deliverance now found in 29:10–14,[26] v. 15 was separated from vv. 8–9 and marked an awkward change of topic, although it continued to provide an appropriate introduction to the critique of false prophets in vv. 21–32, which is still how it functions in the LXX. With the addition of vv. 16–19 in the MT, v. 15 no longer introduces vv. 21–32 and it becomes an awkward intrusion, because its reference to prophets in Babylon has little obvious connection to what precedes or follows. However, in the completed text of the MT, v. 15 now serves to connect vv. 16–19 to the rest of the section by providing a reason for YHWH's punishment of the Palestinian community.[27] This reason is that the *exiles* are heeding their false prophets in Babylon. The larger context has already indicated that false prophets consistently minimize the Babylonian threat and thereby encourage resistance to Babylon (27:9–10, 14–15, 16; 28:2–4, 10–11; 29:8–9). Because the exiles are following their optimistic prophets, YHWH will devastate those Jews remaining in the land (29:16–19). By virtue of its current position, v. 15 includes the exiles in the indictment of vv. 16–19. The hopes of these exiles, encouraged by false prophets, are tied to the continuation of the nation and a speedy return to it (27:16; 28:2–4, 11; 29:8–9). Thus, the destruction decreed for the non-exiles also constitutes a message of judgment for the exiles, because it dashes any dreams of returning soon to resume life in the homeland. There will be nothing worth returning to.

Another way in which the text links exiles and non-exiles is by attaching a final reason for the announcement of YHWH's horrible judgment upon the non-exiles: "because *they* [the non-exiles] did not heed my words, declares YHWH, when I persistently sent to *them* my servants the prophets, but *you* [the exiles] did not listen, declares YHWH" (29:19). The text is awkward and frequently emended by translators, but the pronouns here include both exiles and non-exiles in the indictment of refusing to heed the true prophets. Therefore, the thrust of 29:15–19 is not simply that the exiles stand under the grace of God while the non-exiles

---

25. See McKane, *A Critical and Exegetical Commentary*, 2:739.

26. For my arguments that 29:10–14 are an addition, see the discussion on p. 48 where sections B and B' are compared.

27. Keown et al., *Jeremiah 26–52*, 67.

stand under judgment. What is at stake is the community's response to true prophecy.

Whereas 29:16-19 may have originated as a partisan political claim, the text in its final form relativizes the partisan elements in several ways. One is by downplaying the sharp distinction between the exiles and non-exiles that is such a strong surface feature of the text. Both groups have refused to heed YHWH's prophets and stand under divine judgment, and YHWH's saving actions will restore a much larger diaspora than just the Babylonian *golah* of 598 (29:14). The completed text also downplays the partisan elements with its focus on the community's response to true and false prophecy, which becomes a more important issue than whether or not one belongs to the deportation of 598.

The longer discussion in chapter 4 about the symbolic meaning of exile in Jeremiah 24 also applies to 29:1-19. Because destruction and exile are YHWH's means of wiping the slate clean in order to rebuild on a new foundation, the community must accept exile and all that it symbolizes in terms of a massive break from pre-exilic existence. At the surface level this message stands in some tension with 27:12-15, where Jeremiah offers the non-exiles the possibility of ongoing life in the land if they accept the Babylonian yoke. As discussed previously, the possibility of escaping catastrophe is a "fiction" whereby the book of Jeremiah promotes various ways in which the community must respond to the events of 587, in this case by accepting Babylonian domination. The Palestinian community's horrific fate (29:16-18) indicates that no part of the nation can escape punishment and that clinging to Judah's pre-exilic world is futile. Because exile is central to the divine plan, it is there that hope for the future is most powerfully at work, and so it is the exiles who receive YHWH's promise of deliverance. Even though historically only a minority of Jews experienced a physical exile to Babylon, and even fewer ever returned, in the Second Temple period the story of exile and return became the normative story of Judaism, and the entire community was invited to think of itself as having been in exile.[28] The community even developed the concept of unended exile as a way to make sense of its ongoing hardships, and as a way to claim that the promises of restoration still testified to the faithfulness of God, even though their fulfillment was delayed. Thus, 29:1-19 is less concerned to spell out the fates of different sectors of the community than to provide an interpretation of exile. The

---

28. See Neusner, *Self-Fulfilling Prophecy*, 1-6.

excessive punishment of 29:16–18 is not only directed at one sociological group but functions as a warning to anyone who listens to false prophets, refuses to accept the reality of exile, and clings to Judah's pre-exilic world. YHWH offers deliverance not only to the deportees of 598, but to persons who identify with the story of exile, who heed the call of true prophecy to embrace exile as divine judgment, and who use the interim period as an opportunity to repent and seek YHWH with all their hearts.

9

Section A'

Condemnation of Specific False Prophets (29:20–32)

JEREMIAH'S INSTRUCTION TO THE exiles to hear a new word of YHWH (29:20) signals the beginning of both a new topic and a new section. There is no indication exactly where Jeremiah's letter to the exiles ends. By v. 24 the letter is clearly finished because the focus shifts to Shemaiah's response to it, but there is no other signal regarding the conclusion to the letter. The text is more interested in the content of Jeremiah's message than in preserving the contours of any specific letter. Whereas 29:1–19 focuses on how to live in exile, 29:20–32 focuses on Jeremiah's condemnation of three false exilic prophets. The larger editorial unit begins with a section condemning false prophets in general and predicting a horrible fate for them (23:9–40). It concludes with a shorter section outlining the offenses and resulting fate of three specific prophets who exemplify the kind of false prophecy condemned in a general way in 23:9–40. Both sections use similar vocabulary to depict some of the characteristics of false prophecy, and both prescribe a horrible fate for these prophets who pose such a threat to the community.

Concerning the Prophets

AHAB AND ZEDEKIAH (29:20-23)

Jeremiah calls the exiles to hear YHWH's judgment on the prophets Ahab and Zedekiah, who are prophesying *sheqer* in YHWH's name (29:21). The text says nothing specific about the message of these two prophets, but the larger context has already spelled out what prophesying *sheqer* involves (27:9-10, 14-15, 16; 28:2-4, 11, 15). Ahab and Zedekiah are two examples of those prophets in Babylon who lead the community astray with promises that Babylonian supremacy is temporary and that the exile will soon be over (cf. 29:8-9, 15). The accusation of prophesying *sheqer* also links Ahab and Zedekiah to the anonymous prophets of 23:9-40 who are repeatedly condemned for prophesying *sheqer* (23:14, 25, 26, 32, 32). Scholars frequently interpret the prediction that Nebuchadnezzar will execute Ahab and Zedekiah as evidence that the Babylonian authorities eliminated these prophets because of their seditious proclamation of the empire's imminent collapse.[1] At the historical level this explanation makes good sense, but in the text the fate of Ahab and Zedekiah serves as proof of their falseness, vindicates the contrasting message of Jeremiah, illustrates the miserable end of those who resist YHWH by refusing to submit to Babylon, and highlights the disastrous consequences of false prophecy. The curse that the exiles will derive from these two prophets, "May YHWH make you like Zedekiah and like Ahab whom the king of Babylon roasted in the fire" (29:22), disparages them even further and makes them a gruesome object lesson.

The first part of the oracle concerning Ahab and Zedekiah outlines their punishment (29:21-22) while the last part cites the reasons: "because they have acted disgracefully [עָשׂוּ נְבָלָה] in Israel, and committed adultery with the wives of their neighbors, and they spoke a word in my name *sheqer* which I did not command them" (29:23). The lack of detail regarding the specific actions or words of these prophets illustrates that the text has little interest in providing a realistic portrayal of them but seeks to condemn them only in a stereotypical manner. Ahab and Zedekiah are charged with announcing a false message without having been divinely commissioned. Given the meaning of *sheqer* in the larger context it seems that these prophets too are denounced for contradicting the word of Jeremiah that the exile will be long. The accusation of personal immorality is somewhat unique in 23:9—29:32 and appears only in sections A

---

1. Overholt, *The Threat of Falsehood*, 46; Clements, *Jeremiah*, 172; Roberts, "Prophets and Kings," 342.

and A' (cf. 23:10–11, 14–15). The term "outrage/folly" (נְבָלָה) stands here in connection with adultery, indicating that it probably designates some type of sexual offense as it frequently does elsewhere (Gen 34:7; Deut 22:21; Judg 19:23, 24; 20:6, 10; 2 Sam 13:12), or perhaps the adultery itself is the "outrage/folly." To accuse Ahab and Zedekiah of outrage/folly is a most serious matter, because it is such a heinous offense that whether or not it is sexual, the consequences for the individual and/or community are usually disastrous (Gen 34:7ff.; Deut 22:21; Josh 7:15ff.; Judg 19:23ff.; 20:6, 10ff.; 1 Sam 25:25ff.; 2 Sam 13:12ff.; Isa 9:16 [Heb.]).[2]

Jeremiah also accuses Ahab and Zedekiah of committing adultery, one of the sins condemned most harshly in the *Torah* and elsewhere (Exod 20:14; Lev 18:20; 20:10; Deut 5:18; 22:22). This parallels the association of false prophets and adultery in 23:10, 14, and may well have been triggered by these earlier passages, since the accusation of adultery has little to do with the core of the conflict between true and false prophecy in 29:20–32.[3] In 23:9—29:32 the true prophet is portrayed as standing in the tradition of Moses, summoning the people to repent and obey the *Torah* (25:4–6; 26:4–5). The charge of adultery invalidates a prophet and his message because a prophet cannot promote the *Torah* if his personal life violates one of its fundamental tenets. The condemnation of Ahab and Zedekiah assumes that prophecy is more than a matter of speaking the correct message, but that the message and the messenger form a single entity that must promote faithfulness to YHWH and his will. Thus, congruence of a prophet's lifestyle with the teachings of *Torah* is a fundamental criterion for distinguishing between true and false prophecy.[4]

The text treats Ahab and Zedekiah as stereotypical models of disobedience whose gruesome death is a verdict on their message and lifestyle, thereby confirming Jeremiah as a faithful witness to YHWH's word and will. The punishment of these prophets is so severe because the offense and its consequences are so grave. In 23:9—29:32 the prophets are blamed for bringing doom upon the nation by undermining the moral and spiritual sensitivity of the people and by providing political advice

---

2. For a fuller discussion see Holladay, *Jeremiah 2*, 143–44.

3. See McKane, *A Critical and Exegetical Commentary*, 2:740; Lange, *Vom prophetischen Wort*, 252–53.

4. As discussed in connection with 23:13–15, Moberly sees morality as the primary criterion that the Bible as a whole uses for discerning between the truth and falsehood of a prophet or anyone else who claims to speak for God. See *Prophecy and Discernment*.

that leads to catastrophic consequences. The community is depicted as vulnerable to false prophets who must be eliminated so as to cut the destructive cancer out of the community's midst. In chs. 28–29 YHWH sentences to death Hananiah, Ahab, Zedekiah, and Shemaiah, all four of the specific prophets whom Jeremiah encounters, a rather dire warning to avoid any contact with the *sheqer* of false prophecy.

There is tension in how 23:9—29:32 depicts the power of false prophecy. On one hand the false prophets are extremely weak. For the most part the stereotypical presentation leaves them nameless and faceless. They have no access to YHWH and his word, speak only ineffective words that arise from their own hearts, and are incapable of interceding effectively for the temple utensils and preventing the final destruction of the nation. The harsh judgment of YHWH consistently hangs over their heads, and all four specific false prophets mentioned in 23:9—29:32 meet an untimely end. In contrast, Jeremiah is a colossus of strength, closely in touch with YHWH, whose word he faithfully delivers in the face of hardship and opposition. The word Jeremiah speaks is powerful because it comes from YHWH and corresponds to the reality of God's plans for history. Despite threats to his life Jeremiah survives, an indication that the true prophetic word will also survive the challenges it faces.

While false prophecy is portrayed as extremely weak, on the other hand it is also depicted as powerful. False prophets infect the nation with wickedness (23:10–11), make the people worship Baal (23:13, 27), destroy the moral fabric of the community (23:14–15), prevent repentance with their rosy picture of the nation's moral condition (23:14, 22), and generally lead the people astray (23:16, 32). The prophetic proclamation of *sheqer* promotes a naive optimism that leads to suicidal policies in the face of the Babylonian threat (27:9–10, 14–15, 16–17; 28:2–4, 11). So powerful are these prophets that the text shoulders them with much of the blame for the destruction of the nation. The tension in the portrayal of false prophecy reveals the text's rhetorical goals. On one hand the reader should avoid false prophecy because it is weak, ineffectual, and leads to death. On the other hand the reader should avoid false prophecy because it has the power to promote apostasy, immorality, and a false understanding of reality, all of which also lead to death.

Section A'

SHEMAIAH (29:24-32)

In 29:24-32 Jeremiah engages in a long-distance conflict with Shemaiah the Nehalamite/dreamer (הַנֶּחֱלָמִי), a prophet among the exiles. A construction like הַנֶּחֱלָמִי normally designates place of origin, but the otherwise unknown location "Nehalam" sounds suspiciously like a version of the word "to dream" (חָלַם) and may represent an attempt to portray Shemaiah as a prophet with false dreams in the vein of 23:25-32; 27:9, and 29:8.[5] Shemaiah's specific offense is that he has dispatched a letter[6] to the priests and people of Jerusalem, in which he scolds the priest Zephaniah for not exercising the responsibility that comes with his leadership position in the temple to silence any crazy person (i.e., Jeremiah) who pretends/claims to prophesy (לְכָל־אִישׁ מְשֻׁגָּע וּמִתְנַבֵּא) (29:25-27). Jeremiah poses a threat because he has sent a letter to the exiles stating that their exile will be long and so they should build homes and plant gardens (v. 28). The conflict between true and false prophecy continues to center on the length of the exile and whether or not the exiles should accept Babylonian domination. Shemaiah is depicted in stereotypical form as a concrete example of one of those prophets in exile whom Jeremiah warns about because they refuse to embrace exile as divine judgment (29:8-9, 15). Not only does Shemaiah contradict the message of Jeremiah, he actively seeks to silence the voice of true prophecy.

The priest Zephaniah reads Shemaiah's letter to Jeremiah, which becomes the occasion for YHWH to command Jeremiah to send another message to the *golah* community (29:29-31). This message consists of an invective-threat oracle against Shemaiah that charges him with two offenses: prophesying without being sent, and making the exiles trust in *sheqer* (29:31). These are the same accusations leveled earlier against Hananiah (28:15), and so Shemaiah functions in ch. 29 as Hananiah did in ch. 28, as a Jeremiah anti-type who appeals to the priesthood and people of Jerusalem, leading the community astray with assurances of deliverance.[7] Prophesying without being sent (cf. 23:21, 32) and prophesying

---

5. Lange, *Vom prophetischen Wort*, 256.

6. There is some ambiguity about whether Shemaiah has written several letters or just one. Verse 25 mentions "letters" while v. 29 speaks of "this letter." The LXX has no reference to letters at all in v. 25. Since the meaning of the passage does not hinge on the number of letters, and since it makes a little more sense to think of Shemaiah writing only a single letter, my discussion will assume that there is only one.

7. Leuchter, *The Polemics of Exile*, 46-47.

sheqer (cf. 23:14, 25, 26, 32, 32) are also prominent offenses in section A, indicating that Shemaiah is also a specific example of the false prophets condemned in a general way in 23:9–40.

Shemaiah's fate will be worse than death, in that neither he nor any of his descendants will live to see "the good" that YHWH will do for the people, because Shemaiah "has uttered/urged disloyalty to YHWH [כִּֽי־סָרָ֤ה דִבֶּר֙ עַל־יְהוָ֔ה]" (29:32). This is identical to the verdict on Hananiah (28:16), indicating again how Shemaiah is Hananiah's counterpart among the exiles. As discussed in chapter 8, the accusation that Shemaiah and Hananiah have urged disloyalty to YHWH is lacking in the LXX and is probably an addition to the MT based on Deut 13:2–6 [Heb.], where Moses instructs the community that they must not heed a prophet or dreamer who encourages them to follow other gods, even if the prophet can perform impressive signs. Instead, such a prophet must be killed, "because he has urged apostasy against YHWH your God [כִּֽי־דִבֶּר־סָרָ֜ה עַל־יְהוָ֣ה אֱלֹהֵיכֶ֗ם]" (13:6). Painting Shemaiah with the same brush as the prophets of Deut 13:2–6 indicates that uttering false assurances of divine protection is just as harmful as urging the worship of other gods because both are forms of disloyalty to YHWH.

Section A' and the entire editorial unit end on a note of hope but also of warning. The reader is reminded of "the good" that YHWH will do for the community, referring back to the promises of restoration in 24:4–7 and 29:10–14, which are also designated "the good" that YHWH will do (24:5, 6; 29:10). But Shemaiah and his descendants will enjoy no share of this salvation, because he has sought to silence the voice of true prophecy. Shemaiah and his family serve as object lessons. There is hope for the future, but not for those who trust in *sheqer*, who refuse to embrace divine judgment, who disregard the message of true prophecy, and who are disloyal to YHWH.

Conclusion

JEREMIAH 23:9—29:32 CONSTITUTES A single editorial unit bearing the title, "Concerning the Prophets" (23:9). The concentric structure illustrates that the material in these chapters is not a haphazard collection, as is often suggested, but that 23:9—29:32 is a carefully organized block of text reflecting on the nature of true and false prophecy and the conflict between them. Recognizing the structure has significant hermeneutical implications, because it encourages the interpreter to read the diverse materials in relation to each other, attentive to how the smaller units contribute to the presentation of true and false prophecy in the whole. Tensions need not lead to diachronic dissecting of the text but can pose fruitful questions about the purpose these tensions serve in the completed whole. The concentric structure creates a new literary context for materials in such a way that the earlier meaning of older sources is sometimes changed in significant ways.

Most of the scholarly literature on true and false prophecy in ancient Israel mines the biblical text for information that can illuminate the historical, religious, and social context that gave rise to the text. Given the limited amount of data available, the cumulative results of such investigations are truly impressive. Somewhat lost in the conversation has been attention to the actual biblical portrayal of true and false prophecy, even though this portrayal is so powerful that it sometimes exercises an unconscious influence over scholars (see the discussion of von Rad, Quell, and Crenshaw in chapter 1). My goal has been to describe sympathetically the presentation of true and false prophecy in the largest block of biblical text to focus on the issue. I have not attempted to systematically engage this presentation theologically, nor to suggest which aspects of this portrayal contemporary faith communities can helpfully appropriate and which aspects might be problematic. This important task will have to wait for other studies.[1]

In summing up the presentation of true and false prophecy in 23:9—29:32 it is helpful to view these chapters in light of the nature and purpose of the book of Jeremiah as a whole. O'Connor observes, "Disaster and its survival are its chief subjects. Disaster produces the book. Every poem, narrative, or sermon relates to disaster in one way or another, either announcing it, explaining it, or offering hope for living through it."[2] This disaster entails massive physical losses of life, possessions, infrastructure, and land, but it also involves the collapse of an entire world of meaning and belief that gave order and structure to Judah's pre-587 existence.[3] If the community is to survive it will have to let go of old realities and embrace a new self-understanding, a new worldview, and a new set of social and religious practices. Various sections of the book of Jeremiah engage this collapse of Judah's world from different perspectives. For example, 21:11—23:8 focuses on the nation's kingship, chs. 30–32 speak words of hope into the disaster, and 23:9—29:32 responds to disaster through the lens of true and false prophecy. O'Connor notes how a massive catastrophe may exceed the ability of a community to understand its reality, articulate its pain, and cope with the crisis. By repeatedly revisiting the disaster of 587 the book of Jeremiah helps the community reenter the loss symbolically, and thereby name and express its grief, understand and give meaning to the crisis, and move forward with some level of faith in YHWH and confidence in the future.[4]

In the midst of a catastrophe that shattered the structures of meaning, the book of Jeremiah provides a narrative giving meaning and shape to the chaotic events. This narrative explains that disaster engulfed the nation because it had refused to worship only YHWH and follow his *Torah*, despite the true prophet Jeremiah's endless warnings and calls for repentance. By diagnosing the reasons for 587 and insisting that events could have unfolded very differently, the book also holds out a hopeful future to the community. The repeated possibility of repentance and

---

1. For a very preliminary and partial attempt to begin this task, see my essay, "The LORD Has Truly Sent the Prophet." See also Brenneman, *Canons in Conflict*, and especially Moberly, *Prophecy and Discernment*.

2. O'Connor, "Surviving Disaster in the Book of Jeremiah," 369.

3. For a description of this "cosmic crumbling" see Stulman, *Jeremiah*, 1–2; Stulman, "Conflicting Paths to Hope," 44–48.

4. O'Connor, "Jeremiah's 'Prophetic Imagination,'" 60–61.

YHWH's offer to save Jerusalem, even at the last moment, testify to God's plan to allow a faithful remnant to survive.[5] Promises of restoration are scattered throughout the book (including 23:9—29:32) like oases in a desert of judgment, and chs. 30–33 contain a series of sustained promises of deliverance. The book assures the community of a positive future if it is willing to seize the opportunity to confess its sin, repent, and radically reorient its life.

It is common to point out that both individuals and communities live by some meta-narrative that shapes scattered and particular life experiences into some kind of coherent whole that provides meaning, purpose, a sense of identity, fundamental life convictions, and guidance for what shape life should take. The Babylonian destruction of Judah shattered the community's self-understanding and therefore created the need for a new meta-narrative that could make sense of the catastrophe and also point toward a way through the disaster. Smith-Christopher notes that refugee and disaster studies document how devastated communities commonly forge new histories (narratives) in order to enable them to reconstruct a meaningful new identity in light of their trauma.[6]

The book of Jeremiah is an exercise in meaning-making and offering possibilities for new life in the future. It re-narrates the story of Judah, rejecting some parts of the previous narrative while building on others. Jeremiah is deeply rooted in Israel's traditions of election, covenant-making, *Torah*, and worship of a gracious God, all of which stand front and center in the new narrative. However, other elements of Judah's narrative, most notably the Royal–Zion traditions as promoted by the Jerusalem establishment including the false prophets, are found grossly wanting and are largely rejected. As already mentioned, 23:9—29:32 contributes to the book of Jeremiah's re-narration by telling the story through the lens of true and false prophecy.

At the heart of the new narrative in the book of Jeremiah and also in 23:9—29:32 is blame, or to put it another way, taking responsibility for the disaster. Smith-Christopher observes that self-blame is a common strategy used by traumatized communities to make sense of their disaster.[7] In 23:9—29:32 this self-blame is refracted through the lens of true

---

5. Perdue, *The Collapse of History*, 257.

6. Smith-Christopher, *A Biblical Theology of Exile*, 79–80.

7. Ibid., 80–81. For similar descriptions of the role of self-blame in coming to terms with disaster, see O'Connor, "Jeremiah's 'Prophetic Imagination,'" 61–62; O'Connor, "The Book of Jeremiah," 85–86; Stulman, "Jeremiah as a Messenger of Hope in Crisis," 12.

and false prophecy. Catastrophe befell the nation because it persistently refused to heed the voices of Jeremiah and YHWH's other servants the prophets but instead listened to its false prophets, who were unconcerned about the moral fiber of the community, who failed to call for repentance, who promoted worship of Baal, and who misled the community with assurances of well-being in the face of disaster.

From a contemporary perspective, sensitized as we are to the dangers of blaming the victim, such a narrative seems unhealthy and hugely problematic. Not only does it oversimplify the complexities of history, but it shifts the blame onto the victim and overlooks the cruel and oppressive actions of the Babylonians, thereby promoting the view that suffering people deserve their suffering. Despite the serious problems with a narrative of self-blame, it is worth understanding how it helps a victimized people cope with disaster. Jeremiah's explanation leaves certain core convictions about YHWH intact. Despite what has happened to his people, YHWH is not a weakling but continues to be the sovereign Lord of the universe who controls the destinies of the nations. YHWH continues to be a God of grace who is ultimately favorably disposed toward Israel, but because the community proved so obdurate he had little option but to summon the Babylonians to wipe the slate clean so that he could rebuild the community on the basis of a faithful remnant willing to heed the prophetic summons to faithful living. In the face of chaos and upheaval, Jeremiah's interpretation of disaster allows the community to believe that history is not capricious but that it is both meaningful and predictable.[8] YHWH is a just God who mediates the connection between the actions of his people and the predictable consequences. Thus, the narrative of self-blame functions as a theodicy that provides an explanation for the catastrophe without challenging either the power or goodness of YHWH.

A narrative of blame does not necessarily destroy the self-confidence of a community but can actually help it cope with disaster and move forward with some confidence.[9] If history is totally chaotic and disaster completely the fault of the evil empire, then life is truly precarious, but if history is controlled by a just and reliable God then people have some sense of control over their destiny. Restoration is a much more real possibility if the disaster is due to one's own sin than if it is entirely due

---

8. Stulman, "Jeremiah as a Messenger of Hope in Crisis," 12.
9. See O'Connor, "Surviving Disaster in the Book of Jeremiah," 371–72.

to the power of Babylon's armies, because one can repent of one's sin.[10] The narrative of blame ultimately functions as a call to repentance and moral vigilance, as well as a summons to reconstruct community life on a new foundation.[11] The narrative of 23:9—29:32 assures the community of its survival and imagines the contours of its faithful life in the new post-587 world.[12] The community must heed the true prophet Jeremiah and accept destruction and exile as deserved judgment and as YHWH's short-term plan for them. They must use the interim period of exile as an opportunity to repent and to reorient their lives around exclusive loyalty to YHWH, careful adherence to *Torah*, and avoidance of anything to do with false prophecy.

Much of the scholarship on true and false prophecy has concentrated on examining criteria for discerning between the two. Despite the emphasis in 23:9—29:32 on the critical importance of distinguishing between true and false prophecy, the issue of criteria plays only a minor role. Instead of providing a list of criteria the text approaches the matter somewhat indirectly by establishing paradigms of both true and false prophecy that highlight the central features of each.[13] The text recognizes that during Jeremiah's time the community had great difficulty in distinguishing between true and false, with devastating consequences, but the text does not invite the reader to relive the historical situation of pre-exilic Israel and apply various criteria in order to discern the voice of true prophecy. Rather, the text establishes paradigms that leave no doubt about the nature of true and false prophecy and which prophets represent which. These paradigms serve two important functions. First, they seek to assist the community of faith in discerning the true and the false prophetic word. Future readers can compare the prophets and prophetic

---

10. Smith-Christopher, *A Biblical Theology of Exile*, 81.

11. Ibid., 120–23. Smith-Christopher points out that in some situations modern societies would do well to accept some self-blame. Accepting blame can be an act of honesty and can lead to taking responsibility for the consequences of past sins, such as the dispossession of the indigenous peoples of North America, or the enslavement of African Americans, or various acts of genocide committed by different peoples around the world.

12. For more on how the book of Jeremiah imagines an alternative world, see Brueggemann, *A Commentary on Jeremiah*, 16–18.

13. For a more detailed discussion of paradigms and how they function with respect to biblical materials see Janzen, *Old Testament Ethics*, 26–30; and Wright, *Old Testament Ethics for the People of God*, 62–73. For a discussion of Jeremiah's life as a paradigm, see Polk, *The Prophetic Persona*, 170–74.

claims of their own day with both the true prophet Jeremiah and his message, as well as with the false prophets who opposed him.[14] More importantly, the paradigms indicate how the community is to appropriate the message of true prophecy. True prophecy constitutes a call to acceptance of exile and divine judgment, to moral self-evaluation, to repentance, to exclusive worship of YHWH, and to obedience to *Torah*.

The critique of false prophets for a variety of offenses establishes a paradigm of false prophecy and warns against any association with such prophecy. The distinguishing marks of false prophets include personal immorality (23:10–11, 14–15; 29:23), promoting paganism (23:13, 27), encouraging immorality among the people by failing to call for repentance (23:14, 17, 22, 32; 28:16; 29:32), and attempting to silence the voice of true prophecy (26:8–9, 11; 29:24–32). The false prophets are discredited further by stressing that they lack both divine revelation and divine mandate to prophesy (23:16, 21, 32; 27:15; 28:15; 29:9, 23, 31). In 28:15 Jeremiah announces to Hananiah, "You have made this people trust in *sheqer*." Of all the accusations leveled against the false prophets, promoting *sheqer* is the most frequent and reprehensible (23:14, 25, 26, 32, 32; 27:10, 14, 15, 16; 28:15; 29:9, 21, 23, 29). The prophets gloss over the people's sins and promise them well-being when YHWH's judgment lurks at the door. In this way the prophets contribute to complacency and prevent repentance, the only course of action that can avert catastrophe. One reason the false prophets are condemned so harshly is because their proclamation of *sheqer* has had such devastating consequences, and so the community must forever be on guard lest history repeat itself.

In one sense the issue of criteria for distinguishing between true and false prophecy hardly comes into play in 23:9—29:32, because the text begins with the assumption that Jeremiah is the paradigmatic true prophet and so whatever he says is by definition true. The corollary is that those prophets who oppose him are automatically false. Because Jeremiah is the true prophet par excellence, the text seeks to strengthen his credibility in the eyes of the reader as a way of asserting that his word is authoritative for the community of faith in an ongoing way. The text undergirds Jeremiah's authority by portraying him as the quintessential true prophet who is close to YHWH and proclaims only what he is commanded to speak, who prophecies courageously in the face of persecution, whose insights into YHWH's plans for history allow him to accurately foretell

---

14. See Wolff, "How Can We Recognize False Prophets?" 73.

the future, and whose call for repentance and adherence to *Torah* points the way to deliverance and blessing. The text also enhances Jeremiah's authority by setting up the false prophets as a foil and laying upon them much of the blame for the disaster of 587.

Jeremiah is not the lone true prophet. YHWH has persistently sent his servants the prophets to urge repentance and obedience to the divine will (25:4–6; 26:4–6; 29:19). Unfortunately, as each of these texts stresses, the history of true prophecy has also been the history of rejection of true prophecy. Things are not much different in Jeremiah's day, illustrated in ch. 26 by the sad fate of Uriah and the attempt to execute Jeremiah, although the elders' appeal to the memory of Hezekiah's enthusiastic response to Micah's prophecy serves as a positive counter-example. The history of true prophecy is a history of judgment prophecy. Micah proclaims the destruction of Zion, Jeremiah's dominant tone is judgment, and he specifically tells Hananiah that the prophets of old announced "war, disaster, and pestilence" and that prophecies of salvation must await the test of fulfillment before they can be reckoned as genuine (28:8–9). Ironically, however, prophecies of death and destruction can lead to salvation, whereas salvation prophecy at the wrong time leads to death and destruction because it distorts reality and thereby leads to catastrophe. The Micah story that stands at the center of the concentric structure demonstrates the positive potential of judgment prophecy to inspire a heartfelt repentance that leads YHWH to renounce judgment.

The Micah story also illustrates the significance of "canonical" prophecy. Micah's prophesy predates the historical context of Jeremiah 26 by more than a hundred years, yet his words are directly applicable to Jeremiah's time. Micah is a canonical prophet whose message never loses its power or relevance. The depiction of Jeremiah as the quintessential true prophet represents a similar claim for his message. The emphasis on YHWH's servants the prophets and on Micah and Jeremiah as canonical prophets highlights how the words of true prophets from the past constitute the words of YHWH that speak anew to every generation of the faithful.

As noted above, 23:9—29:32 participates in a larger narrative that seeks to explain and make sense of the destruction of the nation. The conflict between Jeremiah and the false prophets in 23:9—29:32 centers on the Babylonian threat and how to respond to it. The false prophets minimize the threat, declare that exile is but a temporary setback, and urge resistance. They are not willing to relinquish their attachment to

Judah's pre-exilic world, its institutions, religious ideology, and structures of meaning. Jeremiah declares that Judah's pre-exilic world has been shattered and that the only way forward is to embrace this painful reality as divine judgment, make the most of a difficult situation in exile, and use the interim period as an opportunity to reconstitute the community on a new foundation. The emphasis on the exiles as the group that forms the nucleus of God's future restored community indicates that while exile represents judgment, embracing this reality also allows exile to become a new opportunity for deliverance. Already now the community can experience a foretaste of this deliverance, because YHWH is favorably disposed toward them in their suffering. If they pray and turn to him with their whole heart then he will once again make himself accessible (29:12–14). The *shalom* that YHWH has previously withdrawn from the nation is offered to the exiles if they are willing to seek the *shalom* of Babylon (29:7).

Given that 23:9—29:32 is preoccupied with explaining the destruction of the nation and articulating a vision for living in light of the calamity, it is significant that none of the material in these chapters is dated to or explicitly deals with events after the destruction of Jerusalem, even though other parts of the book portray Jeremiah as being quite active after 587 (chs. 39–44). Setting the material "between the times," after YHWH has decreed judgment but before this judgment is fully actualized, adds existential urgency to the text. Jeremiah's announcements of catastrophe and the first deportation of exiles in 598 raise the possibility of a disastrous end for Jerusalem and the nation. If most or some of the material in 23:9—29:32 were set after the destruction of Jerusalem, then all it could do would be to look back and explain what went wrong. In its present form the material maintains the "fiction" that the fate of the people still hangs in the balance and that their future is to some extent in their own hands. The effect is similar to what von Rad has observed about the book of Deuteronomy.[15] Deuteronomy, probably compiled some time in the seventh (or sixth) century, leaps over centuries of Israelite history and "pretends" that Israel is still camped in the land of Moab, poised to cross the Jordan. Deuteronomy invites the implied readers to imagine that they are once again preparing to enter the promised land, and they are granted a new opportunity to be faithful and claim the gift of the land and the blessings that accompany it. If, however, they are unfaithful,

---

15. See von Rad, *Old Testament Theology*, 1:223, 231.

then they must expect the curses of the covenant. Jeremiah 23:9—29:32 takes post-587 Israelites back to the period between the times, when the threat of judgment hangs over their heads but they still have an opportunity to repent and avert catastrophe. Judgment and well-being, life and death hang in the balance, and everything depends on the community's choices. The great enemy is complacency and a false sense of security fostered by prophets who proclaim *shalom* irrespective of the moral state of the nation. The words of Jeremiah, Micah, and the other true prophets are an ongoing reminder that only repentance and faithfulness to *Torah* lead to life, and that choosing this way of life is an ever-present option even in the face of deepest disaster.

Bibliography

Ackroyd, Peter R. *Exile and Restoration: A Study of Hebrew Thought of the Sixth Century B.C.* OTL. Philadelphia: Westminster, 1968.
———. *Israel under Babylon and Persia.* Oxford: Oxford University Press, 1970.
———. "The Temple Vessels—A Continuity Theme." In *Studies in the Religion of Ancient Israel*, 166–81. VTSup 23. Leiden: Brill, 1972.
Aejmelaeus, Anneli. "Jeremiah at the Turning-Point of History: The Function of Jer. XXV 1–14 in the Book of Jeremiah." *VT* 52 (2002) 459–82.
———. "'Nebuchadnezzar, My Servant': Redaction History and Textual Development in Jer 27." In *Interpreting Translation: Studies on the LXX and Ezekiel in Honour of Johan Lust*, edited by F. García Martínez and M. Vervenne, 1–18. BETL 192. Leuven: Leuven University Press, 2005.
Albertz, Rainer. *A History of Israelite Religion in the Old Testament Period.* Translated by John Bowden. 2 vols. OTL. Louisville: Westminster John Knox, 1994.
———. *Israel in Exile: The History and Literature of the Sixth Century B.C.E.* Translated by David Green. Studies in Biblical Literature 3. Atlanta: Society of Biblical Literature, 2003.
Alden, Robert L. "Chiastic Psalms: A Study in the Mechanics of Semitic Poetry in Psalms 1–50." *JETS* 17 (1974) 11–28.
Allen, Leslie C. *Jeremiah: A Commentary.* OTL. Louisville: Westminster John Knox, 2008.
Amaru, Betsy Halpern. "The Killing of the Prophets: Unraveling a Midrash." *HUCA* 54 (1983) 153–80.
Applegate, John. "Jeremiah and the Seventy Years in the Hebrew Bible: Inner-Biblical Reflections on the Prophet and His Prophecy." In *The Book of Jeremiah and Its Reception*, edited by A. H. W. Curtis and T. Römer, 91–110. BETL 128. Leuven: Leuven University Press, 1997.
Auld, A. Graeme. "Prophets and Prophecy in Jeremiah and Kings." *ZAW* 96 (1984) 66–82.
Baltzer, Klaus. *Die Biographie der Propheten.* Neukirchen-Vluyn: Neukirchener, 1975.
Bar-Efrat, Shimon. "Some Observations on the Analysis of Structure in Biblical Narrative." *VT* 30 (1980) 154–73.
Barton, John. *Oracles of God: Perceptions of Ancient Prophecy in Israel after the Exile.* New York: Oxford University Press, 1986.
Berlin, Adele. "Jeremiah 29:5–7: A Deuteronomic Allusion." *HAR* 8 (1984) 3–11.

Bibliography

Berquist, Jon L. *Judaism in Persia's Shadow: A Social and Historical Approach.* 1995. Reprinted, Eugene, OR: Wipf & Stock, 2003.

———. "Prophetic Legitimation in Jeremiah." *VT* 39 (1989) 129–39.

Berridge, John Maclennan. *Prophet, People, and the Word of Yahweh: An Examination of Form and Content in the Proclamation of the Prophet Jeremiah.* Basel Studies of Theology 4. Zurich: EVZ, 1970.

Blackwood, Andrew W., Jr. *Commentary on Jeremiah: The Word, the Words, and the World.* Waco, TX: Word, 1977.

Blank, Sheldon H. *Jeremiah: Man and Prophet.* Cincinnati: Hebrew Union College Press, 1961.

———. "'Of a Truth the Lord Hath Sent Me': An Inquiry into the Source of the Prophet's Authority." In *Interpreting the Prophetic Tradition: The Goldenson Lectures 1955–1966,* edited by Harry M. Orlinsky, 1–19. Library of Biblical Studies. New York: Ktav, 1969.

———. "The Prophet as Paradigm." In *Essays in Old Testament Ethics,* edited by James L. Crenshaw and John T. Willis, 111–30. New York: Ktav, 1974.

Blenkinsopp, Joseph. *A History of Prophecy in Israel.* Philadelphia: Westminster, 1983.

———. *Prophecy and Canon: A Contribution to the Study of Jewish Origins.* Studies in Judaism and Christianity in Antiquity 3. Notre Dame: University of Notre Dame Press, 1977.

Boadt, Lawrence. *Jeremiah 1–25.* Old Testament Message 9. Wilmington, DE: Glazier, 1982.

———. *Jeremiah 26–52, Habakkuk, Zephaniah, Nahum.* Old Testament Message 10. Wilmington, DE: Glazier, 1982.

Bracke, John M. *Jeremiah 1–29.* Westminster Bible Companion. Louisville: Westminster John Knox, 2000.

Breck, John. "Biblical Chiasmus: Exploring Structure for Meaning." *BTB* 17 (1987) 70–74.

Brenneman, James E. *Canons in Conflict: Negotiating Texts in True and False Prophecy.* New York: Oxford University Press, 1997.

Breuer, Joseph. *The Book of Jeremiah: Translation and Commentary.* New York: Feldheim, 1988.

Bright, John. *Jeremiah.* AB 21. Garden City, NY: Doubleday, 1965.

Brueggemann, Walter. "The Book of Jeremiah: Portrait of the Prophet." *Int* 37 (1983) 130–45.

———. *A Commentary on Jeremiah: Exile and Homecoming.* Grand Rapids: Eerdmans, 1998.

———. "An Ending That Does Not End: The Book of Jeremiah." In *Postmodern Interpretations of the Bible: A Reader,* edited by A. K. M. Adam, 117–28. St. Louis: Chalice, 2001.

———. "Meditation upon the Abyss: The Book of Jeremiah." *WW* 22 (2002) 340–50.

———. "Next Steps in Jeremiah Studies?" In *Troubling Jeremiah,* edited by A. R. Pete Diamond et al., 404–22. JSOTSup 260. Sheffield: Sheffield Academic, 1999.

———. *The Theology of the Book of Jeremiah.* Old Testament Theology. Cambridge: Cambridge University Press, 2007.

———. *To Build, to Plant: A Commentary on Jeremiah 26–52.* International Theological Commentary. Grand Rapids: Eerdmans, 1991.

———. *To Pluck Up, to Tear Down: A Commentary on the Book of Jeremiah 1–25*. International Theological Commentary. Grand Rapids: Eerdmans, 1988.
Buber, Martin. "False Prophets (Jeremiah 28)." In *Biblical Humanism: Eighteen Studies*, edited by Nahum N. Glatzer, 166–71. London: Macdonald, 1968.
Büsing, Gerhard. "Ein alternativer Ausgangspunkt zur Interpretation von Jer 29." *ZAW* 104 (1992) 402–8.
Carr, David M. "Moving beyond Unity: Synchronic and Diachronic Perspectives on Prophetic Literature." In *Prophetie in Israel*, edited by Irmtraud Fischer et al., 59–93. Altes Testament und Moderne 11. Berlin: LIT, 2003.
Carroll, Robert P. "The Book of J: Intertextuality and Ideological Criticism." In *Troubling Jeremiah*, edited by A. R. Pete Diamond et al., 220–43. JSOTSup 260. Sheffield: Sheffield Academic, 1999.
———. *From Chaos to Covenant: Prophecy in the Book of Jeremiah*. New York: Crossroad, 1981.
———. "Halfway through a Dark Wood: Reflections on Jeremiah 25." In *Troubling Jeremiah*, edited by A. R. Pete Diamond et al., 73–86. JSOTSup 260. Sheffield: Sheffield Academic, 1999.
———. "Inscribing the Covenant: Writing and the Written in Jeremiah." In *Understanding Poets and Prophets: Essays in Honour of George Wishart Anderson*, edited by A. Graeme Auld, 61–76. JSOTSup 152. Sheffield: JSOT Press, 1993.
———. *Jeremiah: A Commentary*. OTL. Philadelphia: Westminster, 1986.
———. "The Polyphonic Jeremiah: A Reading of the Book of Jeremiah." In *Reading the Book of Jeremiah: A Search for Coherence*, edited by Martin Kessler, 77–85. Winona Lake, IN: Eisenbrauns, 2004.
———. "Prophecy, Dissonance, and Jeremiah xxvi." In *A Prophet to the Nations: Essays in Jeremiah Studies*, edited by Leo G. Perdue and Brian W. Kovacs, 381–91. Winona Lake, IN: Eisenbrauns, 1984.
———. *When Prophecy Failed: Cognitive Dissonance in the Prophetic Traditions of the Old Testament*. New York: Seabury, 1979.
Cassuto, Umberto. "The Prophecies of Jeremiah Concerning the Gentiles." In *Biblical and Oriental Studies*, translated by Israel Abrahams. Vol. 1, *Bible*, 178–226. Publications of the Perry Foundation for Biblical Research in the Hebrew University of Jerusalem. Jerusalem: Magnes, 1973.
Childs, Brevard S. "The Canonical Shape of the Prophetic Literature." *Int* 32 (1978) 46–55.
———. *Introduction to the Old Testament as Scripture*. Philadelphia: Fortress, 1979.
———. "True and False Prophets." In *Old Testament Theology in a Canonical Context*, 133–44. Philadelphia: Fortress, 1985.
Clements, R. E. *Jeremiah*. Interpretation. Atlanta: John Knox, 1988.
———. "Jeremiah's Message of Hope: Public Faith and Private Anguish." In *Reading the Book of Jeremiah: A Search for Coherence*, edited by Martin Kessler, 135–47. Winona Lake, IN: Eisenbrauns, 2004.
———. *Prophecy and Tradition*. Growing Points in Theology. Oxford: Blackwell, 1975.
———. "Prophecy Interpreted: Intertextuality and Theodicy—A Case Study of Jeremiah 26:16–24." In *Uprooting and Planting: Essays on Jeremiah for Leslie Allen*, edited by John Goldingay, 32–44. Library of Hebrew Bible/Old Testament Studies 459. New York: T. & T. Clark, 2007.

Bibliography

Craigie, Peter C. et al. *Jeremiah 1-25*. Word Biblical Commentary 26. Dallas: Word, 1991.
Crenshaw, James L. *Prophetic Conflict: Its Effect upon Israelite Religion*. BZAW 124. Berlin: de Gruyter, 1971.
―――. "Word and Witness: A Note on Jeremiah 29:23." *VT* 27 (1977) 483.
De Boer, P. A. H. "An Inquiry into the Meaning of the Term מַשָּׂא." *OtSt* 5 (1948) 197-214.
De Vries, Simon J. *Prophet against Prophet: The Role of the Micaiah Narrative (1 Kings 22) in the Development of Early Prophetic Tradition*. Grand Rapids: Eerdmans, 1978.
Diamond, A. R. Pete. "Introduction." In *Troubling Jeremiah*, edited by A. R. Pete Diamond, et al., 15-32. JSOTSup 260. Sheffield: Sheffield Academic, 1999.
―――et al., editors. *Troubling Jeremiah*. JSOTSup 260. Sheffield: Sheffield Academic, 1999.
Dijkstra, Meindert. "Prophecy by Letter (Jeremiah XXIX 24-32)." *VT* 33 (1983) 319-22.
Doering, Lutz. "Jeremiah and the 'Diaspora Letters' in Ancient Judaism: Epistolary Communication with the Golah as Medium for Dealing with the Present." In *Reading the Present in the Qumran Library: The Perception of the Contemporary by Means of Scriptural Interpretations*, edited by Kristin De Troyer and Armin Lange, 43-72. Society of Biblical Literature Symposium Series 30. Leiden: Brill, 2005.
Domeris, William R. "When Metaphor Becomes Myth: A Socio-Linguistic Reading of Jeremiah." In *Troubling Jeremiah*, edited by A. R. Pete Diamond et al., 244-60. JSOTSup 260. Sheffield: Sheffield Academic, 1999.
Dubbink, Joep. "Getting Closer to Jeremiah: The Word of YHWH and the Literary-Theological Person of a Prophet." Translated by Martin Kessler. In *Reading the Book of Jeremiah: A Search for Coherence*, edited by Martin Kessler, 25-39. Winona Lake, IN: Eisenbrauns, 2004.
Duhm, Bernhard D. *Das Buch Jeremia*. Kurzer Hand-Commentar zum Alten Testament 11. Tübingen: Mohr/Siebeck, 1901.
Epp-Tiessen, Daniel. "The LORD Has Truly Sent the Prophet." In *Reclaiming the Old Testament: Essays in Honour of Waldemar Janzen*, edited by Gordon Zerbe, 175-85. Winnipeg: CMBC Publications, 2001.
Eslinger, Lyle. "More Drafting Techniques in Deuteronomic Laws." *VT* 34 (1984) 221-25.
Fensham, F. Charles. "Nebuchadrezzar in the Book of Jeremiah." *JNSL* 10 (1982) 53-65.
Fischer, Georg. "Jer 25 und die Fremdvölkersprüche: Unterschiede zwischen hebräischem und griechischem Text." *Bib* 72 (1991) 474-99.
Floyd, Michael H. "The מַשָּׂא (*MAŚŚĀ'*) as a Type of Prophetic Book." *JBL* 121 (2002) 401-22.
Frei, Hans W. *The Eclipse of Biblical Narrative: A Study in Eighteenth and Nineteenth Century Hermeneutics*. New Haven: Yale University Press, 1974.
Fretheim, Terence E. *Jeremiah*. Smyth & Helwys Bible Commentary. Macon, GA: Smyth & Helwys, 2002.
Fuller, Michael E. *The Restoration of Israel: Israel's Re-Gathering and the Fate of the Nations in Early Jewish Literature and Luke-Acts*. Beihefte zur Zeitschrift für die neutestamentliche Wissenschaft und die Kunde der älteren Kirche 138. Berlin: de Gruyter, 2006.

Gowan, Donald E. *Theology of the Prophetic Books: The Death and Resurrection of Israel*. Louisville: Westminster John Knox, 1998.

Habel, Norman C. *Jeremiah, Lamentations*. Concordia Commentary. St. Louis: Concordia, 1968.

———. *The Land Is Mine: Six Biblical Land Ideologies*. OBT. Minneapolis: Fortress, 1995.

Haran, Menahem. "The Place of the Prophecies against the Nations in the Book of Jeremiah." In *Emanuel: Studies in Hebrew Bible, Septuagint, and Dead Sea Scrolls in Honor of Emanuel Tov*, edited by Shalom M. Paul et al., 699–706. VTSup 94. Leiden: Brill, 2003.

Hardmeier, Christof. "Jer 29,24–32—eine geradezu unüberbietbare Konfusion?: Vorurteil und Methode in der exegetischen Forschung." In *Die Hebräische Bibel und ihre zweifache Nachgeschichte: Festschrift für Rolf Rendtorff zum 65. Geburtstag*, edited by Erhard Blum et al., 301–17. Neukirchen-Vluyn: Neukirchener, 1990.

———. "Die Propheten Micha und Jesaja im Spiegel von Jeremia XXVI und 2 Regum XVIII–XX: zur Prophetie-Rezeption in der nach-joschijanischen Zeit." In *Congress Volume: Jerusalem, 1986*, edited by J. A. Emerton, 172–89. VTSup 40. Leiden: Brill, 1988.

Hermisson, Hans-Jürgen. "Kriterien 'wahrer' und 'falscher' Prophetie im Alten Testament: Zur Auslegung von Jeremia 23,16–22 und Jeremiah 28,8–9." *ZTK* 92 (1995) 121–39.

Herrmann, Wolfram. "Jeremia 23,23f als Zeugnis der Gotteserfahrung im babylonischen Zeitalter." *BZ* 27 (1983) 155–66.

Hibbard, J. Todd. "True and False Prophecy: Jeremiah's Revision of Deuteronomy." Paper presented at the annual meeting of the Society of Biblical Literature, New Orleans, November 21, 2009.

Hill, John. "The Book of Jeremiah MT and Early Second Temple Conflicts about Prophets and Prophecy." *ABR* 50 (2002) 28–42.

———. "The Book of Jeremiah (MT) and Its Early Second Temple Background." In *Uprooting and Planting: Essays on Jeremiah for Leslie Allen*, edited by John Goldingay, 153–71. Library of Hebrew Bible/Old Testament Studies 459. New York: T. & T. Clark, 2007.

———. "The Construction of Time in Jeremiah 25 (MT)." In *Troubling Jeremiah*, edited by A. R. Pete Diamond et al., 146–60. JSOTSup 260. Sheffield: Sheffield Academic, 1999.

———. *Friend or Foe? The Figure of Babylon in the Book of Jeremiah MT*. Biblical Interpretation Series 40. Leiden: Brill, 1999.

———. "'Your Exile Will Be Long': The Book of Jeremiah and the Unended Exile." In *Reading the Book of Jeremiah: A Search for Coherence*, edited by Martin Kessler, 149–61. Winona Lake, IN: Eisenbrauns, 2004.

Holladay, William L. "A Fresh Look at 'Source B' and 'Source C' in Jeremiah." *VT* 25 (1975) 394–412.

———. "God Writes a Rude Letter (Jeremiah 29:1–32)." *BA* 46 (1983) 145–46.

———. *Jeremiah 1: A Commentary on the Book of the Prophet Jeremiah, Chapters 1–25*. Hermeneia. Philadelphia: Fortress, 1986.

———. *Jeremiah 2: A Commentary on the Book of the Prophet Jeremiah, Chapters 26–52*. Hermeneia. Minneapolis: Fortress, 1989.

Bibliography

Holt, Else K. "Jeremiah's Temple Sermon and the Deuteronomists: An Investigation of the Redactional Relationship between Jeremiah 7 and 26." *JSOT* 36 (1986) 73–87.

———. "The Potent Word of God: Remarks on the Composition of Jeremiah 37–44." In *Troubling Jeremiah*, edited by A. R. Pete Diamond et al., 161–70. JSOTSup 260. Sheffield: Sheffield Academic, 1999.

Horwitz, William J. "Audience Reaction to Jeremiah." *CBQ* 32 (1970) 555–64.

Hossfeld, Frank Lothar, and Ivo Meyer. *Prophet gegen Prophet: Eine Analyse der alttestamentlichen Texte zum Thema: Wahre und falsche Propheten*. Biblische Beiträge 9. Fribourg: Schweizerisches Katholisches Bibelwerk, 1973.

———. "Der Prophet vor dem Tribunal: Neuer Auslegungsversuch von Jer 26." *ZAW* 86 (1974) 30–50.

Huey, F. B., Jr. *Jeremiah, Lamentations*. New American Commentary 16. Nashville: Broadman, 1993.

Hyatt, J. Philip. "The Deuteronomic Edition of Jeremiah." In *A Prophet to the Nations: Essays in Jeremiah Studies*, edited by Leo G. Perdue and Brian W. Kovacs, 247–67. Winona Lake, IN: Eisenbrauns, 1984.

———. "Torah in the Book of Jeremiah." *JBL* 60 (1941) 381–96.

Jacob, Edmond. "Quelques remarques sur les faux prophètes." *TZ* 13 (1957) 479–86.

Jacobs, Mignon R. "Favor and Disfavor in Jeremiah 29:1–23: Two Dimensions of the Characterization of God and the Politics of Hope." In *Probing the Frontiers of Biblical Studies*, edited by J. Harold Ellens and John T. Greene, 131–55. Princeton Theological Monograph Series. Eugene, OR: Pickwick Publications, 2009.

Janzen, J. Gerald. *Studies in the Text of Jeremiah*. HSM 6. Cambridge: Harvard University Press, 1973.

Janzen, Waldemar. *Old Testament Ethics: A Paradigmatic Approach*. Louisville: Westminster John Knox, 1994.

———. "Withholding the Word." In *Traditions in Transformation: Turning Points in Biblical Faith*, edited by Baruch Halpern and Jon D. Levenson, 97–114. Winona Lake, IN: Eisenbrauns, 1981.

Jones, Douglas Rawlinson. *Jeremiah*. New Century Bible Commentary. London: Pickering, 1992.

Kegler, Jürgen. "The Prophetic Discourse and Political Praxis of Jeremiah: Observations on Jeremiah 26 and 36." In *God of the Lowly: Socio-Historical Interpretations of the Bible*, edited by Willy Schottroff and Wolfgang Stegemann, 47–56. Translated by Matthew J. O'Connell. Maryknoll, NY: Orbis, 1984.

Keown, Gerald L. et al. *Jeremiah 26–52*. Word Biblical Commentary 27. Dallas: Word, 1995.

Kessler, Martin. "The Function of Chapters 25 and 50–51 in the Book of Jeremiah." In *Troubling Jeremiah*, edited by A. R. Pete Diamond, 64–72. JSOTSup 260. Sheffield: Sheffield Academic, 1999.

———. "Jeremiah 25,1–29: Text and Context." *ZAW* 109 (1997) 44–70.

———. "Jeremiah Chapters 26–45 Reconsidered." *JNES* 27 (1968) 81–88.

———, editor. *Reading the Book of Jeremiah: A Search for Coherence*. Winona Lake, IN: Eisenbrauns, 2004.

———. "The Scaffolding of the Book of Jeremiah." In *Reading the Book of Jeremiah: A Search for Coherence*, edited by Martin Kessler, 57–66. Winona Lake, IN: Eisenbrauns, 2004.

Kingsbury, Edwin C. "The Prophets and the Council of Yahweh." *JBL* 83 (1964) 279–86.

Klein, Ralph W. *Israel in Exile: A Theological Interpretation*. Mifflintown, PA: Sigler, 2002.

Kraus, Hans Joachim. *Prophetie in der Krisis: Studien zu Texten aus dem Buch Jeremia*. Biblische Studien 43. Neukirchen-Vluyn: Neukirchener, 1964.

Lalleman-de Winkel, Hetty. *Jeremiah in Prophetic Tradition: An Examination of the Book of Jeremiah in the Light of Israel's Prophetic Traditions*. Contributions to Biblical Exegesis and Theology 26. Leuven: Peeters, 2000.

Lange, Armin. "Reading the Decline of Prophecy." In *Reading the Present in the Qumran Library: The Perception of the Contemporary by Means of Scriptural Interpretations*, edited by Kristin De Troyer and Armin Lange, 181–91. Society of Biblical Literature Symposium Series 30. Leiden: Brill, 2005.

———. *Vom prophetischen Wort zur prophetischen Tradition: Studien zur Traditions- und Redaktionsgeschichte innerprophetisher Konflikte in der Hebräischen Bibel*. Forschungen zum Alten Testament 34. Tübingen: Mohr/Siebeck, 2002.

Lemke, Werner E. "The Near and the Distant God: A Study of Jer 23:23–24 in Its Biblical Theological Context." *JBL* 100 (1981) 541–55.

———. "Nebuchadrezzar, My Servant." *CBQ* 28 (1966) 45–50.

Leuchter, Mark. *Josiah's Reform and Jeremiah's Scroll: Historical Calamity and Prophetic Response*. Hebrew Bible Monographs 6. Sheffield: Sheffield Phoenix, 2006.

———. *The Polemics of Exile in Jeremiah 26–45*. Cambridge: Cambridge University Press, 2008.

Lindblom, Johannes. *Prophecy in Ancient Israel*. Oxford: Blackwell, 1962.

Long, Burke O. "Prophetic Authority as Social Reality." In *Canon and Authority: Essays in Old Testament Religion and Theology*, edited by George W. Coats and Burke O. Long, 3–20. Philadelphia: Fortress, 1977.

———. "Social Dimensions of Prophetic Conflict." *Semeia* 21 (1982) 31–53.

Longman, Tremper, III. *Jeremiah, Lamentations*. New International Biblical Commentary. Peabody, MA: Hendrickson, 2008.

Lund, Nils Wilhelm. *Chiasmus in the New Testament: A Study in Formgeschichte*. Chapel Hill: University of North Carolina Press, 1942.

———. "Chiasmus in the Psalms." *AJSL* 49 (1933) 281–312.

———. "The Presence of Chiasmus in the New Testament." *JR* 10 (1930) 74–93.

———. "The Presence of Chiasmus in the Old Testament." *AJSL* 46 (1930) 104–26.

Lundbom, Jack R. *Jeremiah 1–20: A New Translation with Introduction and Commentary*. AB 21A. New York: Doubleday, 1999.

———. *Jeremiah 21–36: A New Translation with Introduction and Commentary*. AB 21B. New York: Doubleday, 2004.

———. *Jeremiah 37–52: A New Translation with Introduction and Commentary*. AB 21C. New York: Doubleday, 2004.

———. *Jeremiah: A Study in Ancient Hebrew Rhetoric*. SBLDS 18. Missoula, MT: Scholars, 1975.

Macholz, Georg Christian. "Jeremia in der Kontinuität der Prophetie." In *Probleme biblischer Theologie: Gerhard von Rad zum 70. Geburtstag*, edited by Hans Walter Wolff, 306–34. Munich: Kaiser, 1971.

Maier, Christl M. "Jeremiah as Teacher of Torah." *Int* 62 (2008) 22–32.

Man, Ronald E. "The Value of Chiasm for New Testament Interpretation." *BSac* 141 (1984) 146–57.

Bibliography

McCarthy, Dennis J., SJ. "The Inauguration of Monarchy in Israel: A Form-Critical Study of I Samuel 8–12." *Int* 27 (1973) 401–12.

McConville, J. G. *Judgment and Promise: An Interpretation of the Book of Jeremiah.* Leicester, UK: Apollos, 1993.

McEntire, Mark H. "A Prophetic Chorus of Others: Helping Jeremiah Survive in Jeremiah 26." *RevExp* 101 (2004) 301–11.

McKane, William. *A Critical and Exegetical Commentary on Jeremiah.* 2 vols. International Critical Commentary. Edinburgh: T. & T. Clark, 1986–1996.

———. "Jeremiah 27,5–8, Especially 'Nebuchadnezzar, my servant.'" In *Prophet und Prophetenbuch: Festschrift für Otto Kaiser zum 65. Geburtstag,* edited by Volkmar Fritz et al., 98–110. BZAW 185. Berlin: de Gruyter, 1989.

———. "Poison, Trial by Ordeal and the Cup of Wrath." *VT* 30 (1980) 474–92.

———. "משא in Jeremiah 23:33–40." In *Prophecy: Essays Presented to Georg Fohrer on His Sixty-fifth Birthday,* edited by J. A. Emerton, 35–54. BZAW 150. Berlin: de Gruyter, 1980.

Meyer, Ivo. *Jeremia und die falschen Propheten.* Orbis biblicus et orientalis 13. Göttingen: Vandenhoeck &Ruprecht, 1977.

Middlemas, Jill. *The Templeless Age: An Introduction to the History, Literature, and Theology of the "Exile."* Louisville: Westminster John Knox, 2007.

Miller, John W. *Meet the Prophets: A Beginner's Guide to the Books of the Biblical Prophets.* New York: Paulist, 1987.

Miller, Patrick D. "The Book of Jeremiah: Introduction, Commentary, and Reflections." In *The New Interpreter's Bible,* Vol. 6, *Introduction to Prophetic Literature, Isaiah, Jeremiah, Baruch, Letter of Jeremiah, Lamentations, Ezekiel,* edited by Leander E. Keck, 553–926. Nashville: Abingdon, 2001.

Moberly, R. W. L. *Prophecy and Discernment.* Cambridge Studies in Christian Doctrine 14. Cambridge: Cambridge University Press, 2006.

Mottu, Henri. "Jeremiah vs. Hananiah: Ideology and Truth in Old Testament Prophecy." *Radical Religion* 2 (1975) 58–67.

Mowinckel, Sigmund. "The 'Spirit' and the 'Word' in the Pre-Exilic Reforming Prophets." *JBL* 53 (1934) 199–227. Reprinted as "The Spirit and the Word in the Prophets," in Mowinckel, *The Spirit and the Word: Prophecy and Tradition in Ancient Israel,* edited by K. C. Hanson, 83–99. Fortress Classics in Biblical Studies. Minneapolis: Fortress, 2002.

Müller, H.-P. "מַשָּׂא." In *Theologisches Wörterbuch zum Alten Testament,* edited by G. Johannes Botterweck and Helmer Ringgren, 5:220–25. 15 vols. Stuttgart: Kohlhammer, 1984.

Münderlein, Gerhard. *Kriterien wahrer und falscher Prophetie: Entstehung und Bedeutung im Alten Testament.* 2nd ed. Europaîsche Hochschulschriften 23, Theologie 23. Bern: Lang, 1979.

Neusner, Jacob. *Self-Fulfilling Prophecy: Exile and Return in the History of Judaism.* South Florida Studies in the History of Judaism 2. Atlanta: Scholars, 1990.

Nicholson, Ernest W. *The Book of the Prophet Jeremiah.* 2 vols. Cambridge Bible Commentary. Cambridge: Cambridge University Press, 1973–75.

———. *Preaching to the Exiles: A Study of the Prose Tradition in the Book of Jeremiah.* New York: Schocken, 1970.

Niebuhr, H. Richard. *The Meaning of Revelation.* London: Macmillan, 1941.

Nissinen, Martti. "How Prophecy Became Literature." *SJOT* 19 (2005) 153–72.

Nötscher, Friedrich. *Das Buch Jeremias: Übersetzt und erklärt*. Bonn: Hanstein, 1934.
O'Connor, Kathleen M. "The Book of Jeremiah: Reconstructing Community after Disaster." In *Character Ethics and the Old Testament: Moral Dimensions of Scripture*, edited by M. Daniel Carroll R. and Jacqueline E. Lapsley, 81–92. Louisville: Westminster John Knox, 2007.
———. *The Confessions of Jeremiah: Their Interpretation and Role in Chapters 1–25*. SBLDS 94. Atlanta: Scholars, 1988.
———. "'Do Not Trim a Word': The Contributions of Chapter 26 to the Book of Jeremiah." *CBQ* 51 (1989) 617–30.
———. "Jeremiah's 'Prophetic Imagination': Pastoral Intervention for a Shattered World." In *Shaking Heaven and Earth: Essays in Honor of Walter Brueggemann and Charles B. Cousar*, edited by Christine Roy Yoder et al., 59–71. Louisville: Westminster John Knox, 2005.
———. "Lamenting Back to Life." *Int* 62 (2008) 34–47.
———. "The Prophet Jeremiah and Exclusive Loyalty to God." *Int* 59 (2005) 130–40.
———. "Rekindling Life, Igniting Hope." *Journal for Preachers* 30 (2007) 30–34.
———. "Surviving Disaster in the Book of Jeremiah." *WW* 22 (2002) 369–77.
Orlinsky, Harry M. "Nationalism—Universalism in the Book of Jeremiah." In *Essays in Biblical Culture and Bible Translation*, 117–43. New York: Ktav, 1974.
Osswald, Eva. *Falsche Prophetie im Alten Testament*. Sammlung gemeinverständlicher Vortrage und Schriften aus dem Gebiet der Theologie und Religionsgeschichte 237. Tübingen: Mohr/Siebeck, 1962.
Osuji, Anthony Chinedu. "True and False Prophecy in Jer 26–29 (MT)." *ETL* 82 (2006) 437–52.
———. *Where Is the Truth? Narrative Exegesis and the Question of True and False Prophecy in Jer 26–29 (MT)*. BETL 214. Leuven: Peeters, 2010.
Overholt, Thomas W. "Jeremiah 27–29: The Question of False Prophecy." *JAAR* 35 (1967) 241–49.
———. "King Nebuchadnezzar in the Jeremiah Tradition." *CBQ* 30 (1968) 39–48.
———. *The Threat of Falsehood: A Study in the Theology of the Book of Jeremiah*. Studies in Biblical Theology 2/16. Naperville, IL: Allenson, 1970.
Parke-Taylor, Geoffrey H. *The Formation of the Book of Jeremiah: Doublets and Recurring Phrases*. Society of Biblical Literature Monograph Series 51. Atlanta: Society of Biblical Literature, 2000.
Parunak, H. Van Dyke. "Oral Typesetting: Some Uses of Biblical Structure." *Bib* 62 (1981) 153–68.
Pauritsch, Karl. "Gott sendet unermüdlich seine Worte: Zur Botenvorstellung in Jer 26,5." *Kairos* (1975) 100–117.
Peels, H. G. L. "'You Shall Certainly Drink!': The Place and Significance of the Oracles against the Nations in the Book of Jeremiah." *EuroJTh* 16 (2007) 81–91.
Perdue, Leo G. *The Collapse of History: Reconstructing Old Testament Theology*. OBT. Minneapolis: Fortress, 1994.
———. "Jeremiah in Modern Research: Approaches and Issues." In *A Prophet to the Nations: Essays in Jeremiah Studies*, edited by Leo G. Perdue and Brian W. Kovacs, 1–32. Winona Lake, IN: Eisenbrauns, 1984.
Perdue, Leo G., and Brian W. Kovacs, editors. *A Prophet to the Nations: Essays in Jeremiah Studies*. Winnona Lake, IN: Eisenbrauns, 1984.

Bibliography

Person, Raymond F., Jr. "A Rolling Corpus and Oral Tradition: A Not-So-Literate Solution to a Highly Literate Problem." In *Troubling Jeremiah*, edited by A. R. Pete Diamond, 263–71. JSOTSup 260. Sheffield: Sheffield Academic, 1999.

Petersen, David L. *Late Israelite Prophecy: Studies in Deutero-Prophetic Literature and in Chronicles.* Society of Biblical Literature Monograph Series 23. Missoula: Scholars, 1977.

Pixley, Jorge. *Jeremiah.* Chalice Commentaries for Today. St. Louis: Chalice, 2004.

Plant, R. J. R. *Good Figs, Bad Figs: Judicial Differentiation in the Book of Jeremiah.* Library of Hebrew Bible/Old Testament Studies 481. New York: T. & T. Clark, 2008.

Pohlmann, Karl-Friedrich. *Studien zum Jeremiabuch: Ein Beitrag zur Frage nach der Entstehung des Jeremiabuches.* Forschungen zur Religion und Literatur des Alten und Neuen Testaments 118. Göttingen: Vandenhoeck & Ruprecht, 1978.

Polk, Timothy. *The Prophetic Persona: Jeremiah and the Language of the Self.* JSOTSup 32. Sheffield: JSOT Press, 1984.

Porten, Bezalel. "The Structure and Theme of the Solomon Narrative (I Kings 3–11)." *HUCA* 38 (1967) 93–128.

Quell, Gottfried. *Wahre und falsche Propheten: Versuch einer Interpretation.* Beiträge zur Förderung christlicher Theologie, 46. Band, 1. Heft. Gütersloh: Bertelsman, 1952.

Rad, Gerhard von. "Die falschen Propheten." *ZAW* 51 (1933) 109–20.

———. *Old Testament Theology.* Vol. 1, *The Theology of Israel's Historical Traditions.* Translated by D. M. G. Stalker. London: SCM, 1975.

Raitt, Thomas M. "The Prophetic Summons to Repentance." *ZAW* 83 (1971) 30–49.

———. *A Theology of Exile: Judgment/Deliverance in Jeremiah and Ezekiel.* Philadelphia: Fortress, 1977.

Renner, J. T. E. "False and True Prophecy: A Study of a Problem on the Basis of Jeremiah 23 and 28." *RTR* 25 (1966) 95–104.

Reventlow, Henning Graf. "Gattung und Überlieferung in der 'Tempelrede Jeremias,' Jer 7 und 26." *ZAW* 81 (1969) 315–52.

———. *Liturgie und prophetisches Ich bei Jeremia.* Gütersloh: Mohn, 1963.

Rhodes, Arnold B. "Israel's Prophets as Intercessors." In *Scripture in History and Theology: Essays in Honor of J. Coert Rylaarsdam*, edited by Arthur L. Merrill and Thomas W. Overholt, 107–28. Pittsburgh Theological Monograph Series 17. Pittsburgh: Pickwick Press, 1977.

Rietzschel, Claus. *Das Problem der Urrolle: Ein Beitrag zur Redaktionsgeschichte des Jeremiabuches.* Gütersloh: Mohn, 1966.

Roberts, J. J. M. "Prophets and Kings: A New Look at the Royal Persecution of Prophets against Its Near Eastern Background." In *A God So Near: Essays on Old Testament Theology in Honor of Patrick D. Miller*, edited by Brent A. Strawn and Nancy R. Bowen, 341–54. Winona Lake, IN: Eisenbrauns, 2003.

Rofé, Alexander. "The Arrangement of the Book of Jeremiah." *ZAW* 101 (1989) 390–98.

Rudolph, Wilhelm. *Jeremia.* 2nd ed. Handbuch zum Alten Testament, 1. Reihe 12. Tübingen: Mohr/Siebeck, 1958.

Sanders, James A. "Hermeneutics in True and False Prophecy." In *Canon and Authority: Essays in Old Testament Religion and Theology*, edited by George W. Coats and Burke O. Long, 21–41. Philadelphia: Fortress, 1977.

———. "Jeremiah and the Future of Theological Scholarship." *ANQ* 13 (1972) 133–45.

Scalise, Pamela J. "The Way of Weeping: Reading the Path of Grief in Jeremiah." *WW* 22 (2002) 415-22.
Schenker, Adrian. "Nebukadnezzars Metamorphose vom Unterjocher zum Gottesknecht: Das Bild Nebukadnezzars und einige mit ihm zussamenhängende Unterschiede in den beiden Jeremia Rezensionnen." *RB* 89 (1982) 498-527.
Schmidt, Werner H. "Einsicht und Zuspruch: Jeremias Vision und Brief—Jer 24 und 29." In *Textarbeit: Studien zu Texten und ihrer Rezeption aus dem Alten Testament und der Umwelt Israels—Festschrift für Peter Weimar*, edited by Klaus Kiesow and Thomas Meurer, 387-405. Alter Orient und Altes Testament 294. Münster: Ugarit-Verlay, 2003.
Schreiner, Josef von. "Tempeltheologie im Streit der Propheten: Zu Jer 27 und 28." *BZ* 31 (1987) 1-14.
Seebass, H. von. "Jeremias Konflikt mit Chananja: Bemerkungen zu Jer 27 und 28." *ZAW* 82 (1970) 449-52.
Seidl, Theodor. "Datierung und Wortereignis: Beobachtungen zum Horizont von Jer 27,1." *BZ* 21 (1977) 23-44, 184-99.
———. *Formen und Formeln in Jeremia 27-29: Literaturwissenschaftliche Studie, 2. Teil*. Münchener Universitätsschriften. St. Ottilien: EOS, 1978.
———. *Texte und Einheiten in Jeremia 27-29: Literaturwissenschaftliche Studie, 1. Teil*. Münchener Universitätsschriften. St. Ottilien: EOS, 1977.
Seitz, Christopher R. "The Crisis of Interpretation over the Meaning and Purpose of the Exile: A Redactional Study of Jer xxi-xliii." *VT* 35 (1985) 78-97.
———. "The Place of the Reader in Jeremiah." In *Reading the Book of Jeremiah: A Search for Coherence*, edited by Martin Kessler, 67-75. Winona Lake, IN: Eisenbrauns, 2004.
———. "The Prophet Moses and the Canonical Shape of Jeremiah." *ZAW* 101 (1989) 3-27.
———. *Theology in Conflict: Reactions to the Exile in the Book of Jeremiah*. BZAW 176. Berlin: de Gruyter, 1989.
Sharp, Carolyn J. "The Call of Jeremiah and Diaspora Politics." *JBL* 119 (2000) 421-38.
———. *Prophecy and Ideology in Jeremiah: Struggles for Authority in the Deutero-Jeremianic Prose*. Old Testament Studies. Edinburgh: T. & T. Clark, 2003.
Sheppard, Gerald T. "Isaiah 1-39." In *Harper's Bible Commentary*, edited by James L. Mays, 542-70. New York: Harper & Row, 1988.
———. "True and False Prophecy within Scripture." In *Canon, Theology, and Old Testament Interpretation: Essays in Honor of Brevard S. Childs*, edited by Gene M. Tucker, David L. Petersen, and Robert R. Wilson, 262-82. Philadelphia: Fortress, 1988.
Siegman, Edward F. *The False Prophets of the Old Testament*. Washington, DC: Catholic University of America, 1939.
Sisson, Jonathan Paige. "Jeremiah and the Jerusalem Conception of Peace." *JBL* 105 (1986) 429-42.
Skinner, John. *Prophecy and Religion: Studies in the Life of Jeremiah*. Cambridge: Cambridge University Press, 1922.
Smelik, Klaas A. D. "An Approach to the Book of Jeremiah." Translated by Martin Kessler. In *Reading the Book of Jeremiah: A Search for Coherence*, edited by Martin Kessler, 1-11. Winona Lake, IN: Eisenbrauns, 2004.

Bibliography

Smith, Daniel L. "Jeremiah as Prophet of Nonviolent Resistance." *JSOT* 43 (1989) 95–107.

———. *The Religion of the Landless: The Social Context of the Babylonian Exile.* Bloomington, IN: Meyer-Stone, 1989.

Smith-Christopher, Daniel L. *A Biblical Theology of Exile.* OBT. Minneapolis: Fortress, 2002.

Soderlund, Sven. *The Greek Text of Jeremiah: A Revised Hypothesis.* JSOTSup 47. Sheffield: JSOT Press, 1985.

Stevenson, Dwight E. *The False Prophet.* New York: Abingdon, 1965.

Stock, Augustine. "Chiastic Awareness and Education in Antiquity." *BTB* 14 (1984) 23–27.

Stulman, Louis. "Conflicting Paths to Hope in Jeremiah." In *Shaking Heaven and Earth: Essays in Honor of Walter Brueggemann and Charles B. Cousar,* edited by Christine Roy Yoder et al., 43–57. Louisville: Westminster John Knox, 2005.

———. *Jeremiah.* Abingdon Old Testament Commentaries. Nashville: Abingdon, 2005.

———. "Jeremiah as a Messenger of Hope in Crisis." *Int* 62 (2008) 5–20.

———. *Order amid Chaos: Jeremiah as Symbolic Tapestry.* Biblical Seminar 57. Sheffield: Sheffield Academic, 1998.

———. *The Other Text of Jeremiah: A Reconstruction of the Hebrew Text Underlying the Greek Version of the Prose Sections of Jeremiah with English Translation.* Lanham, MD: University Press of America, 1985.

———. "The Prose Sermons as Hermeneutical Guide to Jeremiah 1–25: The Deconstruction of Judah's Symbolic World." In *Troubling Jeremiah,* edited by A. R. Pete Diamond et al., 34–63. JSOTSup 260. Sheffield: Sheffield Academic, 1999.

———. *The Prose Sermons of the Book of Jeremiah: A Redescription of the Correspondences with Deuteronomistic Literature in the Light of Recent Text-Critical Research.* SBLDS 83. Atlanta: Scholars, 1986.

Stulman, Louis, and Hyun Chul Paul Kim. *You Are My People: An Introduction to Prophetic Literature.* Nashville: Abingdon, 2010.

Sweeney, Marvin A. "The Masoretic and Septuagint Versions of the Book of Jeremiah in Synchronic and Diachronic Perspective." In *Form and Intertextuality in Prophetic and Apocalyptic Literature,* 65–77. Forschungen zum Alten Testament 45. Tübingen: Mohr/Siebeck, 2005.

———. "The Truth in True and False Prophecy." In *Truth: Interdisciplinary Dialogues in a Pluralistic Age,* edited by Christine Helmer et al., 9–26. Studies in Philosophical Theology 22. Leuven: Peeters, 2003.

Telcs, George. "Jeremiah and Nebuchadnezzar, King of Justice." *CJT* 15 (1969) 122–30.

Thiel, Winfried. *Die deuteronomistische Redaktion von Jeremia 1–25.* Wissenschaftliche Monographien zum Alten und Neuen Testament 41. Neukirchen-Vluyn: Neukirchener, 1973.

———. *Die deuteronomistische Redaktion von Jeremia 26–52.* Wissenschaftliche Monographien zum Alten und Neuen Testament 52. Neukirchen-Vluyn: Neukirchener, 1981.

Thompson, J. A. *The Book of Jeremiah.* New International Commentary on the Old Testament. Grand Rapids: Eerdmans, 1980.

Tov, Emanuel. "The Book of Jeremiah: A Work in Progress." *BRev* 16/3 (2000) 32–38, 45.

———. "Did the Septuagint Translators Always Understand Their Hebrew Text?" In *De Septuaginta: Studies in Honour of John William Wevers on His Sixty-fifth Birthday*, edited by Albert Pietersma and Claude Cox, 53–70. Mississauga, ON: Benben, 1984.

———. "Exegetical Notes on the Hebrew Vorlage of the LXX of Jeremiah 27 (34)." *ZAW* 91 (1979) 73–93.

———. "The Literary History of the Book of Jeremiah in the Light of Its Textual History." In *Empirical Models for Biblical Criticism*, edited by Jeffrey H. Tigay, 211–37. Philadelphia: University of Pennsylvania Press, 1985.

———. *The Septuagint Translation of Jeremiah and Baruch: A Discussion of an Early Revision of the LXX of Jeremiah 29–52 and Baruch 1:1–3:8*. HSM 8. Missoula: Scholars, 1976.

———. "Some Sequence Differences between the MT and LXX and Their Ramifications for the Literary Criticism of the Bible." *JNSL* 13 (1987) 151–60.

———. *The Text-Critical Use of the Septuagint in Biblical Research*. Jerusalem Biblical Studies 3. Jerusalem: Simor, 1981.

Unterman, Jeremiah. *From Repentance to Redemption: Jeremiah's Thought in Transition*. JSOTSup 54. Sheffield: JSOT Press, 1987.

Vanderhooft, David Stephen. *The Neo-Babylonian Empire and Babylon in the Latter Prophets*. HSM 59. Atlanta: Scholars, 1999.

Vermeylen, Jacques. "Synchronic and Diachronic Perspectives on Prophetic Literature: A Response to David Carr." In *Prophetie in Israel*, edited by Irmtraud Fischer et al., 95–104. Altes Testament und Moderne 11. Berlin: LIT, 2003.

Volz, D. Paul. *Der Prophet Jeremia*. 2nd ed. Kommentar zum Alten Testament. Leipzig: Deichertsche Verlagsbuchhandlung D. Werner Scholl, 1928.

Wal, A. J. O. van der. "Toward a Synchronic Analysis of the Masoretic Text of the Book of Jeremiah." Translated by Martin Kessler. In *Reading the Book of Jeremiah: A Search for Coherence*, edited by Martin Kessler, 13–23. Winona Lake, IN: Eisenbrauns, 2004.

Walker, Norman. "The Masoretic Pointing of Jeremiah's Pun." *VT* 7 (1957) 413.

Walsh, Jerome T. *Style and Structure in Biblical Hebrew Narrative*. Collegeville, MN: Liturgical, 2001.

Walters, Stanley D. "Jacob Narrative." In *The Anchor Bible Dictionary*, edited by David Noel Freedman, 3:599–608. New York: Doubleday, 1992.

Wanke, Gunther. *Untersuchungen zur sogennanten Baruchschrift*. BZAW 122. Berlin: de Gruyter, 1971.

Weippert, Helga. *Die Prosareden des Jeremiabuches*. BZAW 132. Berlin: de Gruyter, 1973.

Weiser, Artur. *Das Buch Jeremia*. 5th ed. Alte Testament Deutsch 20/21. Göttingen: Vandenhoeck & Ruprecht, 1966.

Weiss, Richard D. "Oracle." In *The Anchor Bible Dictionary*, edited by David Noel Freedman, 5:28–29. New York: Doubleday, 1992.

Welch, Adam C. *Jeremiah, His Time and His Work*. Oxford: Blackwell, 1951.

Welch, John W. "Criteria for Identifying and Evaluating the Presence of Chiasmus." In *Chiasmus Bibliography*, edited by John W. Welch and Daniel B. McKinlay, 157–74. Provo, UT: Research Press, 1999.

———. "Introduction." In *Chiasmus in Antiquity: Structures, Analyses, Exegesis*, edited by John W. Welch, 9–16. Hildesheim: Gerstenberg, 1981.

Werblowsky, R. J. Zwi. "Stealing the Word." *VT* 6 (1956) 105–6.
Werline, Rodney Alan. *Penitential Prayer in Second Temple Judaism: The Development of a Religious Institution.* Society of Biblical Literature Early Judaism and Its Literature 13. Atlanta: Scholars, 1998.
Whitley, C. F. "The Term Seventy Years Captivity." *VT* 4 (1954) 60–72.
Willis, John I. "Dialogue between Prophet and Audience as a Rhetorical Device in the Book of Jeremiah." *JSOT* 33 (1985) 63–82.
Wilson, Robert R. *Prophecy and Society in Ancient Israel.* Philadelphia: Fortress, 1980.
———. *Sociological Approaches to the Old Testament.* Guides to Biblical Scholarship. Philadelphia: Fortress, 1983.
Winkle, Ross E. "Jeremiah's Seventy Years for Babylon: A Re-assessment. Part I: The Scriptural Data." *AUSS* 25 (1987) 201–14.
———. "Jeremiah's Seventy Years for Babylon: A Re-assessment. Part II: The Historical Data." *AUSS* 25 (1987) 289–99.
Wolff, Hans Walter. "How Can We Recognize False Prophets?: Criteria for the Difficult Task of Testing the Spirits." In *Confrontations with Prophets: Discovering the Old Testament's New and Contemporary Significance,* 63–76. Philadelphia: Fortress, 1983.
Wright, Christopher J. H. *Old Testament Ethics for the People of God.* Downers Grove, IL: InterVarsity, 2004.
Wright, N. T. *The New Testament and the People of God.* Christian Origins and the Question of God 1. Minneapolis: Fortress, 1992.
Yates, Gary E. "Narrative Parallelism and the 'Jehoiakim Frame': A Reading Strategy for Jeremiah 26–45." *JETS* 48 (2005) 263–81.
Zevit, Ziony. "The Use of עֶבֶד as a Diplomatic Term in Jeremiah." *JBL* 88 (1969) 74–77.
Zimmerli, Walther. "The Fruit of the Tribulation of the Prophet." Translated by Leo G. Perdue. In *A Prophet to the Nations: Essays in Jeremiah Studies,* edited by Leo G. Perdue and Brian W. Kovacs, 349–65. Winona Lake, IN: Eisenbrauns, 1984.
———. "Visionary Experience in Jeremiah." In *Israel's Prophetic Tradition: Essays in Honor of Peter R. Ackroyd,* edited by Richard Coggins et al., 95–111. Cambridge: Cambridge University Press, 1982. Reprinted in Zimmerli, in *The Fiery Throne: The Prophets and Old Testament Theology,* edited by K. C. Hanson, 56–74. Fortress Classics in Biblical Studies. Minneapolis: Fortress, 2003.

www.ingramcontent.com/pod-product-compliance
Lightning Source LLC
Chambersburg PA
CBHW062020220426
43662CB00010B/1411